Unlocking the Ancient Hebrew Alphabet Code

Hebrew in Living Color ™

by

J. Steven Babbit

Gig Harbor, WA
U.S.A.

Unlocking the Ancient Hebrew Alphabet Code

Hebrew in Living Color ™

Unless otherwise noted the Scriptures are taken from the
NEW AMERICAN STANDARD BIBLE®, Copyright © 1960, 1962, 1963,
1968, 1971, 1972, 1973, 1975, 1977, 1995 by the Lockman Foundation.
Used by permission.

Cover, illustrations, and charts by the author.

Unlocking the Ancient Hebrew Alphabet Code, Hebrew in Living Color ™
(3rd edition) by J. Steven Babbit.

ISBN 1-4392-4342-5
EAN-13 is 9781439243428

Copyright © 2009 and 2010, J. Steven Babbit

All rights reserved. Information in this book may be copied for non-profit educational purposes only, without prior permission; however, no chapter(s) can be copied in its entirety without prior written consent from the author. With the exception of reproduction for educational use only, no part of this book may be reproduced, stored in a retrieval system, or transmitted in any form or by any means, electronic, mechanical, recording or otherwise, without the prior written permission of the author, J. Steven Babbit.

Manufactured in the United States of America

Suggested Retail Price:

$19.99 US

Table of Contents

Forward ……………………………………………………………………	- i -
How to Break an Alphabet Code …………………………………………..	- v -
Chapter 1 – Introduction, Quick Reference Chart, and Linguistic Notes…………	- 1 -
Chapter 2 – ALEPH………..	- 9 -
Chapter 3 – BET or BEIT…………………………………………………	- 15 -
Chapter 4 – GIMMEL…………………………………………………..	- 21 -
Chapter 5 – DALETH…………………………………………………..	- 27 -
Chapter 6 – HEY (or HEI)………………………………………………	- 35 -
Chapter 7 – WAW or VAV (in Modern Hebrew)…………………………	- 43 -
Chapter 8 – ZAYIN……………………………………………………...	- 49 -
Chapter 9 – ĤET………………………………………………………..	- 57 -
Chapter 10 – TET………………………………………………………..	- 65 -
Chapter 11 – YOD………………………………………………………..	- 71 -
Chapter 12 – KAPH……………………………………………………....	- 77 -
Chapter 13 – LAMED……………………………………………………	- 83 -
Chapter 14 – MEM………………………………………………………	- 91 -
Chapter 15 – NUN………………………………………………………..	- 99 -
Chapter 16 – SAMEKH…………………………………………………..	- 105 -
Chapter 17 – AYIN………………………………………………………	- 113 -
Chapter 18 – PEH………………………………………………………..	- 121 -
Chapter 19 – PHE………………………………………………………..	- 127 -
Chapter 20 – TZADE…………………………………………………….	- 131 -
Chapter 21 – QOPH……………………………………………………..	- 139 -
Chapter 22 – REISH……………………………………………………..	- 147 -
Chapter 23 – SHIN………………………………………………………	- 155 -
Chapter 24 – SIN (Seen) ………………………………………………..	- 165-
Chapter 25 – THAV or TAV…………………………………………….	- 169 -
Chapter 26 – YAHWEH, the Mysterious Name of God……………………	- 175 -
Chapter 27 – But Wait! There's More… ………………………………..	- 177 -
About the Author ……………………………………………………..........	- 183 -

Forward

I remember the first time I heard Dr. Robert L. Thomas, chief editor of the *New American Standard Bible* translation project, read Biblical passages and translate them into his own words from Greek to English. I was a graduate student at Talbot Theological Seminary at the time. When this man read and translated the Greek text to our second-year Greek class, it was like hearing Biblical passages in color after years of experiencing them only in black and white.

Only a few weeks before, I had been in the first-year Greek class of a professor named Douglas McDougal who was just finishing up his doctoral dissertation. In his dissertation, he posited that the original language from which all Indo-European languages evolved was built upon a set of foundational word stems which had fixed meanings. One particular day that stands out in my mind, he came into class elated that he had discovered a new root stem – *sta*. Our beloved Greek professor excitedly began to write a list of words containing the root *sta*, which indicated a fixed position or fixed measure. **Sta**tion. **Sta**r. **Sta**re. **Sta**dia. **Sta**nd. **Sta**tic. **Sta**tus quo.

These two professors and these two events caused me to wonder for almost a quarter of a century whether or not Biblical Hebrew also had its own root stems which indicated specific meanings. Something deep inside me longed to experience Biblical Hebrew in color, just as Greek had sprung to life that first day in our second-year Greek class; for as Dr. Thomas read to us, the Greek Scriptures seemingly shined and danced in my mind with all of the colors of a rainbow.

Little did I expect to discover that Hebrew not only contains meaningful root stems; something even more glorious was waiting to be rediscovered. Each *letter* of the Hebrew Alphabet has its own set of meanings. In fact, what I discovered is that Professor McDougal's root syllable, *sta*, most likely originated from just one letter of the Phoenician/Hebrew Alphabet: TZADE, which is pronounced *tsa*.

Furthermore, the underlying system of the Semitic pictorial alphabet explained why in Hebrew only consonants seemed to matter; the vowel sounds for the most part were fluid and rather inconsequential. Also answered were my questions regarding the apparent redundancy of certain Hebrew letters, such as SIN and SAMEKH, both of which denote the sound indicated by the English letter *S*. The same is true of TET and TAV, both frequently voiced like the English letter T. I had long wondered to myself, *Why were two letters for identical sounds apparently necessary to the creators of the Hebrew alphabet?*

I found my answer to this question once I understood the fundamental nature of the Hebrew alphabet system. Although some Hebrew and Phoenician letters *sound* the same, they denote different pictorial meanings. Therefore, it was necessary for the creators of the Phoenician and Hebrew alphabets to use a few duplicate-sounding letters in order to denote a full system of useful meanings; the pictorial system needed a few more sets of meanings than there were voiced sounds to represent these meanings. Duplicate-sounding letters became a necessity for the system to carry the full array of meanings that the ancient Phoenician, Babylonian, and Hebrew scribes desired. Even though the voiced sounds indicated by two different pictograms might have been the same, the pictograms of the letters conveyed different meanings. By changing even just a single letter in the 3-consonant stem of a Hebrew word, one could vastly alter the word's meaning.

The system is brilliant in its simplicity. That such complexity could be built upon such a foundation of simplicity is nothing short of awe-inspiring.

Because Hebrew basically ceased to be a spoken language after Titus and the Romans leveled Jerusalem in 70 A.D., the translation of a few Biblical Hebrew words has posed some difficulties for modern scholars. While contextual clues have allowed translators to make educated guess as to the original meanings of unfamiliar words within Biblical texts, today a few Biblical Hebrew words exist for which the exact original meanings have been lost.

Furthermore, pronunciation of Biblical Hebrew words is far from standardized. For example, an initial BET (בּ) is almost always pronounced as a B, but a BET (ב) in the middle or end positions is usually pronounced as a V sound.

Linguistic evidence indicates that the Biblical Hebrew VAV (ו) was actually pronounced as a W, not as a V as it is pronounced in Modern Hebrew. Often I have shown the *Strong's Concordance* pronunciations in my example letter charts, which means BET is more often shown as a B sound rather than a V sound. Readers familiar with Hebrew pronunciation will therefore notice what may appear as oddities (or errors) in my transliterations. If there were a standardized Biblical Hebrew pronunciation, believe me, I would have used it. Unfortunately, there isn't. So... if you think a word should be transliterated differently, let me say here and now that I agree with you.

The scholastic value of understanding the Hebrew pictorial writing system is immense. With a basic understanding of the original meanings of the Hebrew letters, both Hebrew scholars and novice Biblical Hebrew readers alike will be able to look at the letters within Biblical Hebrew words (in addition to using contextual clues) to find the hidden nuances of their original meanings. In short, many Biblical Hebrew words are self-defining, at least to some extent.

This is not the first book to address the possibility that the letters carried unique meanings; however, while gathering the research data which supports my interpretations of the letters' meanings, I have seen no other books or information on the Internet that offer a system of letter interpretation that can pictorially interpret the meanings of all the Biblical Hebrew words which *Strong's Concordance*[1] and the *New American Standard Hebrew-Aramaic and Greek Dictionaries: Updated Edition*[2] list as **primary root words**. In my mind, it is not a true system until it works with at least *every* root word listed in *Strong's Concordance*, not just a few selected words.

In a few cases, previous authors have correctly surmised at least a portion of the meanings denoted by some of the Hebrew letters. I wish to take nothing away from them, as I see their work as ground-breaking. Likewise, I hope they will embrace my research and graciously permit me to contribute to the linguistic

---

[1] The New Strong's exhaustive concordance of the Bible. James Strong. Nashville : Nelson, 1984.

[2] *New American Standard Exhaustive Concordance (with Hebrew-Aramaic and Greek Dictionaries)*. LOCKMAN FOUNDATION; Robert L. THOMAS, General Editor. - Nashville, Holman Bible Publishers, 1981.

process of fully understanding Biblical Hebrew. I look forward to the day when others build upon the work that I, and others before me, have done.

I will leave the bulk of more serious translation and linguistic debate to those linguists and Hebrew scholars who know more than I about the language. I simply offer this research as my contribution to the foundational building blocks upon which Hebrew scholars might build in the future. The scope of this book is to introduce lay people (and curious scholars) to the meanings of the ancient Phoenician, Hebrew and Babylonian pictorial letters, all of which impacted the development of written and spoken Biblical Hebrew. My hope is that even the most basic student of Biblical Hebrew might benefit from the information contained in this book.

I am by no means an "expert" in Biblical Hebrew, but I am learning more all the time. I leave it to those who claim to be Biblical Hebrew and/or Phoenician scholars to refine my rudimentary work here. As for me, I feel blessed that I am now able to read Biblical Hebrew in color.

Lastly, this book is primarily linguistic in its scope, rather than theological. While some of the sayings and parables of Jesus (called Yeshua in Hebrew) are quoted and discussed herein, they are not cited in order to prove or disprove any particular theological point of view; however, I have used several quotes from Judeo-Christian sources to illustrate how the meanings of the letters may have influenced the *turn-of-phrases* the authors chose to use.

Biblical (Tenach) and *New Testament* quotations have been primarily taken from the New American Standard Bible. I am personally acquainted with the skills of two of the primary NASB translators, having been taught by them as a student in their Greek and Hebrew class. I trust the translation abilities of Dr. Robert Thomas and Dr. Richard Rigsby (and their co-workers), so this is the translation I chose.

For further information, to contact the author directly, to see other books by this author, or to get information about booking individual and/or group tours to Israel, please check out the author's website:

http://www.HebrewInLivingColor.com

Grow in Grace,

J. Steven Babbit

* * *

This book is dedicated to all those who teach.

To every teacher who impacted my life…

Thank you!

How to Break an Alphabet Code

Code breakers look for patterns. Instinctively, I felt that both the *doubled-identical-consonants* and the ***Consonant X – WAW - Consonant X*** constructs (with *Consonant X* being 2 identical Hebrew letters) had significant meanings. Since Hebrew is built around 3-consonant roots, the two patterns were a good place to begin, since I would be dealing with only 2 letters when looking at these constructs, and WAW's letter meaning seemed accurately defined by past researchers.

Secondly, a few of the letters' meanings seemed well-defined based on the similarities between their Phoenician pictographs and their post-Babylonian exile pictographs. Among these were BEIT, PEH, and the WAW. Furthermore, many of the letter's names were the same as their pictogram, including Aleph (a *leader*), Bet/Beit (a house), Peh (a mouth), and REISH (a reed, from *ROSH* which is a head). Mem seemed correctly defined by past researchers as *chaos* or *water*, which brings to mind the Hebrew imagery of a chaotic firmament (waters) described in the first chapter of Genesis.

I began by looking at Biblical Hebrew words that were formed by these "known" consonants in a doubled or N-WAW-N (N being a known consonant) construct. Using a *Strong's Concordance* and the *Libronix Digital Library System*, I searched for words that fit these patterns. I also searched for words comprised of the few letters whose meanings were already known to me and others.

The letter name MEM was one of the first words I tried out. I was fairly sure that MEM denoted WATERS, CHAOS, and FIRMAMENT, all of which were Genesis 1 creation story concepts. Eventually, I came to suspect that the word MeM (מם) meant something like FORMS FORM, FORMING, or MATTER EXISTING. I then looked for other words with two MEMs and a third letter as part of their 3-consonant root.

After reading a specific word's definition in a variety of sources, I tried to apply the known letter meanings, such as the meanings of MEM. When I could find a word with two known letters plus one unknown letter, I used a guess-and-check method to look for patterns of similar meanings for the unknown letters, one letter at a time. Often, it was possible to get a *feel* for what the letter might represent, but it usually took days or weeks of studying each letter for me to really understand the array of meanings the alphabet creators might have been trying to convey with a particular letter.

I knew I was close to a reasonable understanding of a letter's meaning set when the unknown Phoenician pictographs and the post-Babylonian letters started to make sense to me as recognizable images. For example, Ayin means *EYE*, but the pictograph showed such a wide-open eye, so I suspected it might mean something even more than just an eye. Eventually, I discovered it denoted an *alert eye* which indicated the *force of alertness* or a *life force*, much like in those horror movies where the dead guy's eyes suddenly pop open so quickly that the audience is startled.

Those who have done crossword puzzles or the number grid game, Sudoku, know that the more blanks you fill in, the easier solving the puzzle becomes. I began trying to crack the Hebrew alphabet code in August of 2008. Working on an average of 10 hours or more a day, I pretty well had the code broken by March of 2009. During the first 4 months I worked on the code, I was totally immersed in Phoenician and Hebrew letter thought. Sometimes I would even wake up in the middle of the night with an "ah-ha" understanding of a letter's meaning which I had previously not been able to grasp.

Another great help was the order of the letters, as they are arranged and listed within the Hebrew alphabet. Often antithetical pairs are located either next to one another or at least within a few of letters of one another. For example, Mem is followed by Nun, and these two letters represent *stillness* and *movement*, respectively. The same is true of Aleph and Beit, which can mean *individual* and a *household community* respectively. Gimmel and Daleth respectively can denote *opposition* and *two gathered*. A studious look at **the quick-reference chart (located on pages 4 and 5)** might be worth your time if you wish to find other examples of antithetical pairs.

I know there will be no shortage of skeptics who think that guess-and-check is not very good science, but after teaching secondary mathematics and algebra to thousands of students over two decades, I know well that guess-and-check solutions do work, in spite of the fact that they can be extremely tedious and time-consuming.

As I prepare this manuscript for publication, I am still in the process of refining the array of meanings some letters convey. Remember, these are word *pictures* (or picture words), so I doubt anyone will ever come up with a definitive list of exact literal translations. Such a task would be like claiming to have a list of the twenty adjectives that best describe the Mona Lisa or a list of the all-time greatest 9 baseball players by position. I expect my claims to spark some debate, but I view that as a positive outcome of my efforts.

Hopefully, others will see my research as a springboard for further research and not as the ravings of a self-proclaimed "expert" on the Hebrew and Phoenician alphabets. In my own defense, I would like to say that perhaps I *could* be considered an *expert*... but only if one uses my favorite definition of the word *expert:* EX (X) being an *unknown quantity* and SPURT being a *drip under pressure*.

* * *

Chapter 1
Introduction

Quick-Reference Chart of Phoenician & Hebrew Letters
Plus Important Linguistic Notes

It is no secret to anyone who has studied Hebrew that most Biblical Hebrew words are built upon three-consonant roots. However, for roughly two millennia, lying hidden and waiting to be re-discovered, was a long-lost system. I have chosen to refer to this system as the *Ancient Hebrew Alphabet Code*, which apparently has existed from Hebrew's inception. Quite possibly, Phoenician pre-dated Hebrew as a written pictographical language similar to the sign language used among fur traders and Native American tribes who needed to communicate ideas between groups with differing spoken languages.

Originally, it would have been possible for those who could read words written in the Phoenician pictographs to understand nuances of meaning within these three-letter Semitic word roots, because each letter of the ancient Hebrew, Phoenician and Babylonian alphabets had its own specific set of meanings. Exactly when the full understanding of the Hebrew alphabet's pictographical meanings was lost is anybody's guess at this point in time. From what information I can find, or cannot find to be more exact, the realization that a pictographical code even existed seems to have faded away hundreds, if not thousands, of years ago.

In other words, many ancient languages were not written with just random combinations of letters; they were written with carefully-chosen pictographs. Each pictograph's meaning (or array of meanings) was understood by those who read the words. This made it possible for ancient Hebrew speakers who knew the pictorial Alphabet Code to roughly decipher the meanings of unfamiliar words, even foreign words. While it may not have been possible to glean the exact meaning of an unfamiliar word, it would have been possible for a person who knew the pictorial code to get a basic feel for what an unfamiliar word meant. Consequently, if a picture is worth a thousand words, one might say that each Hebrew 3-letter root is alive with full-color pictographical meanings.

Knowing this letter code helped early Semitic language readers to grasp the nuances, the flavors… the colors… of the words that comprised the textual passages they were reading. This ability to grasp the nuances of meanings within Hebrew words could be immensely helpful when interpreting the text of the Torah and Tanach, known today by Jews as the Bible or as the Old Testament to Christians.

In learning how Hebrew and Aramaic words were constructed, I have gained a great deal of insight regarding the way the ancient Hebrews thought. Believe me; it's nothing like the linear, step-by-step, thinking of the Greeks with which English speakers are so familiar.

The ancient Greeks and Romans were very left-brained and linear in their thinking. For every effect, there was a prior cause. In their way of thinking, events and beliefs of the modern era all were connected by a long chain of causes and effects, going all the way back to original causality. Such thinking especially permeates the writings of Paul, who refers to himself as a Roman citizen, in the New Testament.

For example, let's examine the Greek concept of *knowing* compared to the Hebrew concept of *knowing*. To the Greeks, one *knew* something if one studied all of its aspects including the cause-and-effect chain which eventually lead all the way back to something's original state. Philosophical debates were built upon this linear style of thinking.

Great Greek orators, such as Socrates and Plato, excelled in this style of thinking, speaking, and writing. In Greek thinking, knowledge is built "line upon line." (See the end of Chapter 7 and the comments regarding the Greek word *sunesis*.) Public orators drew heavily on the words of those orators who came before; consequently, Socrates and Plato remain famous to this day because of the vast numbers of philosophers who have subsequently through the ages drawn so heavily from them.

In sharp contrast, *knowing*, in the mind of a typical ancient Hebrew, really had little to do with learning and embracing lists of information as abstract ideas. Instead, to an ancient Hebrew *knowing* was experiential in its nature. One did not truly *know* something until they had actually experienced it personally. In other words, hypothetical thinking had its small place in Hebrew philosophy, but to the writers of the Bible, *knowing* was equated with *doing*. Take for example the following Hebrew expression found in Genesis 4:1, "And Adam *knew* Eve his wife; and she conceived, and bare Caina." (KJV, author's emphasis added)

As you examine the meanings of the Hebrew letters, keep in mind that Semitic people saw the meanings in pictures, not in linear word definitions. For this reason, there is not always a well-defined one-to-one correlation between the exact meaning of a Hebrew word and its corresponding English term. Westerners will often want a definitive list of meanings, preferably in annotated outline form. Semitic peoples were often content with the feel, the emotions, and the shades of meanings which each Hebrew letter represented.

At this point in our investigation into the pictorial meanings of the various ancient Semitic alphabets, it should be duly noted that Biblical Hebrew's pictorial letter meanings morphed over time. The greatest changes seem to have occurred during the time of the Babylonian exile (during the sixth century B.C.) when the Phoenician pictorial alphabet was abandoned in favor of the Modern Hebrew alphabet, which is basically Babylonian in origin.

Consequently, Hebrew letters will often have both a Phoenician array of meanings and a separate Babylonian array of meanings. Often, these two arrays of meanings are similar, but they *not* always exactly the same. Keep this in mind when you find yourself thinking, *But I thought he said such-and-such Hebrew letter meant X, but here it says it means Y and/or Z.* As much as is possible without being tedious or burdensome, the letter meanings will be given with my best estimation as to whether their meanings are pre-Babylonian exile in origin or post-Babylonian exile in origin.

Furthermore, one must know a bit about the antiquity of a particular Hebrew word in order to know which set of meanings to apply. Often, this task is as simple as looking the word up in a *Strong's Concordance* or similar concordance, where **primary root words** are indicated. The primary root words almost always use the pictographical meanings of the Phoenician letters. For this task I primarily have used the *Libronix Digital Library System* and its updated version of the *Strong's Concordance*. Again, my gratitude goes out to Dr. Robert Thomas and his colleagues for compiling this impressive research tool.

As a word of caution, Modern Hebrew takes many of its words from modern foreign language such as English, German, French and Russian. Therefore, the system shown in this book breaks down when applied to many Modern Hebrew words. However, the system is extremely reliable with the ancient 3-consonant primary root words found in Biblical texts. These are noted within the Libronix Digital Library System's *New American Standard Hebrew-Aramaic and Greek Dictionaries: Updated Edition*.

So, let's get to it. It's time to begin our journey into unlocking the hidden meanings of the ancient pictorial Hebrew and Phoenician alphabets. Hopefully, you too will find the delight I have found in being able to read Hebrew "in color."

QUICK REFERENCE CHART:

On the following two facing pages, you will find a quick-reference chart of the Hebrew and Phoenician letters, along with a basic overview of their "Alphabet Code" meanings. Subsequent short chapters will offer more detailed looks at each of the letters, as well as the suspected evolutionary histories of their meanings.

The Phoenician symbols were taken from a variety of sources, and you will see that there is a variety of ways to write most of these letters. This is due to the fact that writers of Phoenician were separated by significant amounts of both time and geographical distance.

Most Hebrew letters have a Phoenician set of meanings (pre-Babylonian exile) and a Babylonian set of letter meanings (post-Babylonian exile meanings, influenced by the Babylonian writing system and loosely attached to the Babylonian letter derivatives which we now recognize as both the Biblical and Modern Hebrew alphabet.)

In the following quick-reference chart, the older Phoenician alphabet meanings which pre-date the Babylonian exile will be noted by the letters **Pho**. The meanings adopted during and/or after the Babylonian exile will be noted by the letters **Bab**.

Unlocking the Ancient Hebrew Alphabet Code

# Value	Letter Name	Phoenician Pictographs	Modern Symbol	**Pho.** = Phoenician **Bab.** = post-Babylonian Exile Basic Letter Meanings
1	**Aleph**		א	Pho.- (Ox) leader, primary, strong, servant Bab.- (2 yoked oxen) SEPARATE INDIVIDUAL(s) but UNITED or WORKING TOGETHER
2	**Beit (Vet)**		ב ב	Pho.- (tent) HOUSE or BODY (living, organic bodies), family unit, UNITY, HARMONY Bab.- (3-sided dwelling structure) a TABERNACLE
3	**Gimmel**		ג	Pho.- (a foot) TRAMPLE, working in OPPOSITION, Bab.- (prob. a sitting donkey) RESISTANCE AGAINST, ANTI-, UN-, NON-
4	**Daleth**		ד	Pho.- (the horizon – where the earth and sun meet each day) TWO GATHERED to form an EDGE Bab.- SIDE, EXTENSION, HEM, SHARP EDGE
5	**Hei**		ה	Pho.- RAISED UP, REVEALED, BEHOLD! VIOLA! Bab.- MORE THAN, AMPLIFIED, EXHALTED
6	**Waw (Vav)**		ו	Pho.- (streams, tent peg or nail) FORCE of FLOW, TWO FLOWING INTO ONE, CONNECTING, SYNERGY Bab.- "And", PIERCING, SHARP (PAIN)
7	**Zayin**		ז	Pho.- (harvesting tools, axe, sword) ARCING MOTION Bab.- (weapon) VIOLENT FORCE, CUTTING DOWN, DESTRUCTION, CUT A SWATH, to TAKE
8	**CHet (Ĥet)**		ח	Pho.- OPEN SPACE, a VOID defined by limits or walls Bab.- OUTSIDE, SECTION, DIVIDED, SPIRALING, TWISTED, AROUND, PRIVATE, a VOID or CYLINDER shape that cannot hold water
9	**Tet**		ט	Pho.- (coiled basket bottom) COILED LAYERS Bab.- (a clay container that can hold water) TURNING, EXCHANGING, DEFINED & PRECISE LIMITS, to JOIN
10	**Yod**		י	Pho.- (arm & grasping hand) to CREATE, the HAND of the DIVINE CREATOR (the Y hand denotes an OPPOSABLE THUMB and FINGERS) Bab.- (the sun) HIGH ABOVE, SET APART, bright LIGHT, poss. MIGHTY
20	**Kaph**		כ	Pho.- (palm of hand) BLESSING, ABOVE, ANNOINT, poss. DESTINY Bab.- poss. an Oven (denoting HOT) or a hanging WEIGHT used on scales (denoting WEIGHTY, poss. TRIALS)
30	**Lamed**		ל	Pho.- (folds of soft linen) COMFORT-er (e.g. Psalm 23) Bab.- (Butter Churn Handle) GUIDED FLOW (or "*He who* or *that which* guides the flow"), GUIDANCE, CENTRAL POINT, to MILL, TONGUE/RUDDER/STAFF of GUIDANCE

Chapter 1 – Linguistic Notes and Quick-reference Chart

# Value	Letter Name	Phoenician Pictographs	Modern Symbol	**Pho.** = Phoenician **Bab.** = post-Babylonian Exile Basic Letter Meanings
40	Mem		מ	Pho.- ("MEM" as in MEM-brane) Substance or "stuff", fluid, chaos, the firmament, FORMS FORMING Bab.- (a body or herd) any group of similar objects or animals, BEING, STILLNESS, water
50	Nun		נ	Pho.- (sprouting seedling, lightening) LIFE LIVING, FORCE of MOTION or ACTION, to DO Bab.- to MOVE, MOVEMENT, PROCREATION
60	Sameck		ס	Pho.- (fish gaffing tool) to CATCH, SNARE, a THORN Bab.- (fishing net) COMPLETELY ENCIRCLE, GATHER, GROUP TOGETHER, SUM
70	'Ayin		ע	Pho.- (alert eye) LIFE FORCE, ALERTNESS, under Bab.- FORCE OPEN, to SEPARATE, SPARK of LIFE
80	Pey (Peh) Phey		פ ף	Pho.- (blossom with fruit) to BLOOM OUTWARD, to produce fruit. PHEY: to DROP or FALL Bab.- (a MOUTH) to RELEASE, SCATTER. Pictograph may be a side view of curled fingers opening.
90	TSadi		צ	Pho.- (side view of stalking hunter w/spear / barbed gaff or fish hook) to ATTACH to the SIDE, STALK Bab.- (tree with tap root) FIRMLY ROOTED, FIXED IMAGE, WEIGHTY, SOLID, CONSTANT
100	Qoph		ק	Pho.- (neck & back of head) SWELLING, FULLY DEVELOPED/MATURE (swollen fruit), RIPE Bab.- GO AROUND, ACROSS, THROUGH(out), THOROUGHLY, TRANSFORMATION
200	Resh		ר	Pho.- (head's profile) CHARACTERISTIC, TOP, RECOGNIZABLE ATTRIBUTE, OUTLOOK Bab.- (bend reed) CHANGE, INSIDE, CUTTING
300	SHin Sin		שׁ	Pho.- (sun's path of resurrection) RETURN to LIFE, RESURRECTION, RE-OCCURING MOVEMENT. Egyptian – (teeth) BITE, CONSUME, PRESS, GRIND, PROVIDE, GIVE Bab.- (poss. Challah/Braided Bread) to EXPAND OUTWARD like bread rising, BREAK, SEPARATE, PUFF UP, SPREAD OUT
400	Tav (Taw)		ת	Pho.- (crossed sticks) BECOME ONE, mark of PURITY (e.g. 24k stamped on gold) Bab.- COVENENTAL SIGNATURE or SIGN of CERTIFICATION, MARK of AUTHENTICITY

Five of the twenty-two basic Hebrew letters (23 letters counting the letter GHAYIN which was lost from the Hebrew Alphabet) have a unique written form when they appear at the end of a word. In written Hebrew, the final form of these letters is known as their SOPHET form. The following is a list of the letters that have a final SOPHET FORM:

	Basic Form	Final Sophet	Letter's Meaning in Sophet Form
KAPH	כ	ך	A BLESSING from above flowing down
MEM	מ	ם	A BODY of WATER (sea, lake or ocean)
NUN	נ	ן	(raised arm with fist) VICTORY, JOY
PHEY	פ	ף	To DROP, to FALL (like ripe fruit or leaves) To FLOW DOWN, to DRIP, DROPLETS, NECK
TSADI	צ	ץ	Poss. ATTACHED or FORCE of BONDING

Notes Regarding Transliteration of Hebrew Letters into English:

I have randomly chosen $\hat{H}$ as the symbol which stands for Chet (ח) throughout this book. Hebrew has two H sounds. The letter HEI (ה) is voiced similarly to H in the English Alphabet. On the other hand, **CH**et is a **guttural H**, like the CH in the Scottish word LOCH. Chet is often transliterated as CH, but this tends to confuse many English speakers who then want to pronounce CHet incorrectly, incorrectly voicing CH as in CHip or CHeese. A proper voicing of CHET sounds like one might be trying to clear a bit of phlegm from the upper throat or back of the mouth. CHet is the letter which begins the Hebrew words CHanukah and CHutzpah.

The symbol $\hat{I}$ is used to show a long I (long YOD) vowel sound. $\hat{I}$ should be pronounced as a long Ē, similar to the vowel sound found in the following words: tr**ee**, h**i**story, and sk**i**.

Many of the Hebrew letters can be transliterated in a wide variety of ways. I have tried to show these varieties, but constantly indicating them throughout the book would have been too cumbersome.

Important Linguistic Note Regarding Doubled Hebrew Consonants:

Doubling a letter indicates that **-ING** should be added to the word's verbal meaning.

EXAMPLES of DOUBLING a CONSONANT
(NOTE: Dotting a Hebrew letter indicates it is doubled):

LIFT (ה) becomes LIFTING (הה).

COVER (כ) becomes COVERING (כּ = כ כ).

EXTEND (ד) becomes EXTENDING (דּ = דד).

STRONG (ז) becomes STRENGTHENING (ז ז)

Other Preliminary Linguistic Notes:

When interpreting the ancient Hebrew Alphabet code, a few specific linguistic constructs should be noted. When a Hebrew consonant is doubled, it usually indicates the participle (verb + ing) form of its meaning. The letter TET can mean *to COIL*, so a doubled TET could indicate *COIL-ING*. However, TET can also mean to EXCHANGE PLACES or TURN; therefore a doubled TET could also mean EXCHANGING, TRADING or TURNING.

However, as it is with most linguistic "rules," there are apparent exceptions to the doubled-consonant rule. For examples, THAV (TAV) can mean *PURE*. Since the participle form, *PURE-ing,* would make no sense, a doubled THAV in a three-consonant root would probably indicate *amplification of the letter's meaning,* and should be rendered as *MORE PURE*.

It should be noted that Hebrew was written for the first thousand-plus years without the vowel points (called *nikud*). Seldom were doubled consonants actually ever written with two of the same letters side-by-side in the word. The preferred way in Hebrew to double a consonant is to simply place a dot in the center of the letter, but this notation was also introduced with the other nikud markings after centuries of writing Hebrew without nikud notations. Therefore, it becomes very difficult to ascertain with any certainty whether or not an ancient 3-consonant root word might have originally had doubled consonants.

Whenever identical consonants appear with a WAW (Vav) between them, this 3-letter configuration denotes (**the action** indicated by identical first and third letters) ***again***. For example, HEY can denote the action verb, ***to stand***. HEY-WAW-HEY therefore denotes to ***stand again***, which is idiomatically similar to the meaning of the Greek word *anastasis*. *Anastasis* translates into English as *resurrection* but also literally means to *stand again*.

The Hebrew spellings of the Hebrew letter names used in this book have been primarily taken from page 14 of T*he First Hebrew Primer, third edition.*[3] These Hebrew spellings are somewhat standardized, but I have seen a few variances. On the other hand, the English transliterations of the Hebrew letter names vary greatly from source to source.

WAW's Special Functions When Used as a Vowel Marker:

Almost no vowels are marked in Hebrew, especially the vowels A and E. The long Ē sound in Hebrew is usually marked by YOD and is usually transliterated as an I). Also, Ō and Ū are often marked. This is not a random event within the Semitic language system.

Ō and Ū are almost always indicated by the presence of a WAW as an additional **fourth letter** in what is typically a 3-CONSONANT word root. When a four-letter combination is used to form a basic word, it is because the WAW (but sometimes a YOD or ALEPH) functions as a preposition. This pattern will show itself often on the WAW example chart (see following pages).

---

[3] Simon, Resnikoff, Motzkin, *The First Hebrew Primer, Third Edition,* Eks Publishing Co., Berkeley, CA, 2005

Strong's Concordance Numbering on Example Charts:

In the following chapters, example charts show the pictographical meanings of various Hebrew words, their Hebrew spellings and transliteration, and their *Strong's Concordance* number. The *Strong's* numbers can be used for those who wish to look up the example words for themselves in a *Strong's Concordance* to find additional information.

Strong's numbers shown **in bold** indicate **primitive root words**; words which Hebrew scholars have designated as ***primitive root words*** are the oldest and most basic Hebrew words from which other Hebrew words were later formed. These words appear in the earliest forms of Hebrew, which evolved over time.

Some words in *Strong's Concordance* have the notation "**uncl. der.**" This notation indicates that the word's origin is of "unclear determination." However, I believe the words originated due to their pictographical systemic letter meanings. I have tried to include this information on the example charts, whenever space permitted.

The example charts are redundant intentionally. This allows readers to check for letter meanings in the context of other words with similar letters.

Readers can order an interactive spreadsheet of this database in MS Excel format from the author's website

HebrewInLivingColor.com

* * *

Chapter 2

An Ox   -   Yoked Oxen or Hand-in-Hand

SEPARATED but UNITED (adj.), UNITY, SET APART (as in 2 yoked oxen), STAND APART, INDIVIDUAL, UNIQUE, AGAINST, LEADER, PRIMARY, STRENGTH, servant, provider, away, basic, fundamental, pull away, go out.

ALEPH's letter name means:
SEPARATE [independent] INDIVIDUALS (א) –
DIRECTED FLOW (ל) – FLOWING (ף).

The Modern Hebrew letter for ALEPH probably denotes a YOKE of oxen at a grist mill.   ALEPH can denote both UNITED (ASSOCIATED) or SEPARATE INDIVIDUAL... depending upon how an ox behaves when yoked.   The Aleph symbol (א) shows two YODs in the upper-right and lower-left corners with a slanted WAW between. The slanted line in the ALEPH separates the two YODs, like two oxen which are separate but yoked together.
Additionally, Yod (*YAD*) is a hand. The WAW indicates connection, and in Hebrew the WAW literally means *and*; therefore, one could make a strong argument that the letter Aleph symbolizes *hand-in-hand unity*.

The Hebrew word *ALEPH* or *ALUPH* means a *leader*. A good leader is one who unites the people… in contrast to those leaders who rule their subjects with an iron fist or those who divide the people as a result of their self-centered and narcissistic behaviors.

ALEPH

Action or Motion Indicated	Descriptive Form	Noun(s) Denoted	Prepositional Meanings
to Set Apart to Separate Individuals Yoked together, to Work Together	Separate but… United, Unique, Strong, Primary, Set apart	Leader, An individual Separate entities (with something in common to unite them) poss. labor ???	Associated with (yoked) Apart from Separate from,

ALEPH EXAMPLES:

Strong's Number	Hebrew Word	Transliteration	Word Definition	Pictographical Meanings
poss. from 441 (leader) or 504 (herd of oxen)	אֶלֶף	Aleph	1. UNITED INDIVIDUALS (yoked) 2. AGAINST 3. Separated, Individual, Set apart 4. AWAY (prep.) 5. an ox, a leader, strong	SEPARATE INDIVIDUALS (א) -GUIDED/ LEAD (ל) - FLOW [poss. work together?] (ף) Denotes the concept of INDIVIDUALS [in this case, 2 oxen] being YOKED TOGETHER for a common purpose.
225	אוֹת	ŌTH	a mark, a sign, אות is also the Hebrew translation of the Greek: ALPHA & OMEGA [see Revelation 1:8-18]	INDIVIDUAL (א) – OF (ו) – PURITY (ת)
Modern Hebrew	תְאוֹם	Tey-ŌM	symmetry see # 8420b below	CONNECTED (ת) - INDIVIDUATIONS (א) - OF (ו) - SHAPES/FORMS/IMAGES (מ)
5375	נָשָׂא נָסָה	Biblical: NaSA; Modern: nasha (נָשָׂא)	to take away, to bear carried	MOVE (נ) + SUBSTANCE (שׂ) - AWAY (א) = take away
2061	זְאֵב	Z'-eyV	(lone) wolf	TAKE (ז) - SEPARATE (א) - HOUSE (ב) or STRONG (ז) - INDIVIDUAL (א) - BODY (ב) or ARCING (ז) - Tail??? - BODY (ב)
Modern Hebrew	סְלָא	SeeLA	to weigh	BASKET (סל) + SEPARATE (א) = to WEIGH, as in the two separate baskets on each end of a balance scale. It may not be coincidence that SeYL and the English word SALE as the same phonetically.
251	אָח	AĤ (ACK)	1. brother, countryman 2. hearth	INDIVIDUAL (א) - CLOSE / [a part of the family] UNIT (ח) or INDIVIDUAL who is YOKED (א) - to the FAMILY UNIT [section] (ח)
259	אֶחָד	ECHaD	one, each, once	ONE/INDIVIDUAL (א) - PORTION/SEGMENT (ח) - CUT (ד)

Chapter 2 - ALEPH

Strong's Number	Hebrew Word	Trans-literation	Word Definition	Pictographical Meanings
Modern Hebrew	אָחָה	eeĤaH	to stitch together	SEPARATE (א) - SECTION/PARTS/PIECES (ת) + PULLED UP (ה), possibly because thread is pulled through and up to tighten stitches
Modern Hebrew	אָחוּז	AĤŪZ	percentage	SEPARATE (א) - SECTION/PARTS/POTIONS (ח) OF HARVEST (ז)
8382	תָּאַם	Tha-AM	Biblical Hebrew: double, to bear twins; Modern Hebrew: to join, to combine	JOIN(ed)/COMBINE(d)/UNITE(d) (ת) - INDIVIDUAL/SEPARATE (א) - PARTS/COMPONENTS (מ)
589	אֲנִי	A-NI	1st person pronoun I	SEPARATE INDIVIDUAL (א) - LIVING (נ) - PERSON or Creation (י)
738	אֲרִי	ARI	a lion	GREAT/HIGH/MIGHTY (י) ↔ INDIVIDUAL/LEADER (א) - ATTRIBUTES/CHARACTER/REPUTATION (ר)
7006	קִיא	QI	to vomit, that which is vomited up	ACROSS/COMPLETELY (ק) - CAUSE TO BE (י) - SEPARATED (א) [seems to indicate full projectile vomiting]
270	אָחַז	AĤaZ	to grasp, take hold	COMBINED [yoked concept] (א) - AROUND (ח) - FORCIBLY (ז) or GRASP (ח + א) - FORCIBLY (ז)
264	אָחוֹר	AĤŌR	buttocks	SEPARATE (א) - PARTS/SECTIONS (ח) - OF - REAR/BEHIND (ר)
8420b	תּוֹאָם	TŌ-AM	a twin	CONNECTION or ONENESS (ת) - OF (ו) - INDIVIDUALs (א) - IMAGES (מ) poss. meaning "identical"
7585	שְׁאֹל or שְׁאוֹל	SheŌL	underworld, place to where the dead descend	SUBSTANTIAL/EXPANSE (ש) - SEPARATE (א) – of (ו) - COMFORT (ל)
11	אֲבַדּוֹן	AVaD-DON (Abaddon)	(place of) destruction, ruin	SEPARATED [poss. DESOLATE] (א) - DWELLING PLACE (ב) - CUTTING OFF (דד) - OF (ו) - LIFE/LIVING (נ)

Unlocking the Ancient Hebrew Alphabet Code

Strong's Number	Hebrew Word	Trans-literation	Word Definition	Pictographical Meanings
518	אִם / אִים	EeM	if but also indicates: except, or, though	CONNECTION of INDIVIDUAL THINGS (א) - IS CAUSED TO BE (י) - SUBSTANCE/REALITY (מ)
8373	תָּאַב	TA-aB	to long for	MERGED [become one] (ת) - SEPARATE(d) (א) - PERSONS (ב) [to desire to become one]
8376	תָּאָה	TA-Ah	to mark out	MARK (ת) - AWAY/OUT (א) - AMPLIFIED [poss. MADE OBVIOUS] (ה) or INDIVIDUAL/SEPARATE (א) ↔ MARK(s) (ת) - INDICATED (ה)
7121	קָרָא	QaRA	to call, proclaim, read	FULLY DEVELOPED (ק) - INSIDE () - SEPARATING AWAY (א)
3808	לֹא	LO	NO, NOT, without	SPEAK/GUIDE (ל) – AWAY FROM (א) Note: Typically, ALEF is an A or AH sound, not O. Interestingly, LO also appears in the Bible spelled phonetically: לֹה or לוֹא Perhaps the spelling evolved because the pictographical meaning was lost and spelling LO with an ALEPH seemed wrong.
3809	לָא	LA (Aramaic & Arabic)	NO, NOT, without	see above Alt. phonetic spelling: לָה
3811	לָאָה	LA-AH	to be weary or impatient	NO (לֹא) - FURTHER/MORE (ה)
3813	לָאַט	LaAT	to cover	GUIDED FLOW (ל) - SEPARATED INDIVIDUAL [component parts] (א) - CONTAINER (ט)
5003	נָאַף	NaAPH	to commit adultery	MOVEMENT (נ) - INDIVIDUAL (א) - FALLEN (פ) or MOVEMENTs or ACTIONs of (נ) - a FALLEN (ף) ↔ INDIVIDUAL (א)
4998	נָאָה	NaAH	to be comely	LIVING (נ) - INDIVIDUAL (א) - ELEVATED [poss. BEAUTIFUL] (ה)
5006	נָאַץ	NaATS	to spurn, treat with contempt	LIVING (נ) - INDIVIDUAL (א) – CONTEMPT (ץ) or a DESPISED INDIVIDUAL

Chapter 2 - ALEPH

Strong's Number	Hebrew Word	Trans-literation	Word Definition	Pictographical Meanings
5012 or 5030	נָבָא or נָבִיא	NaBA or NABI	to prophesy, prophesy	LIVING TABERNACLE (נב) - SEPARATE INDIVIDUAL (א)
120	אָדָם	ADaM	man, mankind, ADAM [the first man]	YOKED INDIVIDUALS (א) - TWO GATHERED (ד) - BODY/CREATURE (מ) Note 1: The word ADAM denotes the concept of mankind as a creature (MEM) being composed to two basic separate parts combined into one… poss. Seen by the Hebrews as the Physical and Spiritual components. Note 2: MEM denotes a group of the same species of creatures… a body [herd, flock, congregation, assembly, community, etc.]
7582	שָׁאָה	SHaAH	to make a din, crash, rumble	VOICE/NOISE (שׁ) - SEPARATED AWAY (א) - MORE (ה) [intensity elevated]
7580	שָׁאַג	SHaAG	to roar, to roar mightily	VOICE/NOISE (שׁ) - SEPARATE AWAY (א) - TRAMPLEs/PELTS/POUNDS (ג) NOTE: In 7582 and 7583, SHIN denotes the sense of SIGHT, yet in 7580 it clearly indicates SOUND.
2117	זָזָא	ZaZA	descendent of Judah	INDIVIDUAL/SEPARATE/UNIQUE (א) ↔ STRENGTHS (ז)
517	אֵם or אִמָּא	eM or eeM-MA	mother in Hebrew	The Hebrew term for mother comes from the word for a glue-like substance that rises to the surface when hides are boiled. This substance was used for gluing things together.
331	אָטַם	ATaM	to close, shut, shut up	SEPARATED/INDIVIDUAL (א) - CONTAINED (ט) - PLACE/OBJECT (מ)
332	אָטַר	ATAR	to shut up, close, bind	SEPARATED INDIVIDUAL (א) - CONTAINED (ט) - INSIDE (ר)
727	אֲרוֹן	ARŌN	ARK (of the Covenant)	UNIQUE (set apart) (א) – CHARACTERISTIC [ATTRIBUTE INSIDE] (ר) - OF (ו) – LIFE or MOVEMENT (נ) or UNIQUE – CONTENTS – OF – LIFE (mementos)
1	אָב אַב	AB 1 Hebrew 2. Aramaic	father	LEADER of (א) - HOUSEHOLD (ב)

ALEF - Biblical Food for Thought
אָב AB - Father

Household or Family (ב) ↔ Leader (א)

To the ancient Semitic peoples, the father was seen as the head of the house, the leader of the family. In fact, many of the father's family duties were like those of a rabbi. Upon the father's shoulders rested the duty of explaining the nuances of the annual Passover Seder. For that first Passover in Egypt, the father was responsible for slaughtering the lamb and putting the blood on the household's door mantel; failure to do so would have meant the death of first-born males within the homes.

In the last century, the family unit has seen the degeneration of the father's role within the home. Many fathers have abdicated their family responsibilities as leaders, especially in the raising and training up of their sons who desperately need a solid male role model in order to get their bearings in life as young men.

When the household's father does not provide a good role model, it becomes difficult for the children to grow up and develop a proper concept of their Heavenly Father. Children from homes where the father is either physically or emotionally absent will have a much more difficult time perceiving God as actively being involved in the lives of His people. In other words, absent fathers produce children who perceive God as distant and absent from their lives (and the lives of others).

God describes Himself to us as our father. He cares for us, loves us, and provides for our every need (needs are not to be confused here with *capricious desire*s). As the head of every home, He takes responsibility for providing for all of our needs.

I wish I could tell you that I possess such an incredibly strong faith that I have never worried about finances. In truth, I do worry… sometimes a lot! But here is the notable common factor relating to my past worries – I always had all that I *needed* whether I worried or not.

God desires to fulfill His role in your life. Allow Him to be your Heavenly Father, a father who will both provide for you and train you up; it's often a package deal. Only God can maximize each individual's full potential. We all need both provision and discipline to become mature and healthy adults.

* * *

Chapter 3
Bet (also Beit or Beith)

A Nomad's Tent   -   Tabernacle

The Phoenicians wrote the letter Beit with a pictograph of a Bedouin TENT. The Post-Babylonian exile letter form is a TABERNACLE, representing a BODY (used when indicating a "body" that has a soul/spirit within) or HOUSE (used primarily when denoting a temporal structure), HOUSEHOLD, IN, INTO, HOLLOW, EMPTY or INVISIBLE, COME INTO.

Note: VEIT at end of word can denote the front of body or torso/chest

The post-Babylonian symbol denotes a TABERNACLE structure [sukah]; this must be a three-sided structure by definition.

BEIT's letter name means:

BODY/HOUSE (ב) – CAUSED to BECOME (י) - PURE (ת)

BEIT / BEITH   [Sometimes pronounced BEIS by certain Hebrew speakers.]

Action or Motion Indicated	Descriptive Form	Noun(s) Denoted	Prepositional Meanings
to Dwell Together in Harmony	United, Together, Inside, Harmonious	Body, Person, Home, House Congregation Tabernacle Dwelling place Unity, Family	In, Into, Within Against (as used in Zechariah 2:8 before בבות)

BET (BEITH) EXAMPLES:

Strong's Number	Hebrew Word	Trans-literation	Word Definition	Pictographical Meanings
1003	בֵּית	BEIT Beith	TABERNACLE [house or person's body], HOUSE, PERSON, CONGREGATION UNITY, FIELD, UNIFIED GROUP, FAMILY	BEIT denotes a HOME, a PERSON or FAMILY UNIT but also a CONGREGATION or GROUP of same-species living creatures (flock, herd, etc.) a FIELD [of agricultural crops]. NUN + BEITH in some instances represents MOVED the BODY [without a body] and could poss. indicate at times HOLLOW, EMPTY, INVISIBLE, or TRANSPARENT. At other times the combination suggests a rendering of LIVING TABERNACLE. Beit's name is lit. BODY (ב) - BECOMES ONE (ת)
1354 and 1458	גַּב גֵּו	GaV	a person's back	OPPOSING [COUNTERPART] (ג) - [to the front of the] BODY (ב) or NOT the CHEST/TORSO
1366	גְּבוּל	G'VūL	border boundary	GaV (גב) = a person's BACK. G'vūl = BACK (furthest point) OF (ו) UNIFED & CENTRALIZED GROUP (ל) e.g. the English language idiom: "the back 40"
7094	קָצַב	Qa-TZaV	1. to cut off 2. to stipulate, to determine	1. NECK/COMPLETELY (ק) - CHOPPED/CUT (צ) - [from] BODY (ב) or ACROSS (ק) - CUT (צ) - BODY (ב) or possibly 2. [functioning] AROUND (ק) - FIXED [in place] (צ) - BODY/AGREEMENT [a contract?] (ב)
Modern Hebrew	קַצָּב	Qa-TZaV	to butcher	COMPLETELY/AROUND/ACROSS (ק) - CHOP (צ) - BODY (ב)
2895	טוֹב	TŌV	good, to be pleasing	FULLNESS [fully contained] (ט) - OF (ו) - BODY (ב)

Chapter 3 – BEIT

Strong's Number	Hebrew Word	Trans-literation	Word Definition	Pictographical Meanings
966	בָּזַר	BaZaR	to scatter, distribute	BODY (ב) - ARC (ז) - AROUND [bent] (ר)
2270 see also 2266	חָבֵר	ĤaVeR	friend, associate, united	PART/SECTOR [of] (ח) - HOUSE/BODY/ COMMUNITY (ב) - RECOGNIZABLE (ר)
5445	סָבַל	SaVaL	to bear a heavy load, sustain	GATHER/UNIFY (ס) - BODY [BEIT seems to indicate people rather than an inanimate object] (ב) - LEAD/TAKE/SHEPHERD (ל) [Similar to the concept stated in Gal. 6:2 - "Bear one another's burdens…"]
7623	שָׁבַח	SHaVaĤ	Biblical: To soothe, laud, praise Mod. –To grow in value, to improve	EXPAND (שׁ) - PERSON/HOUSE (ב) - ALL AROUND (ח) [e.g. "magnify the Lord" or to enlarge the house]
7725	שָׁב Or שׁוּב	Mod. SHaV or Bib. SHŪV	return, again, bring back,	CONSUMING/DESTRUCTION (שׁ) - OF (ו) - HOUSE (ב) or CHANGE / RETURN (שׁ) - OF (ו) – a PERSON (ב)
Modern Hebrew	שָׁב	SaV	old man	CHANGED/CONSUMED (שׁ) - BODY (ב) or poss. SHARP (שׁ) [wise] PERSON (ב)
7673	שָׁבַת	SHaBaT	Sabbath	PROVISION (שׁ) - for the HOUSEHOLD/FAMILY (ב) - MARKED/OBSERVED (ת)
974	בָּחַן	BaĤaN	to test, examine, prove	BODY (ב) - ALL AROUND (ח) – MOVE (נ)
975	בַּחוּן	BaĤŌN	a tower	HOUSE (ב) - WALLED PLACE (ח) - of (ו) - LIVING (נ)
5380	נָשַׁב	nashav	to blow	MOTION (נ) – EXPANDING / PUFFING UP (שׁ) - BODY (ב)
6025	עֵנָב	ENaV	a grape	(life) FORCE (ע) - LIVING/GROWING (נ) – BODY (ב) [see below: 5107 NŪV]

Unlocking the Ancient Pictorial Code of the Hebrew Alphabet

Strong's Number	Hebrew Word	Trans-literation	Word Definition	Pictographical Meanings
4186	מוֹשָׁב or מֹשָׁב	MoSHaV	a multitude of dwelling places, a communal settlement combining private ownership & communal living	a PLACE OF (מוֹ) - an ABUNDANCE (שׁ) of HOUSES/FAMILIES (ב)
1086	בָּלָה	BaLaH	to become old, to wear out, worn out	PERSON (ב) - USED (ל) - UP (ה)
1104	בָּלַע	BaLA	to swallow down, swallow up, engulf	BODY/PERSON (ב) + throat (לַע) [throat is 930 from 3886 לוּעַ LUA... SWALLOW: "going forth of force"]
11	אֲבַדּוֹן	AVaD-DON (Abaddon)	(place of) destruction, ruin	SEPARATED [poss. DESOLATE] (א) - DWELLING PLACE (ב) - CUTTING OFF (דּ) - OF (וֹ) - LIFE/LIVING (ן)
8373	תָּאַב	TA-aB	to long for	MERGED [become one] (ת) - SEPARATED (א) - PERSONS (ב) [to desire to become one]
3820	לֵב	LeV	heart, mind, will, inner man	THAT WHICH GUIDES (ל) - the BODY (ב)
5014	נָבַב	NaBaB	to hollow out, hollow, idiot	HOLLOW/EMPTY (נב) - BODY (ב) or MOVEment (נ) - WITHIN (ב) - BODY (ב)
5024	נָבַח	NaBaĤ	to bark	HOLLOW/EMPTY (נב) -THROAT (ח) or MOVEment (נ) - WITHIN (ב) - THROAT (ח)
5027	נָבַט	NaBaT	to look	RE-MOVE (נ) - BODY (ב) - CONNECTion (ט) or an INVISIBLE CONNECTION "REMOVED BODY" (נ + ב) denotes hollow, empty, bodiless or invisible [without corporeal form]
5034a	נָבֵל	NaBaL	to be senseless or foolish	HOLLOW/EMPTY (נב) - TONGUE (ל)
1197a	בָּעַר	BaAR	to burn, consume, remove, purge	EMPTY/HOLLOWing/CLEARING OUT (ב) - CONDITION (ע) - INSIDE (ר) or INVISIBLE (ב) - FORCE (ע) - INSIDE (ר)

Chapter 3 – BEIT

Strong's Number	Hebrew Word	Transliteration	Word Definition	Pictographical Meanings
5107	נוּב	NŪV or NŪB	to bear fruit	GROWTH [living] (נ) - OF (ו) - BODY (ב) [BEIT denotes a living body as opposed to an inanimate body which would be denoted by a MEM]
7660	שָׁבַץ	SHaVaTS	to weave in a checkered pattern	ABUNDANT or SYMMETRICAL (שׁ) - [geometric] BODYs (ב) – FIXED POSITIONs (ץ)
7641	שִׁבֹּלֶת	SHiBoLeTH	ears of grain	PUFFED UP SUBSTANCE (שׁ) - BODY/FIELD (ב) - GUIDED FLOW (ל) - BECOME ONE (ת) lit. field of flowing grain heads
2061	זְאֵב	Z'eyV	(lone) wolf	TAKE - SEPARATE - HOUSE or TAKE - HOUSE - APART (Separate)
2071	זָבוּד	Za-VŪD	Bestowed	TAKE(ז) - an OBJECT (ב) - EXTEND (ד) - OVER (ו)
892	בָּבָה	BaBaH	the apple (of the eye)	PEOPLE/FAMILIES (בב) – ELEVATED/FAVORED (ה)
7239	רִבּוֹ or רִבּוֹא	RiBBŌ from 7231 below	ten thousand, myriad	[set] OVER or IN EXCESS OF (ר) - BODY MULTITUDE (ב) - OF (ו) - 1000 INDIVIDUALS (א) Note: Aleph means 1000 in Arabic
7231	רָבַב	RaBaB	to be or become many or much prim root	[set] OVER or IN EXCESS OF (ר) - THOUSANDS or a MULTITUDES (בב)
7227	רַב	RaB	many, much, great, captain, chief	[set] OVER or IN EXCESS OF (ר) - a 1000 or a MULTITUDE (ב)

BEIT - Biblical Food for Thought

NaB or NaV as the root of NaVi (נָבִיא)

Meaning: A prophet or prophets
Moving/Living (נ) – Body/Tabernacle (ב)
The Yod suffix indicates a person (e.g. Israel + Yod = Israeli, a citizen of Israel)

The people in and around Israel during Biblical times saw the prophets as being able to give a *living* word… a message which came directly from God. The letter BEIT is literally a tabernacle, a 3-sided tent or house. From the time of Moses until the destruction of the Second Temple in 70 A.D., the presence of God filled the Holy of Holies. Only once a year could the high priest enter into the Holy of Holies and stand in the presence of God in order to atone for the sins of Israel.

The tabernacle tent was used from the time of Moses until Solomon built the first permanent temple. All along, God wanted the temporary structure of the tabernacle tent to represent His preferred dwelling place – within the temporal physical bodies of men and women who were dedicated to Him. The building of a permanent temple was Solomon's idea, not God's.

Prophets were God's first, and perhaps in some ways preferred, portable dwelling places among the nation of Israel. God's Spirit could direct the prophet to travel all around Israel and even into neighboring countries, and then God would stir the prophet (or prophetess) to speak on His behalf. Thus a *living tabernacle* or *moving tabernacle* (as the pictorial word stem NaV נָב within the Hebrew word for a prophet, NaVi נָבִיא suggests) truly does represent what God had in mind when He called, ordained, and used His prophets.

* * *

Chapter 4
Gimmel

⌐L   ג

(A Leg   -   Opposition)

Gimmel represents OPPOSITION or the OPPOSITE OF (ANTI-).
The Phoenicians used a leg because when we walk, our legs work in *opposition* to one another. When a person is walking and the right leg is forward, the left leg is back. The opposing legs constantly exchange places, maintaining the opposite position of one another.

The post-Babylonian letter for Gimmel appears to be a donkey sitting back on his haunches, refusing to move – opposing the will of his owner. As the owner of a stubborn 130 pound dog that dislikes taking baths; I have seen this body posture many times before.

Gimmel's letter name means
Opposing (ג) – Part(s) (מ) – Wave Motion or Guided Flow (ל)
Gimmel's letter name probably denotes
the back and forth motion of a person's LEG(s) when walking.

The letter Gimmel is used in Hebrew and Aramaic words to denote the negative of the word's pictorial meaning.
For example, in English one might say, *dys*functional is the opposite of functional or that *un*clear is the opposite of clear.
In Hebrew the Gimmel represents the many negative English prefixes such as *NON-*, *UN-*, and *DYS-* (to name a few), as well as words such as *NOT* and *NO*.

Deciphering the pictorial meaning of Gimmel within Hebrew words presents a unique and challenging problem. Somewhere along the evolution of the Hebrew Alphabet, perhaps around the time of the Babylonian captivity, a letter similar to Gimmel (the letter was named GHAYIN) was dropped from the Hebrew Alphabet.

Scholars today know Ghayin existed because it was not dropped from the Arabic Alphabet. The Septuagint Bible, a Greek version of the Bible translated and written by a council of Jewish scholars during the Babylonian exile, also shows evidence that Ghayin existed and was known to these scholars. As a result, some versions of the Bible show identical names beginning with various sounds, specifically: G, A or J. This is because Ghayin's presence in the spelling of Hebrew words was replaced by two various letters, Ayin and Gimmel. The proof that Gimmel was replaced by other Hebrew letters is outside the scope of this book, but a more detailed explanation can be found on the Internet at the web site of author Jeff Benner.[4]

The missing letter Ghayin appears to have denoted *Gathered Together for Good/Enjoyable Purposes*. While Ghayin's phonetic sound may have been similar to Gimmel, Ghayin's pictorial meaning (a HARMONIOUS GATHERING) sharply contrasts with Gimmel's meaning (OPPOSITION or AGAINST). In addition, throw in Ayin's meanings where Ghayin once was, and it becomes quite easy to stumble when trying to decipher the ancient Hebrew letter pictorial code. So, when translating words containing Gimmel (or Ayin), one needs to constantly ask the question, "Was Gimmel the original letter used in this word?"

Fortunately, for the vast majority of the words which *Strong's Concordance* shows as *root words*, the answer to that question is "Yes, the pictorial meaning of Gimmel more often than not is *Opposition*." Gimmel usually denotes the negative of the remaining pictorial meanings.

GIMMEL

Action or Motion Indicated	Descriptive Form	Noun(s) Denoted	Prepositional Meanings
To Oppose	Denotes the NEGATIVE, Non-, Un, No, Not	Opposition Disrespect	- NA -

---

[4] http://www.ancient-hebrew.org/4_missing.html

Chapter 4 – GIMMEL

Gimmel Examples: ‎ג ‎ﺟ ‎𐤂

Strong's Number	Hebrew Word	Trans-literation	Word Definition	Pictographical Meanings
word not in Tenach	גָּמֶל	Gimmel	1. a foot 2. to trample	GIMMEL's name means: OPPOSING (ג) - BODY PARTS (מם) - GUIDED FLOW (ל) THE FEET AND LEGS work in opposition to one another. Gimmel (ג) denotes a negative: NO, NON-, UN- GIMMEL (no) + MEM (thing) = nothing IMPORTANT NOTE: GIMMEL, as written since the Babylonian exile, may NOT be originally the correct letter. An extra letter existed in early Hebrew, but was absorbed by GIMMEL and AYIN. The letter's name was GHAYIN. GHayin was translated sometimes as A and sometimes as G in the Septuagint. GHAYIN still exists today in Palestinian Arabic, and denotes *GATHER TOGETHER for Positive Purposes*.
1354 and 1458	גַּב or גֵּו	GaV	a person's back	OPPOSING [COUNTERPART] (ג) - [front of the] BODY (ב) or NOT the CHEST/TORSO
1366	גְּבוּל	G'VūL	border/boundary	GaV (גב)= a person's BACK. G'vūl = BACK (furthest point) OF (ו) UNIFED & CENTRALIZED GROUP (ל) As in the English language idiom: "the back 40"
4197	מֶזֶג	Mezeg	wine	LIQUID or WINE (מ) - NOT (ג) - STRONG (ז) Note: For easier storage, wine was traditionally condensed after brewing and then diluted with water later when it was to be consumed. MEZEG may denote freshly-made wine in a pre-condensed state.
2085	זָג	ZaG	grape skins	*TAKE (ז) - NOT (ג) *[Grape skins are often discarded after pressing grapes when making wine]
1657	גֹּשֶׁן	Goshen	The land of Goshen in Egypt	GATHER for a POSITIVE PURPOSE (גɁ) - PROVISIONs/SUBSTANCE/BREAD (ש) - LIFE (ן) (גɁ) denotes that Ghayin (the letter which disappeared from the Hebrew Alphabet c. 500 BCE) was probably replaced with GIMMEL in this word.
1660	גַּת GaTh (Biblical) or גֵּת GeTH (modern)		an olive or wine PRESS	UN (ג) + COMBINE (ת) lit. OPPOSING - BEING ONE

- 23 -

Strong's Number	Hebrew Word	Transliteration	Word Definition	Pictographical Meanings
Modern Hebrew from 8409	תִּגֵּר	TheeG-GeR	to haggle, to bargain	UNITY (ת) - RESISTED (ג) - INSIDE (ר) or poss. UNITY (ת) - NOT (ג) - APPARENT (ר)
see 8409 and 1624 below	תִּגֵּר (modern) תִּגְרָה	ThiG-GaR (modern) ThiG-RaH (Biblical)	1. complaint (Modern) 2. contention, strife, hostility, opposition (Bible)	NOT MADE ONE (תג) - APPARENT (ר) [GIMMEL is like the English word NON or NOT] see below and see above`
8409	תִּגְרָה	TheeG-RaH	contention, strife, hostility	NON-UNITY (תג) - MORE (ה) – APPARENT (ר) Note: The Hebrew word for *MORE* (*Mey-OD*) always follows the word it amplifies.
1624	גָּרָה	GaRaH see GUR below	stir up strife, provoke	RESISTs (ג) - MORE/MUCH (ה) - ATTRIBUTE (ר) or NON - (ג) - ELEVATED/HIGH (ה) ↔ CHARACTER (ר) [lit. a person of low character… similar to the English term "a low life"] NOTE: Hebrew adjectives usually follow the word they amplify.
1629a	גָּרַז	GaRaZ	to cut off	lit. NO (ג) - CHARACTER (ר) - STRENGTH (ז) or NOT (ג)- STRONG (ז) –INSIDE / INTERNALLY (ר) [no intestinal fortitude]
5462	סָגַר	Sa-GaR	to close	CLOSED UP (ס) - NOT (ג) - OPEN (ר)
2328	חוּג	ĤUG	to draw around, to make a circle	[SPIRAL ROTATION] TURNING (ח) - OF/UNDER (ו) - FOOT (ג) [picture a person drawing an arc in the dirt using one foot while standing on the other]
6026	עָנֹג	ANoG	soft, delicate, dainty	LIFE FORCE of (ענ) – WEAK/DAINTY/MINIMAL/SMALL ? (ג)
2026	הָרַג	HaRaG	killed, slay	RAISED UP/GREAT [amplified] (ה) - CUT (ר) - AGAINST (ג)
1481a	גּוּר	GUR	to sojourn, strangers, aliens	NOT (ג) - OF/ON (ו) - the INSIDE (ר) lit. not an insider

Chapter 4 – GIMMEL

Strong's Number	Hebrew Word	Trans-literation	Word Definition	Pictographical Meanings
1481b	גּוּר	GUR	to stir up strife, quarrel	NOT (ג) - OF/ON (ו) - the INSIDE (ר) lit. not an insider or OPPOSITION (ג) – OF / ON (ו) – the INSIDE (ר)
1471	גּוֹי	GOY pl. GOYIM	a gentile, a non-Jew gentile nation	TRAMPLE (ג) - UPON (ו) - GOD's Divine HAND/CREATION (י)
1653	גֶּשֶׁם	GeSHeM	torrential rain, downpour	TRAMPLE (ג) - SUBSTANCE (שׁ) - BODY [esp. Body of Water] (ם) prob. Lit. a BODY of WATER that SUBSTANTIALLY TRAMPLES or PELTS the earth... this is definitely a HEAVY RAIN.
7580	שָׁאַג	SHaAG	to roar, to roar mightily	VOICE/NOISE (שׁ) - SEPARATE AWAY (א) – TRAMPLEs / PELTS / POUNDS (ג)
1406	גָּג	GahG or GoG	roof, a top	TRAMPLING (גג) **Doubling a Hebrew letter adds -ING** to the verbal form of its pictographic meaning. Also, this word denotes the area known today as Russia (esp. the area near Moscow)
1408	גָּד	GaD	fortune, good fortune	NO (ג) - LACK (ד)
1642	גְּרָר	GeRaR	A city in Gaza which may have influenced Esau's character	NOT (ג) – INSIDERS / WITHIN (ר ר) GERAR denotes people not like the people of Israel. GER denotes a foreigner... so the town's name could lit. be translated FOREIGNERS [double RESH makes FOREIGNER plural]
2282	חַג	ĤaG	a festival gathering, feast	ALL AROUND (ח) - WALK? [foot] (ג) Poss. Foot Circling Around denotes dance
6313	פּוּג	PŪG	to grow numb, weariness	BLOOM (פ) - of (ו) - RESISTANCE (ג)
5046	נָגַד	NaGaD	To confess, confront, oppose	TAKE up or MOVE to (נ) – OPPOSITE (ג) – SIDE (ד)
6293	פָּגַע	PaGA	1. to meet, encounter, reach 2. attacked, kill and cut down	1. BLOOM [events fully developed] (פ) - GATHER for PLEASURE (GHAYIN) - [state of being: "it happened"] (ע) 2. BLOOM [events fully developed] (פ) - OPPOSITION/AGAINST (GIMMEL) - FORCE (ע)

Strong's Number	Hebrew Word	Trans-literation	Word Definition	Pictographical Meanings
1588	גַּן	GaN	Garden	NOT (ג) - MOVE [moved or moving] (נ) Poss. denotes a stationary place where food may be gathered.
1598	גָּנַן	GaNaN	to surround, to defend	NOT (ג) - MOVING (doubled נ turns MOVE into MOV**ING**)

GIMMEL - Biblical Food for Thought

גוֹי **Goy** (Plural: Goyim גוֹים)

Meaning: A nation other than Israel or a Gentile
Trample (ג) – Upon (ו) – the Divine Hand or Creation of God (י)

Yod has a wide variety of meanings. Most importantly, YOD denotes Creation via the HAND of God (see Ch. 11 for details). Israel and the Hebrew people were seen as God's special creation. To trample upon *YOD* indicates trampling upon that which God has created and cares for greatly... specifically, His chosen people and the nation of Israel.

Jerusalem and Mount Zion were the heart of Israel and the central objects of God's heart's desire. In May of 1948, Israel became a nation again[5], after nearly 2000 years of non-existence. In June of 1967, during the Six Day War, the Old City of Jerusalem was reclaimed by Israeli forces and once again put under the sovereign control of the nation of Israel and the Jewish people. Mount Zion was no longer trampled under the feet of the Gentiles; it was once again a possession of the Jewish people. For 2000 years, Jews have waited for God to restore the nation of Israel. Out of all of the many generations passed, *we* are the generation blessed to see this prophetic miracle being fulfilled!

The ancient pictorial representation for the term GOY means to *trample underfoot the handiwork of God*. Whether one is born a Jew or whether one embraces the handiwork of God as a believing Gentile, we must all be careful to consider our actions on a daily basis, lest we too trample upon the hand of God as He works in our personal lives and in the world around us.

* * *

---

[5] Israel became a nation again in just one day, a miraculous event prophetically foretold in Isaiah 66:8

Chapter 5
Daleth

Two Gathered   -   Edge or Extension

Daleth represents TWO GATHERED…or TOGETHER: The Phoenicians used a horizontal line with either an ellipse or a box below it to represent the horizon and the setting or rising sun. The setting and rising of the sun was seen by the ancients as the daily death and resurrection of the sun. At sunset, the earth and sun were gathered together… the TWO GATHERED.

The post-Babylonian letter for Daleth shows an EDGE or an EXTENSION, something like an awning that might be attached to the front of a Bedouin tent's entrance.

Daleth's letter name means -
Two Gathered at the Edge (horizon) (ד) – Guided Flow (ל) – Become One (ת)

Daleth's original pictograph denoted the horizon, the place where the earth and the sun gathered together. Later, as many Hebrew word pictures indicate, Daleth also began to represent the earth, including the surface of the soil where crops were planted. Post-Babylonian words learn more toward using Daleth to indicate an EDGE or a CORNER, as well as denoting tools and weapons which had a sharp edge, such as an axe or knife.

Daleth

Action or Motion Indicated	Descriptive Form	Noun(s) Denoted	Prepositional Meanings
1. The joining of two objects together 2. To Stand 3. To Cut with a sharp edge, incl. to "cut off" from life or to destroy	1. Two joined together 2. Decrease 3. A 90° angle 4. Extended	1. Togetherness of Two 2. Horizon 3. Surface of the soil. 4. A defined cornered area, such as a door. 5. Edginess (hunger) 6. An advantage or competitive edge. 7. Garment's Edge – a hem	- NA -

Daleth Examples:

Strong's Number	Hebrew Word	Trans-literation	Word Definition	Pictographical Meanings
1817	דֶּלֶת	DaLeTh	1. to extend 2. a defined edge/corner (lit. a doorway) 3. to stand (extend one's body) 4. EDGE as in hunger pangs, denoting LACK or DISCOMFORT 5. to CUT [sharp edge]	GATHER TOGETHER (ד) – at a CENTRAL POINT or FLOWING (ל) – to BECOME ONE (ת) Originally, DALETH probably indicated the GROUND, or EARTH's EDGE [HORIZON] where the SUN and EARTH [the TWO] gathered together at sunset. NOTE: In geometry, where 2 faces (flat planes) join together, an EDGE is formed. This edge can be sharp or not, depending upon the angle of joining. For this reason, DALETH denotes: a CORNER, JOINED TOGETHER (two gathered), or a SHARP CUTTING EDGE as well as an EXTENSION or EXTENDED JOINED PIECE. The EDGE meaning of DALETH (in Hebrew) works in the same way English speakers use the terms EDGY and EDGINESS to denote hunger, angst, discomfort and an advantage.

Chapter 5 – DALETH

Strong's Number	Hebrew Word	Trans-literation	Word Definition	Pictographical Meanings
1717	דַּד	DaD	breast, teat, nipple, bosom	TWO GATHERING (דד) [poss. mother and child for nursing]
2086	זֵד	ZeD	insolent, arrogant	STRONG (ז) - EDGE (ד) [prob. *abrasive*]
1765	דָּחַף	DaĤaPH	to drive, hasten [to PUSH in Mod. Hebrew]	EDGE (ד) - AGAINST (ח) - FLOW DOWN/FALL/PUSH (ף)
1824 from 1820	דְּמִי	Da-Mee	rest, quiet, silence	GATHERED (ד) - GREAT (י) ↔ STILLNESS/QUIET/REST (מ)
4058	מָדַד	MaDaD	to measure, measured, stretched	PLACE of (מ) - GATHERING (דד)
from 5539	סָלֵד	SeeLeyD	to praise, to bounce back, to rebound	COMPLETE-ly (ס) - EXTENDED (ד) ↔ LEG (ל) (Note re Hebrew syntax: an adjective comes after the noun which it modifies)
Word not in the Tenach	מֻקְדָּם	MooQ-DahM	early	a THING (מ) - SWELLs/ WIDENS /DEVELOPS (ק) - but LACKING (ד) - SUBSTANCE (ם) [appearing on the outside to be fully develop but not developing properly inside, like fruit becoming large but remaining pithy] NOTE: The DALET (ד) is dotted [doubled] to indicate LACK-ING
5975	עָמַד	AMaD	to stand, to take one's stand,	TAKE (ע) - PLACE (מ) - STAND (ד) [to take a firm stand in one place]
11	אֲבַדּוֹן	AVaD-DON (Abaddon)	(place of) destruction, ruin	SEPARATED [poss. DESOLATE] (א) - DWELLING PLACE (ב) - CUTTING OFF (דד) - OF (ו) - LIFE/LIVING (ן) Note: DOUBLE DALET indicates *CUTTING*
Modern Hebrew Only	אָחוֹד	AĤŌD	a workers' union	SEPARATE (א) - SECTIONS/UNITS (ח) OF a CUT [division] (ד)

Strong's Number	Hebrew Word	Transliteration	Word Definition	Pictographical Meanings
1921	הָדַר	HaDaR	to honor, to adorn	RAISE UP/HONOR (ה) - EXTEND (ד) - ATTRIBUTED CHARACTERISTICS (ר) or REPUTATION (ר) - EXTENDED (ד) - UPWARD (ה)
1922	הֲדַר	HaDaR	to glorify [God]	RAISE UP/HONOR (ה) - EXTEND (ד) - ATTRIBUTED CHARACTERISTICS (ר) or REPUTATION (ר) - EXTENDED (ד) - UPWARD (ה)
259	אֶחָד	ECHaD	one, each, once	ONE/INDIVIDUAL (א) - PORTION/SEGMENT (ח) – CUT or SLICED (ד)
6805	צָעַד	TSAD	to march, to step	KNEE (ד) ↔ BEING (ע) ↔ at a FIXED PACE (צ)
6718	צַיִד	TSaYiD	hunter, hunter's game, provisions	FIXED PACE (צ) - UPON/OVER (י) - the EDGE (ד) [stalking prey]
5110	נוּד	NŪD	1. to move to and fro, to wander 2. to show grief	def. 1: LIVING / MOVING (נ) – AT or ON (ו) - the EDGE (ד) def. 2: poss. REMEMBERANCE (נ) – On (ו) - the EDGE (ד) [grief]
5750	עוֹד	'ŌD	still, yet, more, again	PRESENCE (ע) - OF (ו) - TWO JOINED (ד) [e.g. on the other hand, in addition] or PREVENTING (עו) – LACK (ד) [lacking nothing]
5736	עָדַף	ADaPH	left over, excess prob. OVERFLOW	SEPARATE/AWAY FROM/BEYOND (ע) - the EDGE (ד) - FLOW (פ)
1818	דָם	DahM	Blood	TWO GATHERED (ד) - liquid BODY (מ) [the 2 parts poss. Being LIFE + BLOOD or from the fact that blood will separate into PLASMA [water] and red SOLIDS [blood].

Chapter 5 – DALETH

Strong's Number	Hebrew Word	Transliteration	Word Definition	Pictographical Meanings
1826a	דָּמַם	DaMaM	to be or grow dumb, silenced	GATHERED TOGETHER (ד) – WORDS (מם) Poss. *at a loss for words*. Note: Notice how 1826a and 1826b seem to be completely opposite meanings. GATHERED TOGETHER - WORDS can be taken two opposite ways.
1826b	דָּמַם	DaMaM	to wail	GATHERED TOGETHER (ד) – WORDS (מם) Note: Notice how 1826 and 1826b seem to be completely opposite meanings, yet GATHERED TOGETHER words can be taken two opposite ways.
1830	דָּמַע	DaMA	to weep bitterly	GATHERED TOGETHER (ד) - WORD/SOUND (מ) - FORCEful (ע)
1847	דַּעַת	DaATH	Knowledge	TWO GATHERED (ד) [man and knowledge] - AWAREness (ע) - BECOME ONE (ת)
3205 3206	יָלַד יֶלֶד	1. YaLaD 2. YeLeD	1. to bear, to bring forth, gave birth 2. child, boy	CAUSE TO BE (י) – DIRECTED FLOW [purpose] (ל) – TWO GATHERED or AT THE HEM (ד)
8435 "fr.3205"	תּוֹלְד-וֹת	TOLeD-OT	Generations	TOLAD: BECOME ONE (ת) – GUIDED FLOW or PRODUCE RESULTS (ל) - OF (ו) - TWO GATHERED (ד)
1408	גַּד	GaD	fortune, good fortune	NO (ג) - LACK (ד) or No Edge [lit. no edge of hunger]
2616a	חָסַד	ĤaSaD	to be good, kind, to show yourself kind	ALL AROUND (ח) - COMPLETELY (ס) - two GATHERED/JOINED (ד)
2616b	חָסַד	ĤaSaD	to be reproached, to be ashamed	ALL AROUND (ח) - COMPLETE (ס) - EDGE [lack] (ד)
4058	מָדַד	MaDaD	to measure, measured, stretched	PLACE of (מ) – GATHERING or EDGES (דד) poss. Measure (מ) – EDGES or SIDES (דד)

Unlocking the Ancient Pictorial Code of the Hebrew Alphabet

Strong's Number	Hebrew Word	Trans-literation	Word Definition	Pictographical Meanings
2071	זָבוּד	Za-VŪD	Bestowed	TAKE(ז) - an OBJECT (ב) - EXTEND (ד) - OVER (ו)
1730	דּוֹד	DŌD	beloved, love, uncle	TWO GATHERED (דד) AGAIN (ו) (WAW between 2 identical letters indicates *again*)
6342	פָּחַד	PaĤaD	to dread, to be in awe, afraid	BLOSSOMing OUT (פ) - ALL AROUND (ח) - EDGE [fear or edginess] (ד)
5749a	עוּד	ŪD	to return, to repeat, go about, do again	FORCE (ע) - OF (ו) - TWO GATHERED (ד)
5749b	עוּד	ŪD	to bear witness, admonish, warn	FORCE (ע) - OF (ו) – TWO GATHERED (ד)
5046	נָגַד	NaGaD	to confess, confront, oppose	TAKE up or MOVE to (נ) – OPPOSITE (ג) – SIDE (ד)
3045	יָדַע	YaDa	to know To experience	CAUSE TO BE (י) - TWO GATHERED (ד) – FORCE of AWARENESS (ע)
3034	יָדָה	YaDaH	to praise, to confess, to cast	HAND (YaD יד) – RAISED UP (ה)
3039	יָדִיד	YaDÎD	Beloved	Grasp (י) – Hem (ד) - Grasp (י) – Hem (ד)
3054	יָהַד	YaHaD	to become a Jew	GRASPING HAND (י) – RAISED (ה) – to the HEM (ד)
- NA -	Arabic	ASWaD	to become BLACK	COMPLETEness (ס) – OF (ו) – (sun and horizon gathered together... TWO GATHERED) SUN SETTING (ד) [sky BECOMES BLACK]
5475	סוֹד	SOD	Counsel, Council, Gathering	COMPLETEness (ס) – OF (ו) - TWO GATHERED (ד)

Daleth - Biblical Food for Thought
YA-**DA** יָדַע
Meaning: To know as a result of experience
CAUSE TO BE (י) - TWO GATHERED (ד) – FORCE of AWARENESS (ע)

As mentioned in the forward of this book, the Hebrew (Semitic) concept of *knowing* differed greatly from our Western (Greek) concept of *knowing*. To the Greeks and the Western cultures which came after them, *knowing* meant studying something, learning its intricacies, and then being able to pass on that knowledge. That definition of *knowing* is the one by which our public schools and universities operate. The *passing on* of knowledge by students is often done in test form; it's not really passed *on*, just passed *back* to the teacher or professor as proof that the student has retained what has been taught.\

The problem with book learning is that it's often not as applicable to real life as experiential learning. If book learning were the equal to experience, students coming directly out of college would have a much easier time finding a good job; however, newly-graduated job seekers frequently are told, "Sorry, but we are looking for someone with a bit more experience."

On the other hand, when a Hebrew sought wisdom, sought to *know* a thing, it usually meant learning by hands-on experience. It is one thing to know theoretically how to build a violin, but it is quite another to create one that sounds and plays like a Stradivarius. In Genesis, it says that Adam knew Eve; they had intimate knowledge of one another. Adam did not go to night school to study all about Eve; he knew her personally.

If we are to *know* God and His ways, then we must personally *experience* God and His ways. No amount of listening to sermons will give us the hands-on experience that is required to know God in an experiential way.

How can we *know* that God is faithful until we trust Him with our circumstances to *be* faithful? Sadly, when it comes to really trusting God, most of the time Westerners would prefer to hedge their BEITs. We'd rather trust in *God and...* God *and...* wealth. God *and...* our own personal wisdom (our plan for success). God *and...* (*you* name the worldly resource to seek other than God).

Knowing, in the Hebrew sense of the word, meant for *TWO to GATHER* so that the *FORCE of AWARENESS might be CAUSED*. This can be *TWO* as in a man and wife. The *TWO* can be a parent and their child. But most of all, the *TWO* could and should be God and man, just the *two gathered together*, meeting and spending quality time alone together. It worked for Moses. It worked for David, and it worked for almost anyone about whom you could say, "That person truly knows God!"

- -

Daleth – More Biblical Food for Thought
Ya-DÎD (ya-**deed**) יָדִיד and YaDaH יָדָה
Meanings: *Beloved, Friend* and *To convert to Judaism*

יָד *Yad* literally means a *hand*, ergo *HAND-in-HAND* is denoted by YaDÎD.
However, could have a second meaning using the ancient Phoenician letter pictures…

Grasp (י) – Hem (ד) – Grasp (י) – Hem (ד) = Grasping the Hem (ongoing action)

The prophet Zachariah wrote that after the Messiah comes, Jerusalem would be the place of his throne. People from all over the world would then want to go to Jerusalem:

> 22 '… many peoples and mighty nations will come to seek the LORD of hosts in Jerusalem and to entreat the favor of the LORD.'
> 23 "Thus says the LORD of hosts, 'In those days ten men from all the nations will **grasp the garment** of a Jew, saying, "Let us go with you, for we have heard that God is with you." ' "
>
> - Zechariah 8:22-23

The word used here for *garment* is **kanaph** (Strong's number 3671), which most often means a *wing*, but secondary meanings include *edge, hem* and *skirt*. It is quite possible that in this passage, *kanaph* denotes the *end* or *edge* of a Jew's talith, the fringed prayer shawl.

In Semitic thought, *grasping the hem* of a garment had special significance. Touching the fringes of a righteous person's talith was thought to have brought a blessing, or if needed… healing.

Furthermore, YaDaH (יָדָה) is the Hebrew word which means *to convert to Judaism*. The word picture for YaDaH means *Grasping Hand - to the Hem - Raised Up*. Perhaps the picture story found in Zechariah's prophecy is that once the Messiah is enthroned in Jerusalem, peoples of all nations will enthusiastically be converting to Judaism and that people from all over the world will be going to seek instruction from their king who rules the world and teaches God's Law from Mount Zion.

* * *

Chapter 6
Hei or Hey

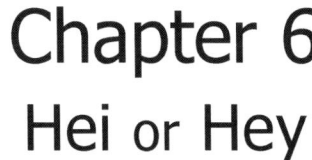

Lifted Up (Revealed) — Elevated Above (More Than)

HEI's Phoenician pictograph denoted:
RAISE UP, LIFT UP, AMPLIFY, EXTOLE, PRAISE, and EXHALT.

The Phoenicians predominantly used the stick figure of a man with his arms lifted up for HEI; this picture tells the whole story. We lift our arms up to put a box on a top shelf, to *elevate* it. We may lift our arms up in *worship*; this too was included in the picture-word's meaning. The other symbol might be a banner or flags raised up.

The post-Babylonian letter for HEI appears indicates ELEVATION ABOVE. The right side and top of the letter form a Daleth (Edge) which is elevated higher than the shorter straight line on the left. The post-Babylonian exile HEI denoted AMPLIFICATION, HIGHER, HIGHER THAN, MORE THAN, ELEVATED ABOVE, and LIFTED UP.

HEI can also represent VOILA or BEHOLD, as in SOMETHING REVEALED.

HEI's pictographical letter name denotes:
RAISED UP (ה) –INDIVIDUAL [or poss. HANDS [6]] (א)

HEI

Action or Motion Indicated	Descriptive Form	Noun(s) Denoted	Prepositional Meanings
Lift, Elevate, Honor, Amplify, Praise HEI + Yod = to grasp	More, Very, Extra, Heaped up higher, Raised up above, Special	Poss. Truth Praise Glory	Up above

---

[6] See Chapter 2, Aleph

HEI EXAMPLES:

Strong's Number	Hebrew	Trans-literation	Word Meaning	Pictorial Meaning
Word not in Bible	הֵא	HEI	1. RAISED UP, UP ABOVE 2. REVEALED 3. INDICATED 4. AMPLIFIED 5. MORE, BEITTER 6. FURTHER... FURTHER-MORE	RAISING UP or REVEALING [Behold! Voila!] **HEI** often shows that something is **ELEVATED in worth**... like the English words **MORE** and **BEITTER**. [YOD indicates MOST and BEST.] A final HEI (ה) sometimes denotes **AMPLIFIED** or **AUGMENTED** [lit. **raised up** to a whole new level, i.e. EXHALTED and like the mathematical term for exponents raised to the power of 2, 3, etc.]. However, a final HEI (ה) most often indicates a feminine (singular) noun.
1888	הַ- [Prefix] ------ הָא [word]	Ha-	1. definite article prefix 2. behold	HEI (ה) is often a prefix attached to nouns; HEI functions as the equivalent of the English definite article, "**the**." HEI indicates a **specific** noun (e.g. **the** house, as opposed to **a** house, which could be any house)
6310	פֶּה	PEY	Mouth, lips, proportion, word	FRUIT (פ) REVEALED/INDICATED (ה) = "mouth"
see PEY	פָה	PHEY	flow/fall/drip down	FLOW/FALL (ף) + INDICATED / REVEALED (ה)
7019	קִץ	QeeTS see Qitsah below	to awake	COMPLETELY (ק) - STIR (צ) [to rouse] See next word:
Modern Hebrew	קִצָּה	QiTSaH	to peel, cut off, scrape, level, destroy	AROUND/COMPLELTY (ק) - CHOP (צ) - VERY MUCH (ה) Note: ה = AMPLIFIED action (lit. raised up or elevated)
6699	צוּרָה	TSŪ-RaH	form, shape, image	FIXED IMAGE (צ) OF (ו) - HIGHLY (ה) ↔ RECOGNIZABLE ATTRIBUTES (ר)

Chapter 6 – HEI

Strong's Number	Hebrew	Transliteration	Word Meaning	Pictorial Meaning
5386b	נָשִׂיא	NASIA	breath, exhale	movement (נ) + puff up (שׂ) + body (מ) + raised / lifted up (יה)
5542	סֶלָה	SeeLaH	to praise	COMPLETEly (ס) – RAISED UP (ה) – STAFF or "Wings" [arms?] (ל) or possibly COMPLETELY- LIFT UP (GLORIFY) – HE WHO GUIDES THE FLOW of all things (God)
Modern Hebrew	הִשִׂיא	Hi-SIA	to give in marriage	RAISED (ה) + LIFTED UP (שׂי) + AWAY (א) (a Jewish bride was traditionally carried to the groom) [שׂ also denotes CHANGE]
Modern Hebrew	הִשִׁיא	Hi-SHIA	to deceive	RAISE (ה) - EXISTENCE [hope?] (שׁ) - HIGH (י) - SEPARATE (א)
2022	הַר	HaR	mountain	RAISED/HIGH (ה) – ATRIBUTE /APPEARANCE / CURVE (ר)
1952	הוֹן	HON	wealthy	ELEVATED/RAISED standard (ה) - of (ו) - LIFE (נ)
1959	הֵידָד	HEDaD	a shout, a cheer	RAISED [loud] (ה) - VOICE (י) - EDGE to EDGE (דד)
1921	הָדַר	HaDaR	to honor, to adorn	[RAISE UP] HONOR (ה) - EXTEND (ד) - ATTRIBUTED CHARACTERISTICS (ר) or REPUTATION (ר) - EXTENDED (ד) - UPWARD (ה)
1922	הֲדַר	HaDaR	to glorify [God]	[RAISE UP] HONOR (ה) - EXTEND (ד) - ATTRIBUTED CHARACTERISTICS (ר) or REPUTATION (ר) – EXTENDED (ד) - UPWARD (ה)
1086	בָּלָה	BaLaH	to become old, to wear out, worn out	PERSON (ב) - USED (ל) - UP (ה)

Unlocking the Ancient Pictorial Code of the Hebrew Alphabet

Strong's Number	Hebrew	Transliteration	Word Meaning	Pictorial Meaning
2532	חֶמְדָּה	CHeMDaH from CHaMaD (2530)	desire, delight, pleasant	HOT/WARM.PASSIONATE (ח) - BODY (מ) - EXTREMELY (ד) - ELEVATED (ה) [This word for "desire" might be best translated idiomatically as having EXTREMELY ELEVATED "HOTS" for someone.]
2026	הָרַג	HaRaG	killed, slay	RAISED UP/GREAT [amplified] (ה) - CUT (ר) - AGAINST (ג)
2040	הָרַס	HaRaS	break down, overthrow… in English: harass	RAISED UP/GREAT [amplified] (ה) - CUT (ר) - COMPLETELY/ALL AROUND (ס)
8409	תִּגְרָה	TheeG-RaH	Strife	NON-UNITY (תג) - MORE (ה) ↔ APPARENT (ר) Note: The Hebrew word for *more* (me-od) always follows the word it amplifies.
Modern Hebrew	הָרָר	HaRaR	a corrupt person	HEI (ה) indicates AMPLIFICATION: **VERY** (ה) - BENT (ר) - INSIDE (ר)
8376	תָּאָה	TA-aH	to mark out	MARK (ת) - AWAY/OUT (א) - AMPLIFIED [poss. MADE OBVIOUS] (ה) or INDIVIDUAL/SEPARATE (א) ↔ MARK(s) (ת) - INDICATED (ה)
8518	תָּלָה	ThaLaH	to hang, hanged	ACTION* (ת) - WAVE-LIKE MOTION (ל) - RAISED UP (ה) [THAV* indicates MOTION poss. due to interchanging meanings with Tet]
1624	גָּרָה	GaRaH	stir up strife, provoke	NON (ג) - ELEVATED/HIGH (ה) ↔ CHARACTER (ר) [lit. a person of low character… similar to the English term "*a low life*"] NOTE: Hebrew adjectives usually follow the word they amplify.

Chapter 6 – HEI

Strong's Number	Hebrew	Transliteration	Word Meaning	Pictorial Meaning
2088	זֶה	ZeH	Biblical Hebrew: this, this one, here, another, one side, same, other. In Modern Hebrew: ZeH is a masc. demonstrative article: **THIS**	Zayin ז is a *RAISED UP ARM* moving in an *ARCING MOTION*. Hei ה denotes *ELEVATED*. Together these letters form a word picture of someone **POINTING** to a thing or place with their arm hand raised high and moving in an arc. See also explanation of ZOH below.
2090	זֹה	ZOH	Similar to 2088 above. A primitive demonstrative pronoun: **THIS**	STRONGLY (ז) - INDICATED [RAISED UP] (ה)
7737a	שָׁוָה	SHaVaH	to agree with, resemble	SYMMETRY/SIMILARITY (שׁ) of LEVEL/ELEVATION/IMPORTANCE (ה) Prob. Much like the English idiom "on the same page"... being "WITH" somebody in thinking
4998	נָאָה	NaAH	to be comely	LIVING (נ) - INDIVIDUAL (א) - ELEVATED [poss. BEAUTIFUL] (ה)
1819	דָּמָה	DaMaH	to be like, to resemble	TWO GATHERED (ד) - BODY (מ) - EVEN MORE (ה) or VERY (ה) ↔ SIMILAR (ד) ↔ FEATURES (מ)
1961	הָיָה	HaYaH	to come to pass, am, was, become	[raised up] MORE (ה) - CAUSING TO BE or COME to BE (י) - MORE (ה) [indicates that *much happens*]
7954	קָמָה	QaMaH	standing grain	AROUND (ק) - PLACE [poss. *field*] (מ) - RAISED ABOVE (ה) Note: ה = lit. indicates *raised up higher than…* or *elevated*
5692 from 5746 to bake	עוּגָה	ŪGaH [ooga]	Cake	NOT (ג) ↔ SEPARATED (עו) + RAISED (ה)
5521	סֻכָּה	SuKKaH	a thicket, Booths, temporary shelter	COMPLETELY (ס) - COVER (כ) – UP ABOVE (ה)
6509	פָּרָה	PaRaH	to bear fruit, to be fruitful	FRUIT (פ) - INSIDE (ר) – REVEALED (ה)

Unlocking the Ancient Pictorial Code of the Hebrew Alphabet

Strong's Number	Hebrew	Trans-literation	Word Meaning	Pictorial Meaning
7953	שָׁלָה	SHaLaH	to draw out, extract	SUBSTANCE (שׁ) – GUIDED FORCE (ל) - UPWARD (ה)
3811	לָאָה	LA-AH	to be weary or impatient	NO (לא) - FURTHER (ה) NO (לא) - MORE (ה)
4296	מִטָּה מִיטָה	MeeTAH [Biblical] MeeTAH [Modern]	bed, couch	REST (מ) - in (י) - ELEVATED (ה) ↔ CONTAINER (ט)
5102 and 5104	נָהָר	NaHaR	river, rivers, stream, canal, current	MOVE (נ) - RAISED UP (ה) – INSIDE (ר) Poss. denotes *Moves Inside RAISED UP* [River Banks]
4229	מָחָה	MaHaH	to wipe, wipe out, wipe away… also to strike	PLACE (מ) - SPACE/VOID (ח) - RAISED UP (ה) lit. *ERASE* Denotes creating a void, emptiness, where previously there was something. OBLITERATE might also work.
2372	חָזָה	ĤaZaH	see, behold	ALL AROUND the SURROUNDING SPACE (ח) - SCAN [sweeping, 180 degree, arcing look] (ז) - BEHOLD (ה) See 4237 below
[4236] 4237	מֶחֱזֶה	MaĤaZaH MeĤaZaH	#4236 - vision #4237 - window	PLACE (מ) - ALL AROUND the SURROUNDING SPACE (ח) - SCAN [sweeping, 180 degree, arcing (look)] (ז) - BEHOLD (ה) See 2372 above
892	בָּבָה	BaBaH	the apple (of the eye)	PEOPLE (בב) – ELEVATED or FAVORED (ה)
3602	כָּכָה	KaKaH	thus, just so, so, like this	HERE (כ) - HERE (כ) - MORE (ה) e.g. "more of the same"
2219	זָרָה	ZaRah	to scatter, disperse, winnow	HARVEST (ז) - CUT (ר) – UP [higher, more, amplified] (ה)

Chapter 6 – HEI

Strong's Number	Hebrew	Transliteration	Word Meaning	Pictorial Meaning
3541	כֹּה	KŌH	thus, here	HERE (כ) - INDICATED (ה)
3542	כָּה	KaH [Aramaic]	here, this point	HERE (כ) - INDICATED (ה)
3543	כָּהָה	KaHaH	1. to be dim, grow dim 2. to rebuke	Def. 1. the COVER of DARKNESS [night] (כ) - RISING (הה) Def. 2: PALM of HAND (כ) - RISING (הה)

HEI - Biblical Food for Thought

HaDaR הֲדַר and הָדָר
Meaning: To glorify (God), to honor, to adorn, majesty

RAISE UP/HONOR (ה) - EXTEND (ד) - ATTRIBUTED CHARACTERISTICS (ר)
or
REPUTATION / ATTRIBUTES (ר) - EXTENDED (ד) - UPWARD (ה)

The Phoenician pictograph for HEI is a stick figure with hands uplifted. This letter is the very representation of praising and worshipping God. HEI is the letter of amplification. Are we not created to amplify God's glory in the world by worshipping Him and doing His will and good deeds (mitzvoth) among men?

King David's Psalm 145 gives a perfect example of the various meanings of *hadar*, which means to *PRAISE, EXTOL* and *GLORIFY* God. In this Psalm, we can see the various attributes and meanings of HEI. David purposes to *RAISE UP* and *HONOR* God. This song *EXTENDS the ATTRIBUTES* of God *upward* and outward; the words of praise magnify the Lord to the surrounding world. They proclaim His faithfulness, His glory, and declare to all that His deeds are mighty:

> 1 I will extol You, my God, O King,
> And I will bless Your name forever and ever.
> 2 Every day I will bless You,
> And I will praise Your name forever and ever.
> 3 Great is the LORD, and highly to be praised,
> And His greatness is unsearchable.
> 4 One generation shall praise Your works to another,
> And shall declare Your mighty acts.
> 5 On the glorious splendor of Your majesty
> And on Your wonderful works, I will meditate.
> 6 Men shall speak of the power of Your awesome acts,
> And I will tell of Your greatness.
> 7 They shall eagerly utter the memory of Your abundant goodness
> And will shout joyfully of Your righteousness.
>
> - Psalm 145: 1-7, NASB

Lastly, the letter HEI is comprised of a DALETH (top and right side) and a WAW (shorter left side). Daleth indicates *TWO GATHERED*, and one of WAW's meanings is *TWO FLOWING INTO ONE*. What a beautiful picture of *praise* is painted by the letter HEI: A MAN PRAISING GOD (ancient pictogram) as the TWO GATHER TOGETHER and FLOW INTO ONE.

* * *

Chapter 7
WAW
(Called VAV in Modern Hebrew)

𐤅 𐤅   ו

Two Rivers Flowing Into One   -   Flowing Into/Tent Peg

WAW represents FLOW.
(WAW is pronounced as *vav* in Modern Hebrew...
Why? The German Jewish scholars who began restoring Hebrew
in the late 19th Century had difficulty pronouncing the *W* sound.)

WAW's pictograph probably depicts *TWO* streams *FLOWING INTO ONE* river
(CONNECTING or SYNERGY).
Some say the meaning of the ancient Phoenician pictograph could be a tent peg or a *nail*. All three of these possibilities indicate the concept of *flowing*: streams flow and connect (turning into rivers), tent pegs flow into the sand, and nails flow into wood.

The post-Babylonian letter for WAW also depicts the original concept of FLOW.
WAW's letter name is a doubled-letter name, containing only two WAWs. Doubling a letter indicates that -*ING* should be added to the word's verbal meaning.

WAW's letter name means: FLOWING or CONNECTING.
WAW as a prefix denotes AND, indicating that one thought flows into the nest.

<u>**WAW's SPECIAL FUNCTIONS WHEN USED AS A VOWEL MARKER**</u>:
    Almost no vowels were marked in ancient Hebrew, especially the vowels A and E. The long E (*ee* as in tree) sound in Hebrew is often marked by the presence of a *YOD* and is transliterated as an **I**. Ō and Ū are also often marked. The marking of some vowels but not others was not a capricious, random event within the Semitic writing system.
    Long Ō and Ū are almost always indicated by the presence of a WAW as an additional **fourth letter** in what is typically a 3-consonant word root. When such a four-letter combination is used to form a basic word, it is because the WAW functions as a preposition, commonly the preposition *of*. This pattern will show itself often on the WAW example chart (see following pages).

WAW

Action or Motion Indicated	Prefix Form	Noun(s) Denoted	Prepositional Meanings when used as a vowel
Continuous or Straight Flow Into, Two Flow Into (one) To Understand	AND	Synergy Nail Pain Suffering Connection Discernment	*Upon* when Ō (וֹ) *On* when Ō (וֹ) *Under* when Ū (וּ) *Of* *From*

WAW EXAMPLES: Y Y ו

Strong's Number	Hebrew	Transliteration	Word Meaning	Pictorial Meaning
2053 a hook, pin, peg	וָו	WAW (Biblical) or VAV (modern) lit. means FLOW-ING INTO	"AND" FLOWING INTO connectedness / relationship	**WAW's** (ו) pictograph was a likely tent stake or nail [which were like perceived as flowed into the sand or wood], but possibly two streams flowing into one. WAW = FLOWING STRAIGHT INTO. WAW as a prefix means **AND**. WAW, therefore, denotes **connectedness & flow**. **WAW** also denoted an action that happened **AGAIN** when placed Between repeated identical consonants. **WAW** Between 2 identical letters which acts as a verb means **Do This Action Again (repeatedly)** Ex. - WAW is placed Between two NUNs: NUN-WAW-NUN = Movement OF Life or Life LIVING **AGAIN**
– NA –	וֹ or וּ	WAW as a vowel: ū (וּ) or ō (וֹ)	of, over, upon and similar prepositions	WAW is a letter which indicates connection; therefore it is frequently used to represent connecting prepositions within Hebrew word pictograms
Modern Hebrew from SAMAR see SAMEKH	סְמַרְ־טוּט	SMaR-TŪT	a rag	GATHER (ס) - LIQUID (מ) - INSIDE (ר) - CONTAIN (ט) AGAIN (טוט) A consonant repeated with WAW in the middle means to do an action AGAIN...TET means to CONTAIN, so TET – *WAW* – TET means to **contain again**... Lit. CONTAIN *AND* CONTAIN [again]

Chapter 7 – WAW

Strong's Number	Hebrew	Transliteration	Word Meaning	Pictorial Meaning
2071	זָבוּד	Za-VŪD	Bestowed	TAKE (ז) - an OBJECT (ב) - EXTEND (ד) ↔ OVER (וֹ)
- NA -	See below:	ŪM	*mother* in Arabic	CONNECTING (וּ) - MEMBER/MEMBRANE (מ) [The *mother* is pictured here as the glue that holds and connects together the family.]
517	אֵם or אִמָּא	eM or eeM-MA	*mother* in Hebrew	The Hebrew term for mother comes from the word for a glue-like substance that rises to the surface when hides are boiled. This substance was used for gluing things together.
1471	גּוֹי	GOY pl. GOYIM	a gentile, a non-Jew gentile nation	TRAMPLE (ג) - UPON (וֹ) - GOD's Divine HAND/CREATION (י)
5750	עוֹד	'ŌD	still, yet, more, again	PRESENCE (ע) - OF (וֹ) - TWO JOINED (ד) [e.g. on the other hand, in addition] or **PREVENTING (עוֹ)** LACK (ד) [lacking nothing]
Modern Hebrew	עוֹנֶן	'ŌNeN	an anchor	SEPARATE (ע) - FROM (וֹ) - MOVING (double נ)
6027	Bib. Hebrew: עֹנֶג Modern: עֹנֶג	'ŌNeG	Bib. Hebrew: daintiness, delight, exquisite; Mod. Hebrew: enjoyment, delight, pleasure	[LIFE] FORCE (ע) - OF (וֹ) - being GATHERED FOR PLEASURE (ג*) NOTE: (ג*) in this case denotes Ghayin, a Hebrew letter that disappeared from use round 500 BCE. It did not mean the same things as GIMMEL nor as AYIN, the 2 letters which replaced it.
5766	עָוֶל	A-VeL	injustice, wrong	SEPARATE (ע) - FROM (וֹ) - LEADERSHIP/CUSTOMS/LAW (ל)
5766	עִוֵּל	Ee-VeL or **EVIL**	to do injustice	SEPARATE (ע) - FROM (וֹ) - LEADERSHIP/CUSTOMS/LAW (ל)
from 5826 and 5828	עוֹזֵר עֶזֶר or עֵזֶר	Ō-ZeR (modern) A-ZER or E-ZER (Biblical)	Helper	SEPARATE (ע) - FROM (וֹ) - AGGRESSION/DESTRUCTION (ז) - [resh] (ר) [The RESH at the end of the word indicates that this is a character trait]

Unlocking the Ancient Pictorial Code of the Hebrew Alphabet

Strong's Number	Hebrew	Transliteration	Word Meaning	Pictorial Meaning
5756	עוּז	ŪZ	to take or seek refuge	SEPARATE (ע) - FROM (ו) - AGRESSION/DESTRUCTION (ז)
5783	עוּר	ŪR	to be exposed, bare	EXPOSE[ing] (ע) - OF (ו) – INSIDE (ר) or FORCE[ing] (ע) - OF (ו) – INSIDE (ר) [poss. forced revelation of the inside]
2895	טוֹב	TŌV	good, to be pleasing	FULLNESS [fully contained] (ט) – OF (ו) - BODY (ב)
3883	לוּל	LŪL	a shaft, enclosed space with steps, winding stairs or spiraling staircase	GUIDED FLOW (ל) - AGAIN (ו) NOTE: WAW (VAV) between repeated identical letters indicates to do that action *AGAIN*. In this case, it seems to indicate a path that repeatedly directs one's way.
2111	זוּע	ZUA	to tremble	**FORCE/SRENGTH (ז) - OF (ו) -** FORCE of ALERTNESS (ע) NOTE: The word prob. denotes the bodily effects of adrenalin
5771	עָוֹן	AŌN	iniquity, guilt, punishment [poss. denotes a death penalty]	SEPARATE (ע) - OF/FROM (ו) – LIFE (נ) or EXPOSURE (ע) - of (ו) - MOVEMENTs (נ)
5486	סוּף	SŪPH	to come to an end, to cease, completely removed	COMPLETENESS (ס) - OF (ו) - DOWNWARD FLOW (ף)
5493	סוּר שׂוּר	SŪR	to turn aside, departed	COMPLETENESS (ס) - OF (ו) - TURNing (ר)
5127	נוּס	NŪS	to flee, to escape	MOVE [flee, escape] (נ) - FROM (ו) - NET (ס)
2056	וָלָד	WALLAD	A child	Note: The use of this Arabic and Aramaic word in Gen. 11:30 shows evidence that the Biblical pronunciation of ו was actually W.

WAW - Biblical Food for Thought

WAW as a Prefix

The Phoenician pictograph for WAW denotes *FLOW* and *CONNECTION*. In Biblical and Modern Hebrew both, a WAW prefix attached to the front of any noun means *AND*. The WAW is actually attached to the noun that follows, such as in the example phrase *"the king WAW-David,"* which would mean "the king *and* David." The Hebrew WAW could represent a nail or a tent peg in the Babylonian pictorial glyphs; nails and tent pegs attached objects to one another-- tents to the ground, boards to other boards, and so on. The Phoenician WAW looks like our modern Y, and Spanish speakers know that a solitary Y means AND, just as a Hebrew WAW (VAV) indicates *and* (kudos to my buddy Dave T. for pointing this out to me).

Perhaps to the ancient Hebrews, everything in life was seen as more connected than we see it today. People were more connected to the land. Fathers were more connected to their families. Members of the community were more connected to one another. There was a natural FLOW to everyday life, and the Creator was certainly a large part of that flow.

To show the connectedness of all of the words of the Torah (5 Books of Moses), each new page on the Torah scrolls begins with a WAW. It is always the first letter at the top of the next page. The pages of the Torah *flow* from one to the next. One cannot pick and choose the parts of the Torah one wishes to hear and obey, for the Torah is all one continuous body of writing. Every page is connected to the one before it.

In the *New Testament* book of *James*, it is written that one must keep the whole Torah (law), not just part of it:

> "For whoever keeps the whole law (Torah) and yet stumbles in one *point,* he has become guilty of all.
> For He who said, 'DO NOT COMMIT ADULTERY,' also said, 'DO NOT COMMIT MURDER.' Now if you do not commit adultery, but do commit murder, you have become transgressor of the law (Torah)."
> - James 2:10 & 11

If our righteousness were based on the sum total of our good and bad deeds, we would never be completely perfect (and therefore *guilt-free*) before a perfect God. We are not righteous before God because we have achieved perfection on our own merits. Even the best of us has his or her shortcomings and imperfections.

However, we **can** stand before our Creator with our scarlet sins washed *white as snow*.[7] What is important is that we repent before the Most High, our Creator, and turn away from our sins. God is merciful to all who come before Him with a humble and repentant heart.

-- -- -- -- -- -- -- -- --

---

[7] Isaiah 1:18

Special Thoughts Regarding WAW (VAV)

| 995 | בִּין | BIN | gain insight to discern, to act wisely | BODY (ב) - GREAT/HIGH (י) - MOVEMENT/FLOW (ן)
In Greek, the term for "understanding" is *sunesis*, which indicates an AH-HA experience of connecting the dots; lit. it means the place where two smaller river join and become a powerfully flowing big river. I believe this is what the Phoenician WAW (VAV) pictograph represents. |

    As a pictogram of two streams flowing into one mighty river, WAW's earliest meaning ancient symbolic meaning might have been *understanding* or *discerning*. This was exactly the meaning of the Greek word *sunesis* (σὐνεσις), which literally meant *running together*, but also denoted *insight, to discern* or *to act wisely*. The Greek word *sunesis* comes from the root word *suniēmi* (συνίημι), meaning *set together* or *to understand;* perhaps from this word we get our word for a massive tidal wave-- *tsunami*.

    Even in today's English we have the idioms *streams of consciousness* and *streams of thought*. It is these connected streams of thought that form a river of wisdom. Learning can be seen as a synergistic event, where small streams form mighty rivers. The sum of the parts is often greater than adding up the individual parts; synergistically speaking, 1 + 1 + 1 can equal 5.

    Is the ancient WAW repeated 3 times inside itself (plus one) to form the menorah candelabra so often seen as a symbol of Judaism? Do all the little things add up to much more than the sum of their parts? Are we, as parts of the community, each a stream flowing into other streams and becoming a mighty river?

    Could this have been the reason WAW (or VAV) was the letter always used by ancient Jewish scribes to begin every new page of a Torah scroll? Certainly it connects all the pages (and often connects multiple verses) of Torah together. Does the letter WAW indicate an ancient concept of connecting together smaller thought streams of information so that they form a large powerful flowing river of knowledge, wisdom and discernment?

* * *

Chapter 8
ZAYIN

⊥ I ↑ Z   ז

Harvesting Tool or Weapon   –   Axe or Weapon

Each of ZAYIN's pictographs represents a HAVESTING TOOL and/or WEAPON. In addition, ZAYIN represents the ARCHING PATH of MOTION of these objects as well as the STRENGTH needed to wield them.

The Phoenicians used pictographs that show what appear to be harvesting tools, but harvesting tools were also used in times of war as weapons.

The post-Babylonian letter for ZAYIN most likely depicts an axe.

ZAYIN's letter name means:
PICK / RAISE (ז) - UP (י) – ARM [poss. MOTION] (נ)

ZAYIN

Action or Motion Indicated	Descriptive Form	Noun(s) Denoted	Prepositional Meanings
Any Arching (or Swinging) Motion To take To swing in a arc To harvest or kill	Violent Aggressive Cut-off or Killed Circular Arcing Strong	Harvesting tool Weapon Death Violent Force Strong Force	- NA -

Unlocking the Ancient Pictorial Code of the Hebrew Alphabet

ZAYIN EXAMPLES:

Strong's Number	Hebrew Word	Transliteration	Word Meaning	Pictorial Meaning
Word Not in Bible	זַיִן Poss. Original Spelling is זיין	Zayin	1. **IRON, STRENGTH** [including weapons & tools of iron], **IRON** also denotes **HARD, INSENSITIVE, UNEMPATHETIC** 2. to HARVEST, KILL, TAKE, SPEND 3. CONTEMPTABLE [deserving of fierce attack or "harvesting"... obviously not in a good sense] 4. FIERCE, AGGRESSIVE, WAR-LIKE incl. AGRESSIVE/DESTRUCTIVE FORCE, LACKING HUMANITY [no softness or compassion]	1. Zayin, in its earliest form, possibly indicated **IRON** tools and weapons. 2. The post-Babylonian meaning of Zayin seems to have morphed to mean PICK or TAKE/RAISE (ז)-UP (י) – ARMs (נ)... an axe, **pick** or weapon [Zayin + Yod = PICK UP, **Yod = UP**] 3. any ARC-LIKE MOTION [such as swinging an ax, any weapon, or **harvesting** tool] ergo... 4. HARVESTING 5. ZAYIN was the symbol of **STRENGTH** but also **WEAPONS, VIOLENCE** and **AGRESSION**. Note: **Nun** can represent **ARM** [just as LAMED = leg]. The strong ARM of the Lord which defends us against our enemies - see Isaiah 53 **Zayin's** letter name, in its earliest pictographic form may have had a doubled YOD, which would have meant IRON (ז)- HAND or FIST (י) – HIGH ABOVE [ruling over] (י) - LIFE (נ)
2107	זוּל	ZŪL	to lavish	**STRENGTH** (ז) - OF (ו) - COMFORT (ל)
2070	זְבוּב	Z'VŪV	a fly, flies	**GREAT/MIGHTY/STRONG** (ז) - BODY [swarm] (ב) - OF (ו) - BODY [indiv. bodies] (ב) Note: Z'VŪV was translated ZeBuB in the KJV version. Baal Zebub or Baal Z'VUV means lord of the flies... prob. the Baal of Death

Chapter 8 – ZAYIN

Strong's Number	Hebrew Word	Trans-literation	Word Meaning	Pictorial Meaning
4197	מֶזֶג	MeZeG	wine (which is finished fermenting and is ready to drink)	LIQUID (מ) - NOT (ג) - STRONG (ז) WINE (מ) - NOT (ג) - STRONG (ז) Note: For easier storage, wine was traditionally condensed after brewing and then diluted with water later when it was to be consumed. MEZEG may denote freshly-made wine in a pre-condensed state.
2088 see also 2090 BELOW	זֶה	ZeH	this, this one, here, another, one side, same, other	Zayin (ז) is a RAISED UP ARM moving in an ARCING MOTION HEI (ה) denotes ELEVATED Together these letters form a word picture of someone POINTING to a thing or place with their arm hand raised high and moving in an arc.
Mod. ARABIC	-- x --	AZZIZ	dear or beloved one... a best friend	Zayin-Yod [denotes sharpened to a point] + Zayin = *IRON SHARPENS IRON* [Prov. 27:17]
6523	פַּרְזֶל	PaRZeL	Aramaic: **IRON**	FACE [prob. denotes **axe head... a "face" with a BLOSSOMING OUT or widened cutting edge**] (פ) - ATTRIBUTE (ר) - IRON (ז) - HANDLE [staff-like] (ל)
1270	בַּרְזֶל	BaRZeL	IRON, axe, axe head	BODY (ב) - INSIDE (ר) - IRON (ז) – [with a] HANDLE (ל) or BODY (ב) - ATTRIBUTE of (ר) - **IRON** (ז) – [with a] HANDLE (ל)
2118	זָחַח	ZaHaH	to remove, displace	FORCE/DESTROY/CHOP/**SMASH** (ז) - into SEGMENTS/PIECES (חח)
Modern Hebrew	זִיף	ZeeF	Mod. Hebrew: bristle	**PICK** (ז) - UP (י) - DROPLETS (ף) [a paint brush in Mod. Heb.] A name of one of Judah's sons: 2128
962	בָּזַז	BaZaZ	take, taking, take as spoils, plunder	BODY (ב) – TAKING (ז ז)
966	בָּזַר	BaZaR	to scatter, distribute	BODY (ב) – TAKE/ARC (ז) - AROUND [bent] (ר)
5797	עֹז or עוֹז	ŌZ	strength, might, power	**STRONG** (ז) ↔ FORCE (ע) or FORCE (ע) - OF (ו) - **STRENGTH** (ז)

Unlocking the Ancient Pictorial Code of the Hebrew Alphabet

Strong's Number	Hebrew Word	Trans-literation	Word Meaning	Pictorial Meaning
4581	מָעוֹז	MaŌZ from 5756 (עוז Ūz) See ŌZ in CH. on Zayin	fortress, strong hold	PLACE OF (מ) - OPENING/SEPARATION (ע) - OF/FROM (ו) - FIERCENESS (ז) Daniel 11:38 says that the anti-Christ will "honor a God of Fortresses (MAOZ)". On the surface, this could be translated as a "GOD WHO SEPARATES [or TAKES AWAY] FIERCENESS"... but the letter Zayin stands for both FIERCENESS and **HARVEST.**
5794	עַז	AhZ	strong, mighty, fierce	FORCE/CONDITION (ע) - STRONG (ז) literally: STRONG (ז) ↔ CONDITION/FORCE (ע)
5810	עָזַז	AZaZ	to be strong	STRENGTHENING (זז) - FORCE (ע) or STRONG FORCE (ע) from WEAPONS or **STRENGTHS** (זז)
2109	זוּן	ZŪN	to feed	STRENGTH (ז) - OF (ו) - LIVING (ן)
270	אָחַז	AĤaZ	to grasp, take hold	COMBINED [YOKED] (א) - AROUND (ח) - **FORCIBLY** (ז) or GRASP (א + ח) - **FORCIBLY** (ז)
2388 **2389**	חָזָק חָזָק	ĤaZaQ	to be strong, to grow strong, strengthen	ALL AROUND (ח) - STRENGTH (ז) - FULLY DEVELOPED (ק)
7806	שָׁזַר	SHaZaR	to be twisted	ABUNDANT (שׁ) - STRENGTH (ז) - BEND (ר)
2085	זָג	ZaG	grape skins	* **TAKE** (ז) - NOT (ג) or poss. NOT (ג) ↔ **STRONG** (ז) *[Grape skins are often discarded after pressing grapes when making wine]
2737	חָרוּז	CHaRUZ	string of beads	SEGMENTS (ח) - INSIDE (ר) - OF (ו) – ARC (ז)
2107	זוּל	ZŪL	to lavish	STRENGTH (ז) - OF (ו) - COMFORT (ל)
2109	זוּן	ZŪN	to feed	STRENGTH (ז) - OF (ו) - LIFE (ן)

Chapter 8 – ZAYIN

Strong's Number	Hebrew Word	Trans-literation	Word Meaning	Pictorial Meaning
2086	זֵד	ZeD	insolent, arrogant	lit. IRON (ז) - EDGE (ד) [prob. denotes uncaring or poss. INSOLENT] ABRASIVE, STRONG or HARD (ז) – EDGE (ד)
3868	לוּז	LUZ	turn aside, depart, devious	GUIDED FLOW [poss. Redirection] (ל) – OF (ו) - STRENGTH (ז) [poss. meaning wasted strength/effort], but LUZ could be interpreted to mean the **GUIDED FLOW of IRON** [iron casting] in its most ancient pictographical meaning.]
2117	זָזָא	ZaZA	descendent of Judah	INDIVIDUAL / SEPARATE/ UNIQUE (א) ↔ STRENGTHS (זז)
2118	זָחַח	ZaĤaĤ	to remove, displace	FORCE/DESTROY (ז) - into SEGMENTS / PIECES (חח)
2076	זָבַח	ZaBaĤ	slaughter for sacrifice	VIOLENT FORCE (ז) - LIVING BEING's BODY (ב) - ALL AROUND (ח)
2071	זָבוּד	Za-VŪD	Bestowed	TAKE (ז) - OBJECT (ב) - EXTEND (ד) - OVER (ו)
2090	זֹה	ZOH	a demonstrative pronoun: THIS	**STRONGLY (ז) - INDICATED [RAISED UP] (ה)**
2082	זָבַל	ZaBaL	to dwell	**STRONG (ז) - HOUSE (ב) - COMFORT (ל)** or possibly **SECURE (ז) - HOUSE (ב) - COMFORT (ל)**
2073	זְבוּל	Z'BŪL or Z'BŪL	elevation, height, lofty, habitation	**STRONG (ז) - HOUSE (ב) - OF (ו) - [COMFORTABLE] HEIGHTS (ל)** or **SECURE (ז) - HOUSE (ב) - ON (ו) - HIGH (ל)**
2219	זָרָה	ZaRah	to scatter, disperse, winnow,	**HARVEST (ז) - CUT (ר) - UP [higher, more, amplified] (ה)**
2372	חָזָה	ĤaZaH	see, behold	ALL AROUND the SURROUNDING SPACE (ח) - SCAN [sweeping, 180 degree, arcing (look)] (ז) - BEHOLD (ה) See 4237 below
[4236] 4237	מֶחֱזָה	MaĤaZaH MeĤaZaH	4236 vision 4237 **window**	PLACE (מ) - ALL AROUND the SURROUNDING SPACE (ח) - SCAN [sweeping, 180 degree, arcing (look)] (ז) - BEHOLD (ה) See **2372** above

Strong's Number	Hebrew Word	Trans-literation	Word Meaning	Pictorial Meaning
2123	זִיז	ZÎZ	moving things, beasts,	STRENGTH (ז) - UPON [above] (י) – STRENGTH (ז)
2213	זֵר	ZeR	circlet, border (round), molding	STRONG (ז) - BEND/ARC (ר) IMPORTANT NOTE: ZER is a 2-consonant root that indicates a **sharp turn or arcing motion** [up to a **180 degree U-turn**]
2232	זָרַע	ZaRA	to sow, to scatter seed	STRONG (ז) - BEND/ARC (ר) - FORCE (ע) See 2213 above. ZER indicates an arc and AYIN denotes a force. Scattering or sowing seed is done by throwing it in an arcing motion.
Modern Hebrew	חֹזֵר	ĤŌ-Zer	to return, to turn around	AROUND (ח) - TURN (זר)
2220	זְרוֹעַ	ZeROA	ARM, shoulder, foreleg of a lamb	RETURN (זר) - of (ו) – LIFE FORCE (ע) Is. 53:1 To whom has the **ARM (zeroah)** of the Lord been revealed?
2094	זָהַר	ZaHaR a) is also for ZoHaR	a) radiant light b) a warning cry	STRONG (ז) – RAISED UP (ה) – RAY (ר) see 7160 below re Resh meaning *RAYS of Light* STRONG (ז) – RAISED UP (ה) – SHOUT (ר)

ZAYIN - Biblical Food for Thought

Mount ZION צִיּוֹן
STRONG (ז or צ) - HOLD (י) – OF (ו) – LIFE (ן)

The Phoenician pictograph ZAYIN denotes *STRENGTH*. The letter THAV indicates *PURE*. I strongly suspect that the combination of **T**AV (or *Thav*) + **Z**AYIN was so common, that the letter *TZadi* was created. *TZADI* (also transliterated into English as *TZADEI* or *TSADI*) is really a contraction of **T**hav and **Z**ayin: *PURE* (ת) + *STRENGTH* (ז) or *GREAT STRENGTH*.

ZION's Hebrew spelling actually begins with a *TZadi*, not a *ZAYIN*. The *TZADI* denotes *GREAT STRENGTH*, not just *STRENGTH* as the letter *Zayin* would denote. Once it became apparent to me that the YOD's hand (showing fingers and an opposable thumb) denoted *grasp* or *hold*, I was able to "translate" the pictographical meaning of the Hebrew word *ZION*.

Chapter 8 – ZAYIN

I suspected that I could verify that Mount *ZION*'s name meant *Strong Hold of Life*. Using a searchable computerized NASB Bible with Strong's Concordance links, I checked for *Zion*'s Biblical spelling. I got a stunning, but very pleasant, surprise. The name Zion first appears in 2 Samuel 5:7, which reads, "Nevertheless, David captured the **stronghold of Zion**, that is the city of David" (author's emphasis added).

I was half expecting that the name *Zion* should be spelled with a *Zayin*, but the *Tzadi* fit well… and in some ways it was actually a better fit than a spelling using the letter *Zayin*. The "stronghold of Zion" must have been a *strongly* fortified place. Upon reading 2 Samuel 5:6, one sees that the Jebusite defenders of this stronghold claimed that the blind and the lame could defend the place against David. Now *that's* fortified! Samuel 5:7 also confirms what the pictographical meaning of the site's name indicates: Mount Zion is a "**stronghold** *of life*."

In the fourth chapter of Isaiah, we read that in some future time, the *Branch* (the Messiah, the Righteous King) will reign from Mount Zion:

> 2 "In that day the Branch of the Lord will be beautiful and glorious, and the fruit of the earth will be the pride and the adornment of the survivors of Israel.
>
> 3 It will come about that he who is left in Zion and remains in Jerusalem will be called holy—everyone who is recorded for life in Jerusalem.
>
> 4 When the Lord has washed away the filth of the daughters of Zion and purged the bloodshed of Jerusalem from her midst, by the spirit of judgment and the spirit of burning,
>
> 5 then the Lord will create over the whole area of Mount Zion and over her assemblies a cloud by day, even smoke, and the brightness of a flaming fire by night; for over all the glory will be a canopy.
>
> 6 There will be a shelter to give shade from the heat by day, and refuge and protection from the storm and the rain."
>
> - Isaiah 5:2-6

The covering cloud of smoke by day and the fire by night indicates that the Tabernacle will likely be re-erected upon Mount Zion, and the Presence of God will once again fill the Holy of Holies. The *smoke by day* and *fire by night* were evidences of God's physical presence that Moses and the Israelites followed during their years of wandering in the wilderness while on their journey from Egypt to the Promised Land.

When will the Tabernacle be rebuilt? To which future point in time does Isaiah 5:5 point? The prophet Jeremiah gives us some additional information to help us recognize when this promised time is near:

> 5 "Behold, the days come, saith the LORD, that I will raise unto David a righteous Branch, and a King shall reign and prosper, and shall execute judgment and justice in the earth.
>
> 6 In his days Judah shall be saved, and Israel shall dwell safely: and this *is* his name whereby he shall be called, THE LORD OUR RIGHTEOUSNESS.
>
> 7 Therefore, behold, the days come, saith the LORD, that they shall no more say, The LORD liveth, which brought up the children of Israel out of the land of Egypt;

8 But, ***The LORD liveth, which brought up and which led the seed of the house of Israel out of the north country, and from all countries whither I had driven them; and they shall dwell in their own land.***"[8]

(Author's emphasis added)

Since 1948, when the nation of Israel was miraculously reborn after being non-existent for nearly 2000 years, Jews from all over the world have been returning to their Promised Land. They have returned from Europe and Russia, *out of the north country*, by the millions. Millions have returned from Africa, Asia and the Americas as well… from every corner of the earth to where God had *driven them*.

Mount Zion has always been God's most special place on earth. In fact, there is only one place on earth the Spirit of God would rather dwell. That place is within the hearts of men and women who have surrendered themselves to the will and guidance of God, and as yielded vessels have become God's holy possession on earth, His living tabernacles.

* * *

---

[8] Jeremiah 23:5-8, King James Version

Chapter 9
ĤET
A Defined Area or Contained Space

ĤET denotes a defined area of SPACE or a SECTION.
ĤET also represents ALL AROUND, much like the English word ENVIRONMENT.
Instead of representing the walls and boundaries that defined the space, ĤET's focus
was on the SPACE itself, the VOID within (or outside of) the defined boundaries.
Ĥet can denote GROW or EXPANSION into the SURROUNDING SPACE

ĤET's secondary meanings include: a tent divider- indicating to *cut in HALF or
DIVIDE*, an *INTERVAL* (evenly spaced *PORTIONS*).   Derivative meanings include:
TURNING (especially in regards to clay pottery creation),
SPIRALING or TWISTING[9] AROUND,
to BRAID, to WEAVE, a CONCEPT, *OTHER*,
HOT or VERY WARM, and poss. PRIVATE.

The Phoenicians used pictographs that show what are most likely to be sections of a
tent, rooms created by hanging up a large curtain between the men and the women.
The post-Babylonian letter for ĤET most likely depicts the SPACE within the tent.

ĤET's letter name means:
SURROUNDING SPACE (ח) – CAUSED to (י) - BECOME ONE (ת)
[Open space becomes one space- a room]

ĤET

Action or Motion Indicated	Descriptive Form	Noun(s) Denoted	Prepositional Meanings
Spiraling - Twisting[12] Divide Braid Weave GROW or EXPAND into SURROUNDING SPACE	Outside Very Warm or Hot All around Private	Interval A Division Section Throat	Around All Around

---

[9] The hieroglyphic **H** sound was represented by **twisted** flax:
http://www.greatscott.com/hiero/hiero_alpha.html

Unlocking the Ancient Pictorial Code of the Hebrew Alphabet

ĤET EXAMPLES:  (Egyptian)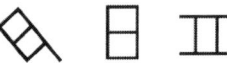

Strong's Number	Hebrew Word	Trans-Literation	Word Definition	Explanation of Pictographical Meanings
- NA -	חֵית	CHeT	a ROOM. The word CHET literally means a **DEFINED AREA** or **SECTOR** [one that is not able to hold water]	**SECTION** (SURROUNDED PORTION / PARTITION) (ח) + JOINED [lit. become one] (ת). CHET's original meaning and pictograph was the empty space defined by the borders of the walls or curtains which SURROUND SPACE within a tent or building. From there, CHET seems to have morphed into meaning a **PARTITION, a SEGMENT, a PORTION**... ANY CLEARLY-DEFINED SPACE which can NOT HOLD WATER (water-holding spaces such as clay pots, jars and cisterns are designated by TET, the letter which follows CHET). The motion denoted by CHET is that of **TWISTING** or **ROTATING on its Y Axis**, including the **SPIRALING** of wind such as a "dust devil" or any spiraling, tornado-like motion. The Egyptian symbol HET was TWISTED flax. CHet can also denote **WARM, HOT, ANGRY** and/or **PASSIONATE**, including violent aspects of extreme passion. CHET means sections in a tent, which were seen as **defined open spaces** (defined by perimeter walls).
2915 from 2902	טִיחַ	Tee-aĤ	to smear or to plaster	FILL (ט) - UP (י) – VOID / EMPTY SPACE (ח) or MOTION [spread] (ט) - OVER (י) - SPIRALING (ח) or LAYER (ט) - ABOVE (י) - **EMPTY SPACE** (ח)
5301	נָפַח נִפַּח	1. NaPHaĤ 2. Ni-PaĤ	1. to blow, breathe, boiling [Bib.] 2. to swell [Mod.]	MOVE (נ) - BLOSSOM out (פ) - into the **SURROUNDING VOID** (ח)
7818	סָחַט	SaĤaT	to wring out	GATHERing (ס) - **TWIST**ing (ח) - ACTION (ט) or GATHER (ס) - **TWIST** (ח) - into a CONTAINER (ט)
1765	דָחַף	DaĤaPH	to drive, hasten [to PUSH in Mod. Hebrew]	EDGE (ד) - **AGAINST** (ח) - FLOW DOWN/FALL/PUSH (ף)
6713 & 6715	צֹחַר	Tsa-ĤaR Mod.Heb TSAĤOR	white	CLEAR (צ) - **EMPTINESS** (ח) – ATTRIBUTE [poss. color] (ר)
6681	צָוַח	Tsa-VaĤ	to scream	MIGHTY FORCE (צ) - OF (ו) - THROAT (ח) Note: CHET denotes the throat because a throat is a place of clearly defined (limited) empty space.
6703	צַח	TSaKH	dazzling, scorching, clearly, pure	FORCE/EXTREME HEAT (צ) - ALL AROUND (ח)
6711	צָחַק	ZaĤaQ	to laugh, entertained, jesting	FORCE (ז) + THROAT (ח) possibly: THROAT FORCE] - SWELLING (ק) = **LAUGH**

Chapter 9 – ḤET

Strong's Number	Hebrew Word	Trans-Literation	Word Definition	Explanation of Pictographical Meanings
251	אָח	AḤ (ACK)	1. brother countryman 2. hearth	INDIVIDUAL (א) - CLOSE/NEAR [a part of the family] UNIT (ח) or INDIVIDUAL who is YOKED (א) - to the FAMILY UNIT [section] (ח)
Modern Hebrew	אֶחָד	eeḤeD	to unite	INDIVIDUAL (א) - SECTIONS (ח) – UNITED (ד) ?
Modern Hebrew	אָחָה	eeḤaH	to stitch together	SEPARATE (א) - SECTION/SEGMENT (ח) + PULLED UP (ה), possibly because thread is pulled through and up to tighten individual segments of stitches
270	אָחַז	AḤaZ	to grasp, take hold	COMBINED [yoked concept] (א) - AROUND (ח) - FORCIBLY (ז) or GRASP (ח + א) – FORCIBLY (ז)
6353	פֶּחָר	PeḤaR	a potter [Aramaic]	BLOSSOM OUT (פ) - ALL AROUND (ח) - the INSIDE (ר) NOTE: Anyone who has watched a potter throw a clay pot on a pottery wheel knows exactly how this word came to be, as it perfectly describes the potter's fingers digging into the inside of the clay lump and the pot BLOOMING ALL AROUND the potter's hands.
264	אָחוֹר	AḤŌR	Buttocks	SEPARATE (א) – PARTS or SECTIONS (ח) - OF - REAR/BEHIND (ר)
2912	טָחַן	TaḤan	to grind, grinder	CONTAIN (ט) - ALL AROUND (ח) - MOVE (נ)
3897	לָחַךְ	LaḤaK	to lick, licked	TONGUE (ל) - ALL AROUND (ח) - COVER (כ)
2270 see also 2266	חָבֵר	ḤaVeR	friend, associate, united	**PART** or **SECTOR** [of] (ח) - HOUSE / BODY / COMMUNITY (ב) - RECOGNIZABLE (ר)
7623	שָׁבַח	SHaVaḤ	Biblical - to soothe, to laud, praise Modern – to grow in value, to improve	EXPAND (שׁ) - PERSON/HOUSE (ב) - ALL AROUND (ח) [e.g. "magnify the Lord" or to enlarge the house]
974	בָּחַן	BaḤaN	to test, examine, prove	MOVE AROUND (נ ↔ ח) - BODY/HOUSE [so as to inspect it] CHET [to twist] + NUN [movement] would denote a **rotating motion on its Y-Axis** [such as a rotating upright cylinder], as opposed to motion on the X-axis, such as the turning of a knob or a movement similar to the hands on a wall clock [which would be TET].

Unlocking the Ancient Pictorial Code of the Hebrew Alphabet

Strong's Number	Hebrew Word	Trans-Literation	Word Definition	Explanation of Pictographical Meanings
975	בַּחוּן	BaĤŌN	a tower	HOUSE (ב) - **WALLED PLACE** (ח) - of (ו) – LIVING (ן)
2706	חֹק	ĤŌQ	1. law, custom, statute, boundary, immutable law 2. portion, share, task	1. PORTION (ח) - JUDGEMENT (ק)* *Qoph, which means **NECK**, often denotes **judgment**. PORTION (ח) ↔ FULL (ק)
2643	חַף	ĤaPH	clean, innocent	**SCRUB** [washing, rubbing motion] (ח) - FACE (ף)
5117	נוּחַ	NŪaĤ	to rest, to wait, to remain, to camp	LIFE (נ) - OF (ו) - **CONTAINMENT** (ח) or LIVING (נ) + WITHIN (ו) a LIMITED RANGE of MOVEMENT (ח)
2525	חַם	ĤaM	hot, warm	**HOT/WARM** (ח) - [physical] BODY (מ)
2527	חֹם	ĤōM	hot, warm	**HOT/WARM** (ח) - [physical] BODY (ם)
2552	חָמַם	ĤaMaM	hot, warm, mated, become warm or heated	**HOT/WARM** (ח) - [physical] BODIES (ממ)
2554	חָמַס	ĤaMaS	treat with violence	PASSIONATE/ANGRY/EXTREMELY HEATED/FORCEFUL (ח) - [physical] BODY (מ) - COMPLETELY (ס)
2532	חֶמְדָּה	CHeM-DaH from CHaMaD (2530)	desire, delight, pleasant	HOT/WARM.PASSIONATE (ח) - BODY (מ) - EXTREMELY (ד) - ELEVATED (ה) [This word for "desire" might be best translated idiomatically: *having EXTREMELY ELEVATED "HOTS" for someone.*]
259	אֶחָד	EĤaD	one, each, once	ONE/INDIVIDUAL (א) - PORTION/SEGMENT (ח) - CUT (ד)
2737	חָרוּז	ĤaRUZ	string of beads	**SEGMENTS** (ח) - INSIDE (ר) - OF (ו) - ARC (ז)
2328	חוּג	ĤŪG	to draw around, to make a circle	[SPIRAL ROTATION TURNING] **CIRCUMSCRIBMENT** (ח) - OF (ו) - FOOT (ג) [picture a person drawing an arc in the dirt using one foot while standing on the other]

Chapter 9 – ĤET

Strong's Number	Hebrew Word	Trans-Literation	Word Definition	Explanation of Pictographical Meanings
4969	מָתַח	MaTHaĤ	to spread out, spreads	PLACE (מ) - JOINED (ת) - **ALL AROUND** (ח) or THING (מ) - JOINED (ת) – **ALL AROUND** (ח)
6743	צָלַח	TSaLaĤ	to break forth, to come upon mightily	GREAT FORCE (צ) - GOing FORTH (ל) – ALL AROUND (ח)
2856	חָתַם	ĤaTaM (Chatham)	sealed, to seal	**ALL AROUND** (ח) - ATTACHED/JOINED (ת) - SUBSTANCE (מ) [i.e. a wax seal]
2388	חָזַק	ĤaZaQ	to be strong, to grow strong, strengthen	ALL AROUND (ח) - STRENGTH (ת) – FULLY DEVELOPED (ק)
2389	חָזָק	ĤaZaQ	strong, stout mighty	ALL AROUND (ח) - STRENGTH (ת) – FULLY DEVELOPED (ק)
7818	שָׂחַט	SaĤaT	to squeeze out	GRASP (שׂ) - ALL AROUND (ח) - MOTION (ט) Note: It is likely that this word was spelled with a SIN instead of a SHIN (with indicates GRASP) to differentiate it from 7819 below.
7819	שָׁחַט	ShaĤaT	to slaughter, beat, slay	GRASP (שׁ) - ALL AROUND (ח) - MOTION (ט) [to seize, to lay hold of, to put one's hand to]
2616a	חָסַד	ĤaSaD	to be good, kind, to show yourself kind	ALL AROUND (ח) - COMPLETELY (ס) - two GATHERED/JOINED (ד) (see below)
2616b	חָסַד	ĤaSaD	to be reproached, to be ashamed	ALL AROUND (ח) - COMPLETE (ס) – EDGE [lack] (ד) (see above)
6743	צָלַח	TSaLaĤ	to break forth, to come upon mightily	GREAT FORCE (צ) - GUIDED FLOW (ל) - ALL AROUND (ח) See 3905 below, for a word which uses the same 3 letters but in a rearranged order.
3905	לָחַץ	LaĤaTS	to squeeze, to press, oppress	GUIDED FLOW / PURPOSEFUL (ל) – ALL AROUND (ח) – SOLID / FIRM / STRONG FORCE (צ) See 6743 above for a word which uses the same 3 letters but in a rearranged order.
2118	זָחַח	ZaĤaĤ	to remove, displace	FORCE / DESTROY / SHATTER (ז) - into SEGMENTS / PIECES (חח)
6703	צַחַח	TsaĤaĤ	dazzling, scorching, clearly, pure	MIGHTY FORCE (ז) - ALL AROUND (ח) - SPACE (ח)

Unlocking the Ancient Pictorial Code of the Hebrew Alphabet

Strong's Number	Hebrew Word	Trans-Literation	Word Definition	Explanation of Pictographical Meanings
2076	זָבַח	ZaBaĤ	slaughter for sacrifice	VIOLENT FORCE (ז) - LIVING BEING's BODY (ב) - ALL AROUND (ח)
7743	שׁוּחַ	SHUaĤ	to sink down	CONSUMED (שׁ) – BY / OF (ו) – SURROUNDINGS (ח)
5024	נָבַח	NaBaĤ	to bark	HOLLOW/EMPTY (נב) -THROAT (ח) or MOVEMENT (נ) - WITHIN (ב) – THROAT (ח)
6315	פּוּחַ	PūaĤ	to breathe, blow	BLOSSOM OUT [exhale] (פ) - OF or INTO (ו) – SPACE (ח)
1272	בָּרַח	BaRaĤ as in Barach Obama	Bib. Heb. – to go through, flee Mod. Heb. - lightening	BODY (ב) - INSIDE/WITHIN (ר) – EMPTY SPACE (ח)
6524a	פָּרַח	PaRaĤ	to bud, sprout, a shoot, blossom, budded	BLOOM/BLOSSOM (פ) - INSIDE (ר) – ALL AROUND (ח) or BLOOM/BLOSSOM (פ) - ATTRIBUTE (ר) – ALL AROUND (ח)
7971	שָׁלַח	SHaLaĤ	to send, sent, go, stretch, spread	EXPANDing (שׁ) - GUIDED FORCE (ל) - [into] VOID/SURROUNDING EMPTY SPACE (ח)
7979	שֻׁלְחָן	SHuLĤaN	table	EXPANDing (שׁ) - GUIDED FORCE [purpose] (ל) - SPACE (ח) - LIVING (נ)
4229	מָחָה	MaĤaH	to wipe, wipe out, wipe away	PLACE (מ) - SPACE/VOID (ח) - RAISED UP (ה) lit. ERASE Denotes creating a void emptiness) where previously there was something.
2372	חָזָה	ĤaZaH	see, behold	ALL AROUND the SURROUNDING SPACE (ח) - SCAN [sweeping, 180 degree, arcing indicating *to look*] (ז) - BEHOLD (ה) See 4237 below
[4236] 4237	מֶחֱזָה	MaĤaZaH MeĤaZaH	4236 vision 4237 **window**	PLACE (מ) - ALL AROUND the SURROUNDING SPACE (ח) - SCAN [sweeping, 180 degree, arcing indicating *to look*] (ז) - BEHOLD (ה) See 2372 above
2397	חָח	ĤaĤ	hook, ring, fetter	SURROUNDINGS (חח)

Chapter 9 – ĤET

Strong's Number	Hebrew Word	Trans-Literation	Word Definition	Explanation of Pictographical Meanings
2336	חוֹח	ĤoaĤ	briar, bramble, thorn bush, hook, fetter, ring	SURROUNDING (ח) of SURROUNDINGS (ח) poss. To be caught or ensnared by one's surroundings [thorn bushes]
2282	חַג	ĤaG	a festival gathering, feast	ALL AROUND (ח) – GATHER TOGETHER for the Purpose of Pleasure (ג*) * The Gimmel here was prob. originally GHAYIN
6779	צָמַח	TSaMaĤ	to grow, spring forth, sprouted (prim root)	ROOTED (צ) - BODY (מ) - GROWTH or GROWS into SURROUNDING SPACE (ח) See 6784 below for 6779's opposite
6784	צָמַק	TSaMaQ	to dry up, to shrivel up (prim root)	ROOTED (צ) - BODY (מ) - **CONTRACTING** or **SHRIVELING SPACE** (ק) See 6779 above for 6784's opposite

ĤET - Biblical (well... Talmudic) Food for Thought

HANUKKAH (Ĥanukah) חנוכה

ALL AROUND (ח) - LIFE (נ) – OF (ו) – BLESSINGS (כ) - REVEALED (ה)

The pictographical letter meanings for the word *Chanukah*, the Festival of Light, denote a *life of blessings* or *living blessings* being *revealed*. Perhaps a *living blessing* might be rendered as a *MIRACLE*. The letters on the dreidel (wooden top which is spun in a children's game where chocolate coins are the prize) are NUN, GIMMEL, HEI and SHIN. These letters begin the four Hebrew words which mean a *GREAT ↔ MIRACLE HAPPENED HERE*.

According to the Talmud, Hanukkah (also spelled Hanukah or Chanukah) celebrates a miracle that happened when the oil lamp in the Temple was re-kindled after the Maccabees defeated the Hellenistic rulers who had defiled the Temple. When the temple was rededicated, the Levitical priests had only enough properly sanctified oil for one day. It took a week to make more oil according to Biblical specifications. Miraculously, the small jar of oil burned for 8 days instead of just one; thus giving the Levitical priests the necessary time to make a proper supply of oil for the temple lamps.

An alternate origin of Hanukkah also exists according to myjewishhistory.com:

> Hanukkah is one of the few Jewish holidays not mentioned in the Bible. The story of how Hanukkah came to be is contained in the books of 1 and 2 Maccabees, which are not part of the Jewish canon of the Hebrew Bible.

> These books tell the story of the Maccabees, a small band of Jewish fighters who liberated the Land of Israel from the Syrian Greeks who occupied it. Under the reign of Antiochus IV Epiphanes, the Syrian Greeks sought to impose their Hellenistic culture, which many Jews found attractive. By 167 B.C.E, Antiochus intensified his campaign by defiling the Temple in Jerusalem and banning Jewish practice. The Maccabees--led by the five sons of the priest Mattathias, especially Judah--waged a three-year campaign that culminated in the cleaning and rededication of the Temple.
>
> Since they were unable to celebrate the holiday of Sukkot at its proper time in early autumn, the victorious Maccabees decided that Sukkot should be celebrated once they rededicated the Temple, which they did on the 25th of the month of Kislev in the year 164 B.C.E. Since Sukkot lasts seven days, this became the timeframe adopted for Hanukkah.

The events described above make no mention of any overt miracle, other than the victory of the Jewish zealots over their oppressors. Perhaps miracles are often in the eyes of the beholder. The ĤET which begins the name of this holiday denotes *ALL AROUND*.

Whether you are a person who believes in overt miracles or not, take a little time in the coming days and weeks to look *all around* you. Blessings from God happen every day. On the other hand, so do hardships. Perhaps the greatest miracle from God I have seen in my own life is that even when life's circumstances seemed too difficult and there seemed to be no way through them, still a way existed. I was able to take that *next step* even when I was incredibly weary.

If you find yourself wondering where the strength for that *next step* will come from, try asking God to help you find it. Like the oil in the Temple lamp that kept burning for *just one more day* for seven days in a row until the problem was solved, God can be the source of miraculous strength for taking that *"next step"* during even the most trying of circumstances.

* * *

Chapter 10
TET

Woven or Wicker Basket - Clay Water Jar
(Joined All Around)

Tet's picture image should bring to mind a potter's wheel and the making of a clay pot.
TET primarily denotes COILING, TURNING or a LAYER.
Secondary meanings include: STRIKE at/out, to SURROUND, PRECISE [WALLED, LIMITED, CONFINED, NARROW, CONTAINED, EXACT, or TIGHT], to SWEEP, a COILED (wicker or woven) BASKET, a CONTAINER that can HOLD WATER, a COILED SNAKE, a turned CLAY POT, INTO.
*INSCRIBE*D and *JOINED* are Thav crossover meanings; note the Phoenician pictograph for THAV (an X) inside of a CIRCLE… possibly indicating BECOME ONE - ALL AROUND or Water-tight.

TET indicates the motion of a potter's wheel, where one side is always moving away while the opposite side is moving toward the potter; therefore, the motions TET can denote are EXCHANGING PLACES, GIVING AND TAKING, or TRADING.

The post-Babylonian letter for TET most likely depicts
a clay water jar (complete with a spout on the left and a handle on the right).

TET's letter name means:
COILs or LAYERS (ט) - CAUSED to (י) - BECOME ONE (ת)

TET

Action or Motion Indicated	Descriptive Form	Noun(s) Denoted	Prepositional Meaning
Coiling Turning or Rotating Braiding Weaving Exchanging Places Trading (Places)	Confined Surrounding Exact or Tight Limited	A clay water jar or wicker basket or A container that can hold water. MOTION (in general)	INTO

TET and THAV seem to have swapped meanings over time. Similar to the problems encountered with GIMMEL (which merged with some meanings from the lost letter, GHAYIN), TET and THAV's pictographical meanings can be problematic and should be closely scrutinized.

THAV or TAV, the final letter of the Hebrew Alphabet, is still pronounced by some Hebrew speakers as a soft *TH*, while TET is the letter that is more closely represented by the English letter T. However, the initial letters of the Hebrew alphabet and Greek alphabet hold similar places. *Aleph, Beit, Gimmel,* and *Daleth* in Hebrew are mirrored by the Greek letters *Alpha, Beta, Gamma,* and *Delta*.

The 7th letter of the Greek Alphabet is *Theta*, a *TH* sound. TET is the Hebrew Alphabet's 9th letter. Near the end of the Greek Alphabet is *Tau*, while Hebrew's last letter is *Thav*. Many linguistic scholars believe that either Greek or Hebrew traded the places of the letters which denoted the *T* and *TH* sounds. In fact, inside the circle of TET's Phoenician letter is an X, which is THAV's pictograph.

Pictographical interpretation of the letters Thav and Tet within Hebrew words provides further evidence that the letter swap was likely made in Hebrew, as the two letters' meanings seem to have been interchanged over time. Consequently, pictographical translation of the words may require determining subjectively using contextual clues as to whether the TET or THAV pictographical meanings apply.

TET EXAMPLES:

Strong's Number	Hebrew Word	Trans-literation	Word Definition	Explanation of Pictographical Meanings
prob. from 2916 mud, clay	טִיט	TET	JOINED, CONNECTING, MOTION [esp. turning], COILED, a CONTAINER, LAYERED, PRESSED, DOWN, [see Thav section re Tet spelled תֵת]	ACTION + Joined = coiled (like a snake), woven or clay basket. ALSO: The word TET or TETH indicates a defined area that *can contain water*, such as a clay jar or pot. TET (Teth) also indicates a turning motion and also is used to indicate clay and mud, which led to the letter Teth further symbolizing COILED [ergo a SNAKE]. Another meaning of TET could easily be CLAY TURNING, which equates to the concept of throwing/turning clay to make containers. The motion of a turning potter's wheel is always one where there is motion away from and motion toward the potter; therefore, TET can denote the motion of EXCHANGING or TRADING places.

Chapter 10 – TET

Strong's Number	Hebrew Word	Transliteration	Word Definition	Explanation of Pictographical Meanings
2916	טִיט	TÎT (teet)	mud, mire, clay	LAYER (ט) - UPON/OVER (י) - LAYER (ט) or COIL (ט) - UPON/OVER (י) - COIL (ט) [as in coiled clay-ropes pottery: LAYERED]
2915 from 2902	טִיָּח	Ti-YaĤ (tee-yaĤ)	to plaster, to coat, to cover over defects	MOTION/ACTION [apply/spread] (ט) - OVER (י) - OPEN SPACE (ח)
Modern Hebrew	טִיֵּל	Ti-Yai L	to walk, stroll, take a hike, go on a trip	MOTION/ACTION [to pick] (ט) - UP (י) - LEG/STAFF (ל)
7818	סָחַט	SaĤaT	to wring out	GATHERing (ס)-TWISTing (ח)-ACTION (ט) or GATHER (ס)-TWIST (ח)- [into a] CONTAINER (ט)
Modern Hebrew from	סְמַר-טוּט	SMaR-TŪT	a rag	GATHER (ס) - LIQUID (מ) - INSIDE (ר) - CONTAIN (ט) AGAIN (טוט) [WAW Between 2 TETs means Tet's pictographical meaning *AGAIN*.]
2927	טְלַל	T'LaL	to have shade	COVER (ט) - WAVING [poss. palm branches] (לל) or BRANCHING (לל) - COVER (ט)
2915 from 2902	טִיחַ	Tee-aĤ	to smear or to plaster	FILL (ט) - UP (י) - VOID/DEFINED EMPTY SPACE (ח) MOTION [LAYER] (ט) – ABOVE / OVER (י) - HOLE / CRACK / IMPERFECTION (ח) [Chet can indicate either a void or a spiraling motion.]
Modern Hebrew only	טָח	TaĤ	to smear or to plaster	FILL/JOIN (ט) - VOID (ח)
3875	לוֹט	LOT	cover, veil, envelope	TOP (ל) - OF (ו) - CONTAINER (ט)
3874	לוּט	LŪT	to wrap up tightly; Mod. Hebrew: cover, cloak	TOP (ל) - OF (ו) - CONTAINER (ט)
Modern Hebrew only	זוּט	ZUT	a bag	TAKE (ז) - within (ו) - CONTAINER (ט)

Unlocking the Ancient Pictorial Code of the Hebrew Alphabet

Strong's Number	Hebrew Word	Transliteration	Word Definition	Explanation of Pictographical Meanings
Modern Hebrew only	זוֹט	ZOT	bottom	BOTTOM (ז) - OF (ו) - CONTAINER (ט)
2895	טוֹב	TŌV	good, to be pleasing	FULLNESS [fully contained] (ט) - OF (ו) - BODY (ב)
2912	טָחַן	TaḤaN	to grind, grinder	CONTAIN (ט) - ALL AROUND (ח) – MOVE (נ)
Modern Hebrew only	טֶקֶס	Te-QeS	ceremony, protocol	ACTIONs (ט) - THROUGHOUT (ק) - GATHERING (ס)
7000	קָטַר	QaTaR	to shut in, enclose	COMPLETELY/SECURELY (ק) - CONTAINED (ט) - INSIDE (ר)
7818	שָׂחַט	SaḤaT	to squeeze out	GRASP (שׂ) - ALL AROUND (ח) – MOTION (ט) Note: It is likely that this word was spelled with a SIN instead of a SHIN (with indicates GRASP) to differentiate it from 7819 below.
7819	שָׁחַט	ShaḤaT	to slaughter, beat, slay	GRASP (שׁ) - ALL AROUND (ח) - MOTION (ט) [to seize, to lay hold of, to put one's hand to]
5027	נָבַט	NaBaT	to look	RE-MOVE (נ) - BODY (ב) – CONNECTion (ט) or an INVISIBLE CONNECTION "REMOVED BODY" (ב + נ) denotes hollow, empty or bodiless/invisible
2927	טְלַל	T'LaL	to have shade	COVER (ט) - WAVING [palm branches] (לל) or BRANCHING (לל) - COVER (ט)
3813	לָאַט	LaAT	to cover	GUIDED FLOW (ל) - SEPARATED INDIVIDUAL [component parts] (א) - CONTAINER (ט)
331	אָטַם	ATaM	to close, shut, shut up	SEPARATED/INDIVIDUAL (א) - CONTAINED (ט) - PLACE/OBJECT (מ)
332	אָטַר	ATAR	to shut up, close, bind	SEPARATED INDIVIDUAL (א) - CONTAINED (ט) - INSIDE (ר)

Strong's Number	Hebrew Word	Trans-literation	Word Definition	Explanation of Pictographical Meanings
6362	פָּטַר	PaTaR	to separate, remove, set free, open	RELEASE (פ) - that which is CONTAINED (ט) - INSIDE (ר)
4296	מִטָּה מִיטָה	1. [Bib.] MeeTAH 2. [Mod.] MeeTAH	bed, couch	REST (מ) - in (י) - ELEVATED (ה) ↔ CONTAINER (ט)
2902	טוּחַ	TUAĤ	to overlay, to over-spread, to coat	LAYER (ט) – OVER (ו) – OUTSIDE OF (ח)
2901	טָוָה	TaVaH	to spin	TURN (ט) – FLOW TOGETHER (ו) – RAISE UP (ה) [denoting a potter's wheel perhaps?]

TET - Biblical Food for Thought

TET
COILs (ט) - CAUSED to (י) - BECOME ONE (ת)

The name of the letter TET means both TURNING and COILING. During my first couple of years of grade school, I greatly enjoyed the days when we got to make art projects with clay. Typically the first thing most of the boys made was clay snakes... nothing but uninspired, long ropes of clay. Eventually, however, our art teacher taught us to stack these coils upon one another to make containers.

The post-Babylonian exile meanings of TET seem to have been all about working with clay and building containers that were capable of holding water. Anyone who has seen a potter work with clay turning upon a potter's wheel has seen how marvelously beautiful pottery pieces rise up under the careful and skilled guidance of the potter's hands.

Isaiah 64:8 uses this imagery to remind us that God is in control of our lives; it is He who forms us and shapes us:

> "But now, O Lord, You are our Father,
> We are the clay, and You our potter;
> And all of us are the work of Your hand."

What have we to fear if we allow the Master Potter to work with us freely? Yet, all too often I find myself like a piece of unshaped clay fighting the Master Potter at every turn. All that I gain for my ill-advised struggling is more time on the potter's wheel.[10]

On the other hand, when I do relax and let the Creator do what He does best… rule over His Creation, I am rewarded with unimaginable beauty and goodness coming into my life and character. God's hand can make all things beautiful… thankfully, that means even me.

* * *

---

[10] See also Isaiah 45:9

Chapter 11
YOD

GRASPING HAND - HAND of GOD
Forked Hand represents an Opposable Thumb for Holding Tools...
indicating to Create

YOD primarily denotes TO CAUSE TO BECOME, to GRASP (especially a tool), to HOLD, to CLUTCH, to CREATE, and the CREATOR's HAND.

Secondary meanings of YOD include the following:
BRIGHT, RISE UP, UPWARDS, ABOVE, LIGHT, the SUN, CLEAN, SHINING, QUICK, a SHARP POINT,
and to RETURN (the Sun returned each morning).

The Phoenician pictograph depicts an arm with a closed hand (for GRASPING). The Y-shaped hand denotes an opposable thumb and fingers, needed for grasping tools. Being able to *grasp tools* made possible the human (and god-like) ability *to create*.

The post-Babylonian letter for TET most likely depicts the SUN or SUN GOD. The SUN was seen as the CREATOR by many ancient cultures.

YOD's letter name means:

CAUSING to BE, CREATION or CREATOR (י) - OF (ו) – TWO GATHERED (ד)
[TWO GATHERED probably denotes HEAVEN and EARTH]

YOD

Action or Motion Indicated	Descriptive Form	Noun(s) Denoted	Prepositional Meanings
Causing to Be to Create, to Hold, to Grasp, to Clutch	Bright Shining Clean Most High	the Creator's Hand, the Sun, Light	On, Up, Upon, Above, Over, Of

YOD is the only Hebrew letter which is suspended and unsupported above the line of writing, just as the sun stands unsupported above the earth below. Most ancient cultures thought that the primary ruler of the gods was the sun god. The sun god Ra reigned supreme in Egypt, and Zeus rode his fiery chariot across the sky according to the Greeks. *Shemesh* is the Hebrew word for *sun;* the Canaanite sun goddess was named *Shemesh*, and "*Shamash* was the common Akkadian name of the sun god as well as the name of the god of justice in Babylonia and Assyria."[11]

YOD EXAMPLES:

Strong's Number	Hebrew Word	Trans-Literation	Word Definition	Explanation of Pictographical Meanings
Word not in Tenach	יוֹד	Yod	RISE-OVER-GROUND 1. Sun 2. to CREATE, CREATION, God's CREATIVE Hand 3. ABOVE, HIGH, UP EXHALTED. 4. BRIGHT 5. to Hold or Grasp or Clutch 7. "I AM"	Y(י)- O(ו) - D(ד) is YOD, which means RISE-OVER-GROUND or the HORIZON, originally indicating the **SUN**, but later referring to **God the Creator** [specifically, God's divine HAND over His creation]. Other meanings for YOD are CREATE [*cause to come to be*], BRIGHT / SHINING (like the sun), **poss. INDIVIDUAL, ABOVE ELEVATED, AMPLIFIED, MORE, HIGHer, OF/ON/UP/UPON, a GRASPING HAND, to STRIKE** [with the hand], a **SIGN** [Note: Gen. 1:17 states that the sun and moon were set in the heavens as *signs.*]
2915 from 2902	טִיחַ	Ti YaCH	to smear, to plaster, to cover over defects	FILL (ט) - UP (י) - VOID/DEFINED EMPTY SPACE (ח) MOTION [LAYER] (ט) – ABOVE / OVER (י) - HOLE / CRACK / IMPERFECTION (ח) [Chet can indicate either a void or a spiraling motion.]
Modern Hebrew	טִיֵל	Ti-Yai L	to walk, stroll, take a hike, go on a trip	MOTION [to pick] (ט) - UP (י) – LEG/STAFF (ל)
5869 & 5870	עַיִן	Ayin	EYE	EYE (ע) - BRIGHT (י) - and IN (י) - MOTION (ן) = signs of being alert & alive
6735b	צִיר	TSeeR	Swivel	FIXED (צ) - BECOMES [is caused to be] (י) - BENT [bendable] or CHANGED (ר)

---

[11] Wikipedia.com article on Shamash

Chapter 11 – YOD

Strong's Number	Hebrew Word	Trans-Literation	Word Definition	Explanation of Pictographical Meanings
1824 from 1820	דָּמִי	Da-Mee	rest, quiet, silence	poss. EXTEND (ד) - STILLNESS/QUIET/REST (מ) - MORE (י)
6529	פְּרִי	Pri [Pree]	fruit, result, offspring	FRUIT (פ) - INSIDE (ר) - CREATED/CAUSED TO BE/DEVELOPS (י)
3423	יָרֵשׁ	YaReSH	to seize, take possession, inherit, dispossess	CAUSE (י) - CHANGE (ר) - of WEALTH/SUSTENANCE/PROVISION (שׁ)
Not in Tenach	זיין	Zayin	to TAKE UP ARMS	1. Zayin means *PICK* or *TAKE* or *RAISE* (ז) - UP (י) – ARMs (ן). 2. an axe, **pick** or weapon [Zayin + Yod = PICK UP, **Yod = UP**] **Nun** stands for **ARM** [just as Gimmel and Lamed can = leg]
Modern Hebrew	זיף	ZeeF	Modern Hebrew: bristle (i.e. the bristles of a paint brush)	PICK (ז) - UP (י) - DROPLETS (ף) [a paint brush in Mod. Heb.] Strong's # 2128: "A name of one of Judah's sons" Listed as being of "unclear der."
2915 from 2902	טִיחַ	Tee-aĤ	to smear, to plaster, to cover over defects	FILL (ט) - UP (י) - VOID/DEFINED EMPTY SPACE (ח) MOTION [LAYER] (ט) – ABOVE/OVER (י) - HOLE / CRACK / IMPERFECTION (ח) [Chet can indicate either a void or a spiraling motion.]
1471	גוֹי	GOY pl. GOYIM	a gentile, a non-Jew a gentile nation	TRAMPLE (ג) - UPON (ו) – GOD's Divine HAND/CREATION (י)
3220	יָם	YaM	a sea, a lake	**HIGH/DEEP** (י) - **WATER** (מ) or *CAUSE to BE* or **INDIVIDUAL** or **Unique** (י) - Body of **WATER** (מ)
3117	יוֹם	YŌM	a period of time [translated in Genesis 1 as a "DAY" but in no way does the word YOM indicate a time period of exactly 24 hours]	**CREATION** (י) - of (ו) - MATTER/SUBSTANCE/BEING/BEINGS (מ)

Unlocking the Ancient Pictorial Code of the Hebrew Alphabet

Strong's Number	Hebrew Word	Trans-Literation	Word Definition	Explanation of Pictographical Meanings
589	אֲנִי	ANI (uh-nee)	The 1st person pronoun: **I**	SEPARATE INDIVIDUAL (א) - LIVING (נ) - PERSON or CREATION (י)
738	אֲרִי	ARI	a lion	GREAT/HIGH/MIGHTY (י) ↔ INDIVIDUAL/LEADER (א) - ATTRIBUTES/CHARACTER/REPUTATION/PERSONALITY (ר)
3027	יָד	YaD	hands, strength, authority, command, against, to afford, Mod. Hebrew: a memorial, a place of remembrance	EXTEND (ד) - **MORE** (י) or EXTEND (ד) - **GREATLY** (י) or EXTEND (ד) - HIGH ABOVE (י)
3444	יְשׁוּעָה	Yeshuah	salvation, deliverance	is CAUSED TO BE (י) - ABUNDANCE (שׁ) - OF (ו) - SEPARATION/DELIVERANCE/LIFE (ע) ↔ GREAT (ה)
3443	יֵשׁוּעַ	Yeshua	Hebrew name [translated into Greek as Jesus]	CAUSE to BE (י) - the SUBSTANCE (שׁ) – of (ו) - LIFE FORCE or AWAKENING (ע)
7105	קָצִיר	Qa-TSeeR	to mow, to harvest	ACROSS (ק) - STATIONARY OBJECTS (צ) - MAKE (י) - CUT (ר)
7006	קִיא	QI (KIA?)	to vomit, that which is vomited up	ACROSS/COMPLETELY (ק) - **CAUSE TO BE** (י) - SEPARATED (א) This word seems to indicate forceful, full projectile vomiting... **SPEW**
6718	צַיִד	TSaYiD	hunter, hunter's game, provisions	FIXED PACE (צ) - UPON/OVER (י) - the EDGE (ד) [stalking prey]
Not in Tenach see 6734	צַיֵּת	TSee-YeT	(to) OBEY! (imperative) [poss. from TSITSIT = tassels on Jewish prayer shawls]	PERMANENTLY/CONSISTENTLY (צ) - **HIT [strike]** (י) - the MARK (such as a *bull's-eye*) (ת) **NOTE:** in the ancient pictographs: **HAND** (י) - PERMANENTLY AFFIXED (צ) – to PURITY (ת)

Chapter 11 – YOD

Strong's Number	Hebrew Word	Trans-Literation	Word Definition	Explanation of Pictographical Meanings
3426	יֵשׁ	YeSH uncl. der.	1. being, existence, fact, substance 2. there is/are	CAUSE to BE (י) - EXISTENCE / SUBSTANCE (שׁ)
4325	מַיִם or מַיִם	Biblical: MaYiM Modern: MaY-YiM	water, waters	WATER (מ) - **DEEP/HIGH or RISE (י)** - **CAUSING** to BE (י) - a BODY [of water] (מ)
1961	הָיָה	HaYaH	to come to pass, am, was, become	[raised up] MORE (ה) - CAUSING TO BE/COME to BE (י) - MORE (ה) [lots happens]
7636	שָׁבִיס	SHaBIS	A headband [listed as unc. der.] See 3847 above	PUFF UP (שׁ) - BODY (ב) - UP/HIGH, ABOVE (י) - ENCIRCLED (ס) [PUFF UP BODY is prob. an idiom for PUTTING ON CLOTHES for warmth]
3915	לַיִל לֵיל לַיְלָה	layil leyl laylah	Night	COMFORT (ל) - UPON [lit. *OVER and ABOVE*] (י) - COMFORT (ל) spelling #3: COMFORT (ל) - UPON (י) - GREAT (ה) COMFORT (ל)
2916	טִיט	TÎT	mud, mire, clay	LAYER (ט) - UPON [over / above] (י) - LAYER (ט) or COIL (ט) - UPON/OVER (י) - COIL (ט) [probably denotes primitive pottery similar to the pottery which is made by 1st graders out of coiled clay ropes ☺]
2123	זִיז	ZÎZ	moving things, beasts, everything that moves OR abundance, bountiful	STRENGTH (ז) - UPON [over and above] (י) - STRENGTH (ז)

YOD - Biblical Food for Thought

YOM יוֹם
CREATION (י) – OF (ו) – MATTER or SUBSTANCE (מ)

The first chapter of Genesis gives the creation account. Each day God created something new, and on the 7th day He rested (the Jewish sages say He created *REST* of the 7th day). For centuries theologians and philosophers have debated the question, "Exactly how long is a Biblical day?"

YOM is the word used in the original Hebrew which translated as *day* in most English versions of Genesis. Many scholars agree that *YOM* could be rendered as *A PERIOD OF TIME*.

Based on the pictographical meanings of the letters YOD – WAW - MEM, I would like to suggest another meaning for the word *YOM: CREATION (י) – OF (ו) – MATTER or SUBSTANCE (מ)*. *Yom* seems to denote an undefined and open-ended period of time during which each phase of creation occurred. First God created the heavens, then the earth and so on. Each *PHASE of CREATION* was a *YOM*. Needless to say, these P*HASES of CREATION* could have been as short as a millisecond. On the other hand, the various phases might have been 24 clock hours… or even countless millennia in length.

In short, to argue whether God created the universe in a *week*'s time, as measured by today's standard clock hours, is fruitless. The original pictographical Hebrew word *YOM* offers no *proof* what-so-ever towards establishing the exact length of a Genesis *day*. It should be enough that we embrace the concept of the Lord God as the Divine Creator. Science and the Bible are only at odds when we force them to become so by rigid and narrowly defining how God chose (and chooses still) to behave. As the Psalmist once wrote, "God is in the heavens; He does what *He* wants." [12]

* * *

---

[12] Psalm 115:3, author's paraphrase and emphasis

Chapter 12
KAPH

Palm of the Hand - Oven, *KA*[13]  or Hanging Weight (?)

KAPH denotes the Palm of an Open Hand.
The outstretched HAND OVER denotes a COVERING as well as
a HAND HOLDING and BESTOWING a BLESSING.
The Palm of the Open Hand with Fingers SPREAD OUT poss. denotes DIVERSITY

Secondary meanings of KAPH include the following:
to SEEK, to SEARCH, to REACH OUT, to EXTEND, to FIND and GRASP, to COVER, to allow, to GIVE, to RISE, to BESTOW, to BECOME, to PUT, to PLACE, GENEROUS, EASY, SPACIOUS, MANY, MAY BECOME, the HEAVENS (because they cover the earth), SPREAD OUT OVER / ABOVE (the position of the heavens)

The post-Babylonian letter for KAPH possibly depicts an oven or furnace (seen as holding and producing blessings of cooked food & refined metal), or possibly related to the Egyptian symbol KA[13] (which stood for one's conscience or one's soul)
… but possibly the Post-Babylonian pictogram for Kaph could be a hanging weight used on a balance scale (these scales are still in use today in the Old City of Jerusalem).

KAPH denotes WEIGHTY, HEAVY, GREAT or HONOR.

KAPH's letter name means:
HAND (כ) - FULL (ף)

KAPH

Action or Motion Indicated	Descriptive Form	Noun(s) Denoted	Prepositional Meanings
to cover, to hold, to give, to allow, to seek, to find, to bestow (blessing) to put, may become	Weighty, Heavy, Great, Covered, Dark, Hidden, Spacious, Generous, Fullness. Here (adv.)	Lit. a Handful, Covering, Darkness, Destiny, Heavens, Weight	Over (like a covering)

---

[13] http://www.egyptianmyths.net/section-symbols.htm

Unlocking the Ancient Pictorial Code of the Hebrew Alphabet

KAPH EXAMPLES: (Egyptian **KA**)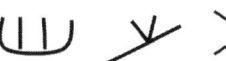

Strong's Number	Hebrew Word	Trans-literation	Word Definition	Explanation of Pictographical Meanings
3709	כַּף	KaPH	1. lit. a HANDFUL: KAPH [Palm of HAND combined with PHEY [drops flowing down denoting FULL] = HAND-FULL	1. HAND (כ) - FULL (ף) [lit. a HANDFUL or FULLNESS] 2. COVER OVER 3. Weighty, Heavy, Great, Honor 4. Destiny (*KA*) 5. HERE A) Kaph can denote the heavens and anything that is above or covers over. Kaph, being a hand, also denotes HOLDing B) KAPH denotes COVERING and the outstretched HAND OVER denoting BLESSING.
Modern Hebrew	סָכֵף	SaKeF	to discourage	COMPLETELY (ס) - HOLD (כ) - DOWN (ף)
5534a	סָכֵר Modern סָכַר Biblical	SaKeR (modern) SaKaR (Biblical)	a dam (modern) to shut up, stop up (Biblical)	GATHER (ס) - HOLD (כ) - INSIDE (ר)
5391	נָשַׁךְ	Nashak	to bite, to take interest (on a loan), creditors	TAKE (נָשַׁ)+ a HANDFUL (ך)
7899	שֵׂךְ	SeKH	Thorn	SHARP/POINTED (שׂ) - FINGERs (ך)
5521	סֻכָּה	SuKKaH	a thicket, Booths, temporary shelter	GATHER (ס) - COVERING (כ כ) - UP ABOVE (ה)
Modern Hebrew	שִׂכָּה	SuKHaH	barb, thorn, spear	SHARP/POINTED (שׂ) - FINGERs (כ) - RAISED UP/ELEVATED (ה) (poss. a pitchfork?)
1719	שָׂכֵל	Sa-KHeL	to be prudent, wise, to have insight	SHARP [clever] (שׂ) - OUTSTRETCHED HAND (כ) - LEADING/GUIDING (ל)
modern Hebrew	כִּבְשָׁן	Kiv-SHaN	Oven	OVEN (כ) - THREE-SIDED HOUSE [lit. TABERNACLE] (ב) - PUFF UP (שׁ) - MOTION (ן)

Chapter 12 – KAPH

Strong's Number	Hebrew Word	Transliteration	Word Definition	Explanation of Pictographical Meanings
3897	לָחַךְ	LaĤaK	to lick, licked	TONGUE (ל) - ALL AROUND (ח) - COVER (כ)
5480a	סוּךְ	SŪK	to pour (in anointing), anointed	COMPLETENESS/GATHERED (ס) - OF (ו) - BLESSING/ANOINTING (כ)
4371	מֶכֶס	MeKes	tax, levy, proportion to be paid	COLLECT (מ) - [a "COVER" charge] ABOVE (כ) - what has been GATHERED (ס) or WEIGHTY "STUFF" GATHERED
4364	מַכְמֹר	MaK-MoR	a net or snare	PLACE (מ) – to HOLD (כ) - OBJECT/BODY (מ) - INSIDE (ר)
3602	כָּכָה	KaKaH	thus, just so, so, like this	HERE (כ) - HERE (כ) – MORE REVEALED (ה) e.g. " more of the same"
3548	כֹּהֵן	KŌHeN	High Priest	GREAT (כ) – RAISED ABOVE (ה) – LIFE / ACTIONS / RESPONSIBILITIES (?) (נ) As in "a life of a special and great high calling & duties"
3542	כָּה	KaH [Aramaic]	here, this point	HERE (כ) - INDICATED (ה)
3543	כָּהָה	KaHaH	1. to be dim, grow dim 2. to rebuke	1. the COVER of DARKNESS [night] (כ) – RISING (הה) 2. PALM of HAND (כ) - RISING (הה)
3678	כִּסֵּא and כִּסֵּא	Biblical and Modern	a throne, a chair	HOLD (כ) - UP (י) - GATHERED [non-standing] (ס) - INDIVIDUAL (א)
3680	כָּסָה	KaSaH (casa = house in Spanish)	cover, covered, hidden, refuge	COVER (כ) - GATHERED/COMPLETELY (ס) - RAISED UP (ה)
3683	כָּסַח	KaSaĤ	to cut off or cut away	HOLD [take?] (כ) - GATHERED/COMPLETELY (ס) - ALL AROUND (ח)
3688	כָּסַל	KaSaL	to become foolish, stupid	COVER (כ) - COMPLETELY (ס) - That Which GUIDES THE FLOW (ל)
3697	כָּסַם	KaSaM	to shear a sheep, clip	TAKE (כ) - COMPLETELY/GATHER (ס) – the BODY (מ)

Unlocking the Ancient Pictorial Code of the Hebrew Alphabet

Strong's Number	Hebrew Word	Trans-literation	Word Definition	Explanation of Pictographical Meanings
3699	כָּסַס	KaSaS	to compute, to divide	TAKE (כ) - GATHERED (ס) - **GATHERINGS** (ס) prob. To GROUP or TAKE GROUPINGS
3700	כָּסַף	KaSaPH	to long for greatly, to be eager, shame	TAKE (כ) - COMPLETE (ס) - FALL (ף) or TAKE (כ) - COMPLETELY (ס) - DOWN (ף)
- NA -	Yük	Turkish: yook	bulk, load, burden, weight, charge, strain, tax	Causing /Applying (Y comes from Yod) – of (ü) – WEIGHT (K comes from Kaph כ)
3513	כָּבֵד	KaVaD	heavy, honored (prim. root)	WEIGHT (כ) - BODY (ב) - EXTENDED (ד) This is a word-picture of a balance scale with hanging weights.
3515	כָּבֵד	KaVeD	Heavy	WEIGHT (כ) - BODY (ב) - EXTENDED (ד) This is a word-picture of a balance scale with hanging weights.
3510	כָּאַב	KaAV	Pain	HEAVY (כ) – AGAINST (א) - BODY (ב)
3512a	כָּאָה	KaAH	to be disheartened	HEAVY (כ) – AGAINST (א) – RAISED ABOVE [encouraged, uplifted] (ה)
3527	כָּבַר	KaBaR	to be much, or many, abundance	HEAVY/WEIGHTY/GREAT Weight of Abundance (כ) – BODY (ב) – in CHARACTER (ר)
- NA -	AKBaR	Arabic: AKBaR	great – as in "Allah AKBaR" See 3513 above	HEAVY/WEIGHTY (K for כ) – BODY/PERSON (B from Bet ב) – in CHARACTER / REPUTATION (R from Resh ר)
3557	כּוּל	KŪL	comprehend, contain, sustain	FULLNESS/ABUNDANCE (כ) – OF (ו) – GUIDANCE or COMFORT (ל)
3559	כּוּן	KŪN	to be firm, prepared, ready	FULLNESS/ABUNDANCE (כ) – OF (ו) – LIFE (נ)
3789	כָּתַב	KaTaV	to write	HEAVY (כ) – MARK (ת) – on BODY (ב) Prob. denotes writing upon a clay tablet.
3799	כָּתַם	KaTaM	to stain	HEAVY (כ) – MARKing (ת) – *SUBSTANCE (מ) *MEM most likely denotes a LIQUID substance here

Chapter 12 – KAPH

Strong's Number	Hebrew Word	Transliteration	Word Definition	Explanation of Pictographical Meanings
3800	כֶּתֶם	KeTHeM	Gold	HEAVY (כ) – PURE (ת) – SUBSTANCE (מ)
3804	כֶּתֶר	KeTHeR	a crown	GREATNESS (כ) – MARKED (ת) – WITHIN (ר)
3807	כָּתַת	KeTHaTH	to beat, to crush by beating, hammered	HEAVY (כ) – PRESSING (ת ת) * *The doubled THAV makes PRESS into PRESS**ING**
3780	כָּשָׂה	KaSaH	to be gorged, satiated	GREAT (כ) – ABUNDANCE (שׂ) – MORE THAN (ה)
4908	מִשְׁכָּן	MiSHKaN	Tabernacle	PLACE of (מ) – GREAT/GLORIOUS (כ) ↔ ABUNDANCE (שׁ) – of LFE ... or poss. MOVING [portable] (נ) or Moveable Place of Abundant Glory
3733	כַּר	KaR	1. a basket-saddle 2. a pasture Listed as "of unc. der." in Strong's and Libronix's concordance	HOLD (כ) – INSIDE (ר)
3615	כָּלָה	KaLaH	completed, accomplished, finished	COMPLETE or COMPLETED (כ) – GUIDED FLOW (ל) – BEHELD or REVEALED (ה)

KAPH - Biblical Food for Thought

SUKKAH סֻכָּה - Plural: SUKKOTH
Meaning: A Booth or Tabernacle

GATHER (ס) - COVERING (כּ = כ ך) - UP ABOVE (ה)

    Every year in the fall, Jews all over the world celebrate SUKKOTH, also known as the Feast of Tabernacles. Sukkoth (or Sukkot) was one of the three feasts (along with Passover and Shavuot in the spring) where Israelites from all of the country would make a pilgrimage to Jerusalem in order to worship.

    Traditionally, temporary, 3-sided shelters, *sukkoth* or *tabernacles*, are built upon rooftops or in the yard and the family has their evening meal (some also sleep in them) every night for the festival week. To most Jews, this festival commemorates the 40 years that Moses and the Israelites spent in the wilderness before coming into the land of Israel. The highlight of the Feast of Tabernacles is the blessing and waving of branches from four species of tree (date palm, myrtle, willow and citrus). Prayers for sufficient rainfall in the coming year are also made. Fall is a time in Israel when temperatures cool down enough that it is quite pleasant to eat and/or sleep outside, and the making of the Tabernacle booths is fun for the family, especially for the children.

    For me, Tabernacles means something even deeper than all of this. I believe that we are God's living tabernacles. God has chosen to tabernacle among us and within us. His Spirit indwells, inspires and transforms those who are yielded to His will and to His ways.

    Like the temporary tabernacles built upon rooftops and in back yards, our bodies are temporal. Nobody lives forever within the tabernacle of our mortal bodies. For this, I am truly thankful, because with age mine has begun to show some serious signs of wear and tear.

    But... more than that, for me the essence of Tabernacles is a great yearning within. Like the Israelites in the wilderness and like the nation of Israel during nearly 2000 years of Diaspora, I feel deep within me that I am a stranger in a strange land, a sojourner while living out my life here on this earth.

    Someday, hopefully very soon, Messiah will come and bring unity among His people and among all peoples of the earth. Where I will be at that time in history, only God knows, but perhaps then this earth will finally feel like home.

* * *

Chapter 13
LAMED

l L

Folds of Fine Line - poss. Shepherd's Staff
Butter Churn Handle (or Rudder)
Anything that Waves Back & Forth

LAMED's Phoenician pictogram denotes a FOLD of fine linen, symbolic of COMFORT.

The post-Babylonian pictogram for Lamed denotes
GUIDANCE (lit. THAT WHICH GUIDES the FLOW), GUIDED FLOW
such as a SHEPHERD's STAFF, BUTTER CHURN, or a BOAT's RUDDER.

LAMED's wide-ranging list of meanings includes the following:
FOLDS or WAVES, GUIDED FLOW, to MILL, a SHEPHERD leader,
CENTER (also central reference point), to BUILD UP,
BOUNDARY (defined by the waving back and forth to show set limits), to PIVOT,
to GUARD, to CONTROL or to TEND, COMFORT (many soft FOLDS of bedding),
HEIGHTS, a WING or BRANCH (anything that WAVES).

Secondary meanings include the following:
VOICE, CRY OUT, MAST, WING, TONGUE, FIRE, TASTE, GO FORTH, TOWARD,
LL = that which lies between the folds [NOTHINGNESS]

LAMED's letter name literally means a SHEPHERD:
HE WHO GUIDES THE FLOW (ל) + a BODY [flock of sheep] (מ) –
TWO GATHERED (ד)   [the shepherd + his flock = *2 gathered*]

LAMED

Action or Motion Indicated	Descriptive Form	Noun(s) Denoted	Prepositional Meanings
to Guide, to Mill to Comfort, to Guard Over, to Limit, to Tend, Wagging or Waving	Folded, Central, Guided, Waving Milled	Comfort, Directed Flow, Guiding Boundaries, Wave motion	To, Toward

Unlocking the Ancient Pictorial Code of the Hebrew Alphabet

LAMED EXAMPLES:

Strong's Number	Hebrew Word	Trans-Literation	Word Definition	Explanation of Pictographical Meanings
- NA -	לָמֶד	LaMed	1. FOLDS of soft linen [denoting **COMFORT**] 2a. GUIDANCE, **GUIDED FLOW**: e.g. boat rudder, Shepherd's staff, a tongue, including a tongue of flame, Central Figure 2b. LAWS, CUSTOMS and RULES 2c. any folding, wave-like, flapping or waving motion 2d. Movement or flow toward a fixed point [guided movement] 2e. a Monument, marker or rallying point 3. PERMA-NENTLY ESTABLISHED 4. INTENDED, for the PURPOSE of GUIDED FLOW* (*GUIDED FLOW can be due to circumstances controlled by either God or man or by the natural flow of time &/or circumstantial events.)	Lamed stands for a variety of guiding factors [**GUIDED FLOW, INTENTIONAL PURPOSE**]: a Shepherd, a boat's rudder, the banks of a river. The first two letters, LAMED and MEM, can denote any of the following (as examples): **SHEPHERD** [the central figure] (ל) + BODY [Flock of sheep] (מ) or RUDDER (ל) + BODY [boat] (מ) or RIVER BANKS (ל) + a **BODY** of WATER [a RIVER] (מ) + the **DALETH** at the end of the word denotes that the **TWO** (are) **GATHERED TOGETHER** (ד) PICTOGRAPHS: 1. Early Phoenician: **FOLDS** of **SOFT LINEN** 2. Post-Babylonian: poss. a **Shepherd's staff** or a **Butter Churn Handle**: to **Mill**, to **Churn**, GUIDED FLOW, a **CENTRAL POINT** or **CENTRAL FIGURE,** a **gathering or rallying point** (like the Shepherd in the midst of the flock) The person or factor which determines the main direction of flow: probably quite literally coming into English as "**MAIN-STREAM**" Therefore, LAMED represents CUSTOMARY, CUSTOMS and SOCIETAL LAWS Note: Social Customs also have boundaries and defined limits... so LAMED = LAW [perhaps LAW-med became shortened, morphed into LAW and eventually made its way into the English language.] See Proverbs 3:6 and James 3: 3-6 3. a leg (nun = arm; yod = hand; etc.) 4. any WAVE-like (FOLDING) MOTION 5. Anything that waves side to side, flaps or wags and determines the direction of flow or motion: a tongue, rudder, Shepherd's staff, a bird's wings, etc. 6. PERMANENT, ESTABLISHED, CUSTOMARY [Lamed likely took on this meaning because God, who was seen as our Shepherd, established His laws as a "permanent ordinance". The SHEPHERD's STAFF denotes a sure state of security as well as everlasting comfort.] See Lev. 16 [re permanent statutes] and Isaiah 9: 6-7

Chapter 13 – LAMED

Strong's Number	Hebrew Word	Trans-Literation	Word Definition	Explanation of Pictographical Meanings
3888	לוּשׁ	LUSH	to knead bread	**GUIDED FLOW** (ל) - OF (וּ) – BREAD/PROVISION (שׁ)
Modern Hebrew	טַיֵּל	Ti-Yai L	to walk, stroll, take a hike, go on a trip	MOTION [to pick] (ט) - UP (יֵ) – LEG / STAFF (ל)
3897	לָחַךְ	LaĤaK	to lick, licked	**TONGUE** (ל) - ALL AROUND (ח) – COVER (ך)
5537	סֶל סַל	SeL (modern) or Sal (Biblical)	basket	GATHER (ס) + to a CENTRAL POINT [or in one place] (ל) = BASKET
Modern Hebrew	סְלָא	SeeLA	to weigh	BASKET (סֶל) + SEPARATE (א) = to WEIGHT, as in the two separate baskets on each end of a balance scale. It may not be coincidence that *SeyL* and the English word *SALE* are the same phonetically.
from 5560	סֹלֶת	SoLeTh	milled or refined flour	COMPLETE ly (ס) - MILL (ל) - BECOME ONE/PURIFIED/REFINED (ת)
5557	סָלַף	SaLaPH	to pervert	GATHER (ס) - LEAD/TAKE (ל) - DOWN (ף)
Modern & 5559	סִלֵק Modern סְלִק Biblical	SeeLeQ (modern) SLeQ (Biblical)	Modern: to lift, to move, to put away Biblical: to come up, taken	GATHER (ס) - LEAD/TAKE (ל) - ACROSS/AROUND (ק)
Modern Hebrew	נָשׁוּל	Nashul	eviction, ousting	nun + shin = take possession, nash: TAKING + OF (וּ) + **COMFORT** (ל)
5445	סָבַל	SaVaL	to bear a heavy load, sustain	GATHER/UNIFY (ס) - BODY [BEIT seems to indicate a person rather than an inanimate object] (ב) - LEAD/TAKE/SHEPHERD (ל) [similar to the concept stated in Gal. 6:2 - "Bear one another's burdens..."]
7965	שָׁלוֹם	Sha-LŌM	peace, completeness, soundness, safely	ABUNDANT (שׁ) - COMFORT (ל) - OF (וֹ) - QUIET BEING [STILLNESS] (ם)

Unlocking the Ancient Pictorial Code of the Hebrew Alphabet

Strong's Number	Hebrew Word	Trans-Literation	Word Definition	Explanation of Pictographical Meanings
3813	לָאַט	LaAT	to cover	GUIDED FLOW (ל) - SEPARATED INDIVIDUAL [component parts] (א) - CONTAINER (ט)
3874	לוּט	LŪT	to wrap up tightly	**TOP (ל)** - OF (וּ) - CONTAINER (ט)
8518	תָּלָה	ThaLaH	to hang, hanged	ACTION* (ת) - **WAVE-LIKE MOTION (ל)** - RAISED UP (ה) * [THAV indicates MOTION probably as a result of interchanging meanings with Tet]
5766	עָוֶל	A-VeL	injustice, wrong	SEPARATE (ע) - FROM (ו) – **LEADERSHIP / CUSTOMS / LAW (ל)** or NOTHING (עוֹ) + LEADERSHIP/LAW (ל) [lawlessness]
5766	עָוִל	Ee-VeL or EVIL	to do injustice	SEPARATE (ע) - FROM (ו) - CUSTOMS/ESTABLISHED LAW (ל)
7031	קַל	QaL	easy, swiftly	[move] ACROSS (ק) – **COMFORTABLY (ל)** or possibly FULLY/THOROUGHLY (ק) - GUIDED (ל)
5769	עוֹלָם or עֹלָם	OLAM	perpetual, permanent, from antiquity, ancient	TAKEing (ע) OF (ו) – **CENTRAL** [established or permanent] (ל) - PLACE (מ) or TAKE (ע) - CENTRAL [established/permanent] (ל) - PLACE (מ)
6963	קוֹל	QOL	sound, voice	MOVE ACROSS (ק) - WITH (וֹ) - EASE (ל) or possibly the MOVING ACROSS / FULLNESS (ק) of **GUIDANCE (ל)**
1086	בָּלָה	BaLaH	to become old, to wear out, worn out	PERSON (ב) and poss. USED (ל) UP (ה) LaH = USED UP ?
6743	צָלַח	TSaLaĤ	to break forth, to come upon mightily	UNBENDING/UNSTOPPEABLE/GREAT FORCE (צ) - GUIDED FLOW (ל) - ALL AROUND (ח) See 3905 below, which uses the same 3 letters but in a rearranged order.
3905	לָחַץ	LaĤaTS	to squeeze, to press, oppress	GUIDED FLOW/PURPOSEFUL (ל) - ALL AROUND (ח) - SOLID/FIRM/DESTRUCTIVE FORCE (צ) See 6743 above, which uses the same 3 letters but in a rearranged order.

Chapter 13 – LAMED

Strong's Number	Hebrew Word	Trans-Literation	Word Definition	Explanation of Pictographical Meanings
2107	זוּל	ZŪL	to lavish	STRENGTH (ז) - OF (ו) - COMFORT (ל)
3820	לֵב	LeV	heart, mind, will, inner man	THAT WHICH GUIDES (ל) - the BODY (ב) or [FOR THE PURPOSE OF] INTENDED to GUIDE the BODY
3808	לֹא	LO	NO, NOT, without	SPEAK / GUIDE / LEAD (ל) - AGAINST (א) Note: Typically, ALEF is an A or AH sound, not O. Interestingly, LO also appears in the Bible spelled phonetically: לֹה or לוֹא Perhaps the spelling evolved because the pictographical meaning was lost and spelling LO with an ALEPH seemed wrong.
3809	לָא	LA (Aramaic & Arabic)	NO, NOT, without	see above Alt. phonetic spelling: לָה
3811	לָאָה	LA-AH	to be weary or impatient	NO (לֹא) – FURTHER (ה) NO (לֹא) – FURTHER MORE (ה)
5034a	נָבֵל	NaBaL	to be senseless or foolish	HOLLOW/EMPTY (נב) [NUN+BEIT indicates a MOVED BODY... a hollowed out place] - TONGUE (ל)
2927	טְלַל	T'LaL	to have shade	COVER (ט) - WAVING [branches] (לל) or BRANCHING (לל) - COVER (ט)
3205 3206	יָלַד יֶלֶד	1. YaLaD 2. YeLeD	1. to bear, to bring forth, gave birth 2. child, boy, youth	CAUSE TO BE (י) - DIRECTED FLOW [purpose] (ל) - TWO GATHERED (ד)
3868	לוּז	LUZ	turn aside, depart, devious	GUIDED FLOW [poss. Redirection] (ל) - OF (ו) - STRENGTH (ז)
3885a	לִין or לוּן	LIN or LŪN	to lodge, pass the night, spend the night, remain overnight	FOLD (ל) - UP (י) - LIFE (ן) or COMFORT/FOLD (ל) - OF (ו) - LIFE (ן) Note: The earliest pictograph for LAMED was a fold of fine linen. Many FOLDS of linen represented a thick cushion of comfort for one's bedding.
3883	לוּל	LŪL	a shaft, enclosed space with steps, winding stairs or spiral staircase	GUIDED FLOW (ל) - AGAIN (ו) NOTE: WAW (VAV) between repeated identical letters indicates to do that action AGAIN. In this case, it seems to indicate a path that repeatedly directs one's way.

Unlocking the Ancient Pictorial Code of the Hebrew Alphabet

Strong's Number	Hebrew Word	Trans-Literation	Word Definition	Explanation of Pictographical Meanings
1719	שָׂכֵל	Sa-KHeL	to be prudent, to be wise, to have insight	SHARP [clever] (שׂ) - OUTSTRETCHED HAND (כ) - LEADING/GUIDING (ל)
6321	פּוֹל	PŌL	green beans Listed as "of unc. der."	BLOSSOM [produce "fruit"] (פ) – on (ו) – a POLE (ל) [Lamed represents a staff-like support.]
7945	שֶׁל	SHeL	SHEL indicates ownership, e.g. That is the house SHEL David.	POSSESSION (שׁ) - GUIDED FLOW/CONTROLLED (ל) [denoting anything of value under the control or ownership of a person]
2073	זְבוּל	Z'BŪL or Z'BŪL	elevation, height, lofty, habitation (poss. to dwell in high places)	STRONG (ז) - HOUSE (ב) - OF (ו) - [COMFORTABLE] HEIGHTS (ל) or SECURE (ז) - HOUSE (ב) - ON (ו) - HIGH (ל) See MaAL below re LAMED (ל) indicating HIGH
5769	עוֹלָם or עֹלָם	OLAM	perpetual, permanent, from antiquity, ancient	TAKEing (ע) OF (ו) - CENTRAL [established/permanent] (ל) - PLACE (מ) or TAKE (ע) - CENTRAL [established/permanent] (ל) - PLACE (מ)
3915	לַיִל לֵיל לַיְלָה	LaYiL LeYL LaYLaH	Night	COMFORT (ל) - UPON [lit. OVER and ABOVE] (י) - COMFORT (ל) spelling #3: COMFORT (ל) - UPON (י) - GREAT (ה) COMFORT (ל)
5549	סָלַל	SaLaL	to lift up, to cast up, highway, prize	COMPLETELY (ס) - BUILDING UP (ל)
5095	נָהַל	NaHaL	to lead or guide to a watering place, bring to a place of rest, refresh	MOVE to (נ) - GREAT (ה) – COMFORT (ל)
5140	נָזַל	NaZaL	to flow	MOVEment of (נ) - STRONG (ז) – GUIDED FLOW (ל)

LAMED - Biblical Food for Thought

The name of the letter LAMED refers to a SHEPHERD:
HE WHO GUIDES THE FLOW (ל) + a BODY [herd of sheep] (מ) –
TWO GATHERED (ד)

Shepherd: *Ra-AH* רעה
WATCHFUL (ר) - FORCE (ע) - AMPLIFED or AUGMENTED (ה)
Indicating a state of high alert, keen watchfulness

One cannot discuss the Biblical concept of SHEPHERD without discussing WATCHFULLNESS as well. The Hebrew word for a shepherd, *RA-AH*, comes from a word stem which means to *WATCH OVER*. Have you ever wondered how God sees us? Psalm 100: 5 tells us clearly who we are to God and who God is to us:

> "Know that the LORD Himself is God;
> It is He who has made us, and not we ourselves;
> *We are* His people and the sheep of His pasture."

Of all the Hebrew letter's, LAMED is the easiest letter for most beginning Hebrew students to spot. Because of its height, Lamed stands out clearly right there in the middle of the alphabet, just the way a shepherd and his staff might be easily spotted in the midst of a herd of sheep. Similarly, sheep can spot the shepherd, or at least his tall staff, from anywhere in the herd. God has called us to be His sheep, the sheep of His pasture. God Himself is our *shepherd*, our *Ra-ah*.

RA-AH means *HE WHO WATCHES OVER*. There is great *COMFORT* (the Phoenician meaning attached to Lamed's pictograph) in having someone watch over you, especially when you perceive them as having more strength than yourself. However, the shepherd's protection of the herd and his guidance to water and food only happens when the *TWO are GATHERED* together. Any sheep that strays too far from the fold can quickly put himself into great danger.

Sometimes shepherds have a particular sheep which is prone to wandering away from the herd. If the problem is so severe that the shepherd fears for the sheep's safety and well-being, one of the more extreme remedies to the problem is for the shepherd to break one of the sheep's legs. After breaking the leg, the sheep is carried upon the shepherd's shoulders until the leg heals.

During the time of healing, the sheep learns to depend upon his shepherd for its every need. Once the leg has healed, the shepherd is able to put the fully-restored sheep back on its own four feet. Thereafter, this sheep will be the one sheep that never leaves the shepherd's side.

The shepherd then puts a bell around this sheep's neck. Other sheep in the flock will follow the sound of the bell and can know without looking that they are following their shepherd.

Via its bell, this unique sheep leads the flock and keeps it together, and shepherds refer to this special sheep as the *bell sheep*. Even today, one can see flocks of sheep grazing on the hills around Jerusalem, and among them is always one special sheep with the bell dangling from its neck.

Scripture frequently refers to the Messiah as a *shepherd*. The prophet Micah (chapter 5) says this about the coming *shepherd* and ruler of Israel:

> 3 Therefore he will give them up until the time
> When she who is in labor has borne a child.
> Then the remainder of his brethren
> Will return to the sons of Israel.
> *4 And he will arise and shepherd his flock*
> In the strength of the Lord,
> In the majesty of the name of the Lord his God.
> And they will remain,
> Because *at that time he will be great*
> *To the ends of the earth.*
> 5 This one will be our peace..."
> - Micah 5:3-5, NASB, author's emphasis added

Verse 3 above has special significance for our current point in history. Micah clearly states that God would begin to shepherd the sheep (Israel), but then *give them up until the time* when a birth takes place. I believe that the birth being spoken of here refers to the re-birth of the nation of Israel in May of 1948. For half a century now Jews from all over the world have been returning to the Promised Land.

If the current return of Jewish people to Israel is one and the same as the historical event foretold in Micah 5:3, then we should soon expect the fulfillment of verses 4 and 5. God will no longer hid His face from mankind, but will instead arise and shepherd his sheep forever. We very well could soon see the greatness and glory of the Messiah here on earth when he comes to reign as king over Israel and all of his people... even *to the ends of the earth.*

Verse 2 (not shown above) tells us that this ruler's *"goings forth are from long ago, from the days of eternity."* Clearly, this is no ordinary king. Such a man must be the long-awaited Messiah. How wonderful it will be when these prophetic words concerning the Shepherd of Israel are fulfilled in full!

* * *

Butter churn with LAMED-shaped handle.

Photo taken by author
Sutter's Mill museum,
California, USA

Churn Handle
Cropped and Rotated 180°

Chapter 14
MEM
CHAOS or a CHAOTIC MASS - a BODY

MEM's Phoenician pictogram probably denotes a CHAOTIC or FORMLESS MASS.

The post-Babylonian pictogram for MEM denotes a BODY. For the most part, the BODY represents a BODY of WATER, but it can also represent a BODY as in a CONGREGATIONAL BODY of PEOPLE or SIMILAR-SPECIES GROUP.

Secondary meanings include the following:
CHAOS, LIQUID, FIRMAMENT, FLUID [water, wine, blood], a FORM, an IMAGE, MORE (added), MUCH, MANY, THING, OBJECT, WORD, ELEMENT(al), a PORTION, a WORD, SUBSTANCE, MASS, MASSIVE, STILLNESS, a PLACE WISDOM (a body of knowledge), FORMING, BEING, a BODY
(Note: BEIT indicates a person's body, but MEM denotes a BODY or OBJECT in the heavens. MEM also denotes a GROUP of people or a HOMOGENOUS GROUPING of SIMILAR ANIMALS such as a herd, flock, school, etc.)

MEM's letter name means:
WATERS (מם) or BODY (מ) of WATER (מ) [lit. Water Body]
or FORMING: FORM (מ) + FORM (מ) = FORMING

MEM

Action or Motion Indicated	Descriptive Form	Noun(s) Denoted	Prepositional Meanings
to FORM, to EXIST in STILLNESS	Formed, Chaotic, Fluid, MASSive	A Group or Layer of Similar SUBSTANCE Matter / "Stuff" Liquid Chaos	From

Note: **MŪ, MŌ** or *Mi* as a **prefix** indicates
a person of... or *a place of...*
Example: **Tz**ur = *Treat as a Foe* or *Harass*   Mi**tz**raim = Egypt

MEM EXAMPLES: מ מ ש

Strong's Number	Hebrew Word	Trans-Literation	Word Definition	Explanation of Pictographical Meanings
not a Biblical word	מֵם	MeM	1. THING, OBJECT, PARTICLE, COMPONENT PART, ELEMENT, WORD, FORM or SHAPE, LIQUID, IMAGE, SUBSTANCE of REALITY, BEING (v.) or a BEING (n.) 2. QUIET (NUN's opposite) or STILLNESS in the plural (ממ) [lit. resting quietly] 3. COLLECT (a tax, dross from smelting)	1. FORMs (מ) or FORMING or IMAGES (EXISTING or BEING STILL)… RESTING QUIETLY 2. COLLECTING [i.e. the waters collecting in the heavens to form rain or collecting to form bodies of water] MEM denotes a BODY, but not human bodies nor congregations of people (that is BEITH's function). Rather, MEM denoted a BODY of WATER [in its most primitive and original form], but also a BODY in the heavens, a BODY such as a herd of sheep or cattle, or a WORD, FORM, IMAGE, PARTICLE, SUBSTANCE, LIQUID or SOLID MATTER… in short the equivalent of the English words: THING or STUFF. A secondary meaning of MEM is STILLNESS, RESTING quietly, or simply EXISTING.
7954	קָמָה	QaMaH	standing grain	AROUND (ק) - PLACE [poss. field] (מ) - RAISED ABOVE (ה) Note: ה = lit. *raised up higher than…* or *elevated*
1826a	דָּמַם	D'MaM	to be still, silent	EXTEND (ד) - STILLNESS (מ מ) [Mem + Mem = quiet + resting]
4197	מֶזֶג	Mezeg	Wine (poss. fresh wine, not condensed)	LIQUID / WINE (מ) - NOT (ג) ↔ STRONG (ז) (*Not Strong* prob. denotes *not condensed*, as was the custom of the day to aid is storage and shipping)
4058	מָדַד	MaDaD	to measure, measured, stretched	PLACE of (מ) - GATHERING (דד)
4969	מָתַח	MaTHaĤ	to spread out, spreads	PLACE (מ) - JOINED (ת) – ALL AROUND (ח) or THING (מ) - JOINED (ת) – ALL AROUND (ח)
6685	צוֹם	TSŌM	to fast, fasting	DIFFICULTY [poss. EMPTINESS] (צ) - OF (ו) - STOMACH or BODY (מ) [MEM poss. denotes the stomach because MEM means a part of the whole or a part of the body. TSOM came into Greek as SOMA… which means "body" and into English as part of the word chromoSOME.]

Chapter 14 – MEM

Strong's Number	Hebrew Word	Trans-Literation	Word Definition	Explanation of Pictographical Meanings
8382	תָּאַם	Tha-AM	Biblical Hebrew: double, to bear twins Modern Hebrew: to join, to combine	JOIN(ed) / COMBINE(d) / UNITE(d) (ת) - INDIVIDUAL/SEPARATE (א) - PARTS/COMPONENTS (מ)
Modern Hebrew From 8389 fr. 8420b	תְאוֹם	Tey-ŌM	Biblical: twins, to bear twins Mod. Hebrew: symmetry	CONNECTED (ת) - INDIVIDUATIONS (א) - OF (ו) – SHAPES /FORMS / IMAGES (מ)
see 517	see below:	ŪM	mother in **Arabic**	CONNECTING (ו) - MEMBER/MEMBRANE (מ) [the person who holds and connects together the family]
517	אֵם or אִמָּא	EM or EeM-MA	EM: Biblical Hebrew Eemah: Mod. Hebrew	The Hebrew term for mother comes from the word for a glue-like substance that rises to the surface when hides are boiled. This substance was used for gluing things together.
2856	חָתַם	ĤaTaM Chatham	sealed, to seal	ALL AROUND (ח) - ATTACHED/JOINED (ת) – SUBSTANCE (מ) [i.e. a wax seal]
518	אִם אִם	EeM	if but also indicates: *except, or, though*	INDIVIDUAL/SEPARATE [possibility] (א) - IS CAUSED TO BE (י) - SUBSTANCE/REALITY (מ)
7965	שָׁלוֹם	Sha-LŌM	peace, completeness, soundness, safely	ABUNDANT (ש) - COMFORT (ל) - OF (ו) - QUIET BEING [STILLNESS] (מ)
3117	יוֹם	YŌM	a period of time	CREATION (י) - of (ו) – MATTER / SUBSTANCE / BEING / BEINGS (מ)
3220	יָם	YaM	a sea, a lake	HIGH/DEEP (י) - WATER (ם) or CAUSE to BE (י) - a Body of WATER (ם)
5975	עָמַד	AMaD	to stand, to take one's stand, to stand in place	TAKE (ע) - PLACE (מ) - STAND (ד) [to take a firm stand in one place]

Unlocking the Ancient Pictorial Code of the Hebrew Alphabet

Strong's Number	Hebrew Word	Trans-Literation	Word Definition	Explanation of Pictographical Meanings
4581	מָעוֹז	MaŌZ from 5756 עוז Ūz See ŌZ in CH. on Zayin	a fortress or strong hold	PLACE OF (מ) - OPENING/SEPARATION (ע) - OF/FROM (ו) - WEAKNESS [possibly those who are WEAK] (ז) In Biblical Hebrew, MEM at the beginning of a separate 3-consonant word indicates either a PLACE OF___ or a PERSON OF___. ŌZ means TAKE REFUGE, so MaŌZ means a PLACE [or person] of TAKING REFUGE.
4186	מוֹשָׁב or מֹשָׁב	MoSHaV	a communal settlement with a blend of private ownership and communal living	MO (a place) + SHAV (to dwell) a **PLACE OF** (מוֹ) - ABUNDANT (שׁ) - HOUSES/FAMILIES (ב)
2525	חַם	CHaM	hot, warm	HOT/ PASSIONATE (ח) – [physical] BODY (מ) HOT (ח) - STILLNESS (מ) [hot with no breeze as in sweltering heat?]
2552	חָמַם	CHaMaM	hot, warm, mated, become warm or heated	HOT/WARM/PASSIONATE (ח) - [physical] BODIES / WATERS (מם = plural: BODIES or WATERS)
4191	מוּת	MŪTH	died, to put to death	PLACE (מ) - OF (ו) - CROSSing or PURITY (ת) [poss. meaning "crossing over" to death]
5276	נָעֵם	NaEM	to be pleasant	LIFE (נ) + PRESENCE (ע) - PERSON (מ) [poss. Meaning an VIVATIOUS Person]
5568	סָמַר	SaMaR	to bristle up	GATHER (ס) - LIQUID (מ) - INSIDE (ר) [denotes the bristles of a brush]
7061	קָמַץ	QaMaTS	to **enclose** with the hand, to grasp	WRAP AROUND (ק) - OBJECT (מ) - FORCEFULLY (צ)
5001	נָאַם	NaAM	utter a prophecy	LIVING (נ) – INDIVIDUAL or UNIQUE (א) - WORD (מ)
1653	גֶּשֶׁם	GeSHeM	torrential rain, downpour	TRAMPLE (ג) - SUBSTANCE (שׁ) - BODY [esp. Body of Water] (מ) prob. Lit. a BODY of WATER that SUBSTANTIALLY TRAMPLES or PELTS the earth… this is definitely a HEAVY RAIN.
1818	דָּם	DahM	Blood	TWO GATHERED (ד) - liquid BODY (מ) [the 2 parts poss. being LIFE + BLOOD or from the fact that blood will separate into PLASMA [water] and red SOLIDS [blood].

Chapter 14 – MEM

Strong's Number	Hebrew Word	Trans-Literation	Word Definition	Explanation of Pictographical Meanings
1826a	דָּמַם	DaMaM	to be or grow dumb, silenced	GATHERED TOGETHER (ד) – WORDS (מם) Note: Notice how 1826 a and 1826b seem to be completely opposite meanings, yet *GATHERED TOGETHER WRODS* can be taken two opposite ways.
1826b	דָּמַם	DaMaM	to wail	GATHERED TOGETHER (ד) – WORDS (מם) Note: Notice how 1826a and 1826b seem to be completely opposite meanings, yet GATHERED TOGETHER words can be taken two opposite ways.
1830	דָּמַע	DaMA	to weep bitterly	GATHERED TOGETHER (ד) - WORD/SOUND (מ) - FORCEful (ע)
1824 from **1820**	דֳּמִי	Da-Mee	rest, quiet, silence	GATHERED (ד) - GREAT (י) ↔ STILLNESS/QUIET/REST (מ)
4325	מַיִם or מַיִם	Biblical: MaYiM Modern: MaY-YiM	water, waters	WATER (מ) - DEEP/HIGH or RISE (י) - CAUSING to BE (י) – a BODY [of water] (מ) [poss. a lake or sea]
8064 8065	שָׁמַיִם	Shamayim in both Hebrew and Aramaic	heaven, sky	ABUNDANT or SPREAD OUT/EXPANSE (שׁ) - Body of Water [moisture?] (מ) - CAUSES to BE (י) - WATER/RAIN (מ) or ABUNDANT (שׁ) - GREAT/HIGH (י) - BODY of WATERS (מם)
1826	דְּמַם	D'MaM	to be still, silent	EXTEND/GATHER (ד) - STILLNESS (מ) [Mem + Mem = quiet + RESTING]
8537	תֹּם	THoM or TOM	completeness, integrity	PURE (ת) - BODY/OBJECT (מ)
331	אָטַם	ATaM	to close, shut, shut up	SEPARATED/INDIVIDUAL (א) - CONTAINED (ט) - PLACE/OBJECT (מ)
4296	מִטָּה מִיטָה	1.Mee-TAH (Bib. spelling)	bed, couch	REST (מ) – IN or UPON (י) - ELEVATED (ה) ↔ CONTAINER (ט)

Strong's Number	Hebrew Word	Trans-Literation	Word Definition	Explanation of Pictographical Meanings
4524	מֵסַב	MaSaV	that which surrounds or is round, surrounding area, table	PLACE (מ) - SURROUNDING/ENCIRCLED (ס) - PERSON/HOUSE/LIVING BODY (ב)
4229	מָחָה	MaĤaH	to wipe, wipe out, wipe away… also to strike	PLACE (מ) - SPACE/VOID (ח) - RAISED UP (ה) [poss. lit. to ERASE] Denotes creating a void, emptiness, where previously there was something… OBLITERATE might also work.
4371	מֶכֶס	MeKes	tax, levy, proportion to be paid	[collect] a PORTION (מ) - ABOVE (כ) -what has been GATHERED (ס)
4330	מִיץ	MITS (MeeTS)	To press, to squeeze, to wring	BODY (מ) – GREATLY/HIGHLY (י) - PRESSED (ץ)
4843	מָרַר	MaRaR	to be bitter or troubled	BODY (מ) - BITTER / TROUBLED (ר) - INSIDE (ר)
4784	מָרָה	MaRaR	to be contentious or rebellious	BODY (מ) - BITTER or TROUBLED (ר)- MORE (elevated) or REVEALED (ה)
4786	מֹרָה	MoRaH	bitterness, grief	BODY (מ) - BITTER or TROUBLED (ר)- MORE (elevated) or REVEALED (ה)
4753	מֹר	MOR	Myrrh Myrrh was used for embalming and burned as a fragrance at funerals	BODY (מ) - BITTER (ר)
4179	מוֹרִיָּה	(Mount) Moriah	The mountain where Abraham offered up Isaac as a potential sacrifice.	BODY or Place (מ) - OF (ו) – TROUBLE or CHARACTER (ר) ↔ GREAT (י) - REVEALED (ה)

MEM - Biblical Food for Thought
Mount Moriah מוריה

Mount Moriah's name means:
Place (מ) - OF (ו) - GREAT (י) ↔ CHARACTER (ר) - REVEALED (ה)

Or perhaps
Myrrh (MOR: מור) of God (YAH: יה)

Mount Moriah is the name of the mountain that Abraham climbed with his son, Isaac, with the intention of offering up Isaac as a sacrifice. The last five words on the example chart above are all related, having the root stem of MEM-RESH, meaning BITTER ↔ BODY. It is this same root stem from which we get the English word *myrrh*.

Myrrh is a fragrance primarily made from the sap that comes from a small, bush-like tree with thorny branches, the *Commiphora myrrha*. It is used both for embalming and for burning as incense during funerals. Myrrh's symbolism and it's relation to death is well-known to Middle Eastern cultures.

The MEM-RESH root stem also means BITTER or BITTERNESS. The sting of death and grief are also closely connected with the concept of BITTERNESS.[14] Mount Moriah was the location of Solomon's Temple in Jerusalem, where the Western Wall (Wailing Wall) still stands today. It was always at the Temple where the Levitical priest made the atoning sacrifices for the nation of Israel.

Leviticus, chapter 6:1-7, explains why the guilt offering was made and how it was to be done:

> "When a person sins and acts unfaithfully against the LORD, and deceives his companion… then he shall bring to the priest his guilt offering to the LORD, a ram[15] without defect from the flock, according to your valuation, for a guilt offering, and the priest shall make atonement for him before the LORD…" (NASB)

According to tradition, Abraham's offered up of Isaac on (or very near) Mount Moriah. Some rabbinical commentaries say that Abraham was willing to offer up his son, Isaac, because Abraham believed God would raise Isaac from the dead, even if Abraham had gone through with the sacrifice and plunged the knife into his son's heart. Regardless of one's level of buy-in to the historical accuracy of this Biblical event, there is a lesson to be learned on

---

[14] See Ezekiel 21:6 Here, the term "bitter grief" comes from one Hebrew word, *meriruth*, which contains the root stem MEM-RESH.

[15] Lev. 5:15

Mount Moriah. In the moment of great trials, especially when facing death, one's character is laid bare for all to see.

Rabbi Akiva (Akiba), one of Judaism's greatest sages, was killed by the Romans for taking part in the Bar Kochba revolt (132-135 C.E.). At the moment of his tortuous death, Akiva proclaimed, the "*Shema Yisroel* ("Hear O Israel, the Lord thy God, the Lord is one!" from Deuteronomy 6:4). May our character, when it is revealed, be as righteous!

* * *

Chapter 15
NUN
SPROUTED SEED, LIGHTENING - LIFE

NUN was represented by two Phoenician pictograms:
The LIGHTENING BOLT denoted LIFE FORCE.
The SPROUTING SEED represented RE-CREATION and PROCREATION.

The post-Babylonian pictogram for NUN is uncertain, but it could be the side view of the thumb and index finger spread apart indicating a MEASURE or SPAN of life.

Secondary meanings include the following:
LIFE, to LIVE, to DO, MOTION or MOVEMENT

NUN's letter name means:
LIFE (נ) - LIVES (נ) ↔ AGAIN (indicated by the WAW between the 2 NUNs)

NUN

Action or Motion Indicated	Descriptive Form	Noun(s) Denoted	Prepositional Meanings
to Live, to Move, to Do, to Procreate, poss. to Work	Living, Moving, Free	Life Force, Life, The *MOVEMENT* of living creatures.	Below, At the bottom of

NOTE: The WAW placed between any two identical letters indicates *AGAIN*.

NUN's pictograph means LIFE; therefore, NUN's letter name, NUN – WAW – NUN, means *LIFE AGAIN*… or PROCREATION

NUN EXAMPLES:

Strong's Number	Hebrew Word	Trans-literation	Word Definition	Explanation of Pictographical Meanings
5125	נוּן	Nūn to Propagate	LIFE LIVING AGAIN [to propagate] MOVEMENT of LIVING CREATURES also: MOVE, DO, poss. WORK	LIFE (נ) LIVING (נ) AGAIN (ו) ... the Nun-VAV-Nun construct indicates LIFE (NUN) AGAIN. Tet denotes inanimate objects moving, while Nun usually denotes the movement of living things: LIFE, MOVEMENT, and poss. WORK Nun Sophet (ן) can indicate BOTTOM in some words, especially in words that end with WAW NUN (וֹן), pronounced "ŌN"
5301	נָפַח נָפַח	1. NaPHaĤ (Biblical) 2. Ni-PaĤ (Modern)	1. to blow, breathe, boiling (Bib. Hebrew) 2. to swell (Mod. Hebrew)	MOVE or LIFE (נ) - BLOSSOM out (פ) - into the SURROUNDING VOID (ח)
2-letter root	נ + שׁ	nas or nash	to take	MOVE + DISPURSE = to take
5378	נָשָׂא	Nasha	1. to lead astray 2. to exact payment	1. MOVEMENT (נ) - PUFF UP (שׁ) - SEPARATE/AWAY (א) also 2. MOVEMENT (נ) - DISBURSE (שׁ) - SEPARATE/AWAY (א)
Modern Hebrew	נָשׁוּל	Nashul	eviction, ousting	nun + shin = take possession, nashul = TAKING + OF (ו) - COMFORT (ל)
5391a	נָשַׁךְ	Nashak	to bite, to take interest (on a loan)	TAKE AWAY (נָשׁ) + a SCOOP/HANDFUL (כ) "Take a cut" is the equivalent idiom in modern English.
5386	נָשִׁי	n'shi	to loan, a debt	DISBURSE (נשׁ) + YOD = disbursed with interest Note: YOD often denotes "more, high or above"
5387	נָשִׂיא	Nashiah	lifting up, carrying, raising, leaders, prince, chief	TAKE (נָשׂ) + ABOVE/HIGH (י) + AWAY (א) + RAISED UP (ה)
7160	קָרַן	QaRaN	to radiate light, beam of radiant light	ACROSS [radiating] (ק) - APPEARANCE (ר) - MOVE (נ) or DEVELOP (ק) - MOVING (נ) ↔ APPEARANCE (ר)
5380	נָשַׁב	NaSHaV	to blow	MOTION (נ) – EXPANDING / PUFFING UP (שׁ) - BODY (ב)

Chapter 15 – NUN

Strong's Number	Hebrew Word	Trans-literation	Word Definition	Explanation of Pictographical Meanings
974	בָּחַן	BaĤaN	to test, examine, prove	MOVE AROUND (נ ↔ ח) - BODY/HOUSE [so as to inspect it]
2912	טָחַן	TaĤan	to grind, grinder	CONTAIN (ט) - ALL AROUND (ח) - MOVE (נ)
5276	נָעֵם	NaEM	to be pleasant	LIFE (נ) - FORCE (ע) - PERSON (ב)
Modern Hebrew	עוֹנֶן	'ŌNeN	an anchor	SEPARATE (ע) - FROM (ו) - MOVING (Double NUN: נן) or PREVENTING (עו) MOVING (נן)
see 5771 below	עוֹנה	'ŌNaH	Sin	SEPARATION/TAKING (ע) - OF (ו) – LIFE (נ) Plus (ה) [indicating *amplified*]
5117	נוּחַ	Nuach	to rest, to wait, to remain, to camp	LIFE (נ) - OF (ו) - CONTAINMENT (ח) or LIVING (נ) + WITHIN (ו) a LIMITED RANGE of MOVEMENT (ח)
589	אֲנִי	A-NI	1st person pronoun I	SEPARATE INDIVIDUAL (א) - LIVING (נ) - PERSON or CREATION (י)
6025	עֵנָב	ENaV	a grape	LIFE FORCE (ע) - LIVING/GROWING (נ) - BODY (ב) [See also 5107 *NŪB*]
1952	הוֹן	HON	wealthy	ELEVATED/RAISED standard (ה) - of (ו) - LIFE (נ)
6725	צִיּוּן	TSIYŪN	a signpost, a monument, marker	PERMANENT (צ) - SIGN (י) - OF (ו) - REMEMBERANCE (ן) Note: NUN means "living again"… so REMEMBERANCE equates to RE-LIVING an event
6726	צִיּוֹן	TSIYŌN	Mt. **Zion**, God's Holy Mtn.	PERMANENT (צ) - SIGN [the sun and moon were set by God as permanent signs] (י) - OF (ו) - REMEMBERANCE (ן) See 6725 above

Unlocking the Ancient Pictorial Code of the Hebrew Alphabet

Strong's Number	Hebrew Word	Trans-literation	Word Definition	Explanation of Pictographical Meanings
5107	נוּב	NŪV or NŪB	to bear fruit	GROWTH [living] (נ) - OF (ו) - BODY (ב) [BET denotes a living body as opposed to an inanimate body which would be denoted by a MEM]
5110	נוּד	NŪD	1. to move to and fro, to wander 2. to show grief	def. 1: LIVING/MOVING (נ) - AT (ו) - the EDGE (ד) def. 2: poss. REMEMBERANCE [re-living] (נ) - OF (ו) - the EDGE (ד) [grief]
6026	עָנֹג	ANoG	soft, delicate, dainty	LIFE FORCE of (ענ) – WEAK/DAINTY/MINIMAL/SMALL ? (ג)
11	אֲבַדּוֹן	AVaD-DON (Abaddon)	(place of) destruction, ruin	SEPARATED [poss. DESOLATE] (א) - DWELLING PLACE (ב) - EDGES (ד) - OF (ו) - BELOW/BOTTOM/the ABYSS (נ)
5771	עָוֹן	AŌN or AVŌN	iniquity, guilt	FORCE (ע) - OF (ו) – BOTTOM / LOWEST (נ) [behavior caused by **basest** motives] or EXPOSURE (ע) - OF (ו) - MOVEMENTs [poss. DEEDS] (נ)
2109	זוּן	ZŪN	to feed	STRENGTH (ז) - OF (ו) – LIVING/LIFE (ן)
5003	נָאַף	NaAPH	to commit adultery	MOVEMENT (נ) - INDIVIDUAL (א) - FALLEN (ף) or MOVEMENTs or ACTIONs of (נ) - a FALLEN (ף) ↔ INDIVIDUAL (א)
4998	נָאָה	NaAH	to be comely	LIVING (נ) - INDIVIDUAL (א) - ELEVATED [poss. indicating *BEAUTIFUL*] (ה)
5014	נָבַב	NaBaB	to hollow out, hollow, idiot	HOLLOW/EMPTY (נב) - BODY (ב) or MOVEment (נ) - WITHIN (ב) - BODY (ב)
5024	נָבַח	NaBaĤ	to bark	HOLLOW/EMPTY (נב) - THROAT (ח) or MOVEment (נ) - WITHIN (ב) - THROAT (ח)
5027	נָבַט	NaBaT	to look	RE-MOVE (נ) - BODY (ב) - CONNECT (ט) or an INVISIBLE CONNECTION "REMOVED BODY" (ב + נ) denotes hollow, empty or bodiless/invisible
5034a	נָבֵל	NaBaL	to be senseless or foolish	HOLLOW/EMPTY (נב) - TONGUE (ל)

Chapter 15 – NUN

Strong's Number	Hebrew Word	Trans-literation	Word Definition	Explanation of Pictographical Meanings
5012 or 5030	נָבָא or נָבִיא	NaBA Or NABI	to prophesy, prophesy	LIVING TABERNACLE (נב) - SEPARATE INDIVIDUAL (א)
8566	תָּנָה	ThaNaH	to hire	BECOME ONE (ת) - MOVE [poss. WORK or DO] (נ) - MORE (ה) "Many hands make light work."
5127	נוּס	NŪS	to flee, to escape, fugitive	MOVE [flee, escape] (נ) - FROM (ו) – NET (ס)
5102 and 5104	נָהָר	NaHaR	river, rivers, stream, canal, current	MOVE (נ) - RAISED UP (ה) - INSIDE (ר) Poss. denotes MOVES INSIDE RAISED UP [BANKS]
202	אוֹן	ŌN	vigor, wealth strength	Note: This word looks as if it should have originally been spelled AYIN (ע) -WAW-NUN, which would then denote FORCE (ע) - OF (ו) - **LIFE (נ)**.
5577	סַנְסִן	SaNSiN	fruit stalk of the date tree, a fruit stalk	GATHER (ס) – MOVE (נ) - GATHER (ס) – MOVE (נ) or Gathering and Moving
Modern Hebrew	סִנְנֵן	SeeNaN	to formulate, to arrange a text	GATHER (ס) – MOVE (נ) – MOVE (נ) – MOVE (נ)
5095	נָהַל	NaHaL	to lead or guide to a watering place, bring to a place of rest, refresh	MOVE to (נ) - GREAT (ה) – COMFORT (ל)
5040	נָזַל	NaZaL	to flow	MOVEment of (נ) - STRONG (ז) - GUIDED FLOW (ל)

NUN - Food for Thought
NAHAR: LIVING or MOVING (נ) - MOUNTAIN (הַר)

"Faith that can Move Mountains"

It is highly likely that we have all heard the phrase, "Faith that can move mountains" at one time or another. It comes from a saying ascribed to Yeshua (Jesus), who himself was Jewish. He told his followers that if they had faith as small as a mustard seed (one of the smallest seeds known to them), they tell a mountain to cast itself into the sea. That has always struck me as a strange thing to say, as nobody seems to have ever mustered up (pun intended) that kind of faith... as far as I know. But maybe what this Jewish teacher was really saying made more sense in Aramaic, especially when one knows the meanings of the ancient Phoenician letters.

The Hebrew word NAHAR, which means a *RIVER*, could be rendered as follows: **LIVING** or **MOVING** (נ) - **MOUNTAIN** (הַר) HAR (הַר) is the Hebrew word for mountain [*raised up - inside*]. Adding a NUN at the beginning of HAR to change it into NAHAR נָהָר would indicate a **living** mountain or ***moving*** mountain.

Perhaps the Hebrew word for mountain (NAHAR) really indicates a mountain or any place with a river flowing down off of it. *LIVING water* was an idiom for *moving* or *flowing water* in Biblical Hebrew [see Jer. 17:13, Zach. 14:8 & John 7:38]. A *moving* or *living mountain* might be an idiomatic term for a mountain that *flowed with water*.

If this is so, perhaps this idiomatic expression might explain what Yeshua meant when he talked about telling a mountain *to move* or *cast itself into the sea* (Matthew 21:21). Perhaps *FLOW* (and not *cast*) was the meaning of the original Aramaic or Hebrew word that Yeshua used when he said spoke this parable to the Israelite crowd in their native language.

So then, what is needed to turn a *MOUNTAIN* (HAR) into a *FLOWING RIVER* (**Na**HaR)? Just a NUN... which was represented by the Phoenician pictograph of a sprouting seed. We only need a SEED of faith the size of a mustard seed to change a *mountain* (HaR) into a *river* (**Na**HaR) which flows to the sea. But along with faith, we also need patience, for rivers flowing down the side of even the most imposing mountain will eventually erode that mountain into the ocean.

* * *

Chapter 16
SAMEKH

FISH GAFF (poss. a SUPPORT)   -   CASTING NET

SAMEKH's pictograph probably represented a TOOL for GAFFING FISH,
but numerous sources claim it to be representative of a SUPPORT.
In Arabic and Phoenician, SAMEKH means FISH;[16]
while in HEBREW, SAMAKH means a SUPPORT.
Without a doubt, SAMEKH's pictograph translates as GATHERING;
therefore, a FISH GAFFING TOOL seems the more likely object represented.

The post-Babylonian pictogram for SAMEKH appears to be a CASTING NET,
complete with the upper-left swoosh which denotes
the line that a fisherman would have attached to his wrist.

Both early and latter pictographs indicate the following meanings:
GATHER, ENCIRCLE, ENCLOSE COMPLETELY (SURROUND), CONTAIN.

Secondary Pre-Babylonian meanings included: THORN, MAKE A TURN (directional change
to a new heading), SUPPORT, SLAVERY or BONDAGE.

Post-Babylonian derivative meanings include a TOTAL or COMPLETE GROUP (SUM), as
well as: closed system, the womb (e.g. cistern, cyst, system).

SAMEKH's letter name means:
GATHER/ ENCLOSE COMPLETELY (ס) –

BODY [i.e. a school of fish] (מ) - HOLD (כ) [as in gathering fish in a NET]

SAMEKH

Action or Motion Indicated	Descriptive Form	Noun(s) Denoted	Prepositional Meanings
to Gather, to Catch, to Ensnare	Gathered, Surrounded Completely	the Catch, the Grand Total, Addition or the **S**UM Some say a Support	AROUND (the perimeter)

---

[16] See www.phoenicia.org/tblalpha.html

SAMEKH EXAMPLES:

Strong's Number	Hebrew Word	Trans-Literation	Word Definition	Explanation of Pictographical Meanings
from Arabic	סָמֶךְ (fish) - Not סָמַךְ (support)	סָמֶךְ (Samekh) means FISH in Arabic - not to be confused with 5564 סָמַךְ (Samakh) which in Hebrew means a SUPPORT	SAMEKH lit. means a FISH in Arabic and Phoenician. The letter's pictographical name, SAMEKH, means GATHER (ס) + BODY or a SCHOOL of FISH (מ) + HOLD (ך), denoting a FISHING NET	GATHER (ס) - BODY (ב) - HOLD (כ) to GATHER, DRAW TOGETHER [the way a cast net is closed], the CATCH (lit. FISH) from the NET, the BOUNTY, the SUM TOTAL, to GROUP by gathering parts, the TAKE [profit], COMPLETE, SURROUND, ENCIRCLED, ENCLOSE/ENCLOSED NOTE: The "gather" concept of SAMEKH in Hebrew can denote a secondary meaning similar to the English use of the word when describing the "gathering step" of a high jumper, which is the final step before leaping upward. It denotes contracting the body so that it may direct the energy of expansion upward and/or outward. A horse in full gallop moves by "gathering" its front and rear legs and then expanding. Gimmel denotes walking with legs in opposition, so the horse's style of running would have been unusual and therefore descriptively noteworthy. The antithetical counterparts to SAMEKH's "GATHER" meaning would be QOPH's "SWELL" [expand in less than a 360 degree direction] or SHIN [EXPAND OUTWARD equally in all directions simultaneously].
Modern Hebrew only	סָכֶף	SaKeF	to discourage	COMPLETELY (ס) - HOLD (כ) - DOWN (ף)
5534a	סֶכֶר modern סָכַר Biblical	SaKeR (modern) SaKaR (Biblical)	Mod. - a dam Biblical - to shut up, stop up	GATHER (ס) - HOLD (כ) - INSIDE (ר)
5564	סָמַךְ	SaMaKH	To lay, support	GATHER/COMPLETEly (ס) – BODY (מ) - HOLD (ך) Perhaps the word SAMAKH originally meant *a gaff*.
7818	סָחַט	SaĤaT	to wring out	GATHERing (ס)-TWISTing (ח)- ACTION (ט) or GATHER (ס)-TWIST (ח)- [into a] CONTAINER (ט)
Modern Hebrew	סְמַרְ-טוּט	SMaR-TŪT	a rag from 5568 below	GATHER (ס) - LIQUID (מ) - INSIDE (ר) - CONTAIN (ט) AGAIN (טוט)

Chapter 16 – SAMEKH

Strong's Number	Hebrew Word	Trans-Literation	Word Definition	Explanation of Pictographical Meanings
5568	סָמַר	SaMaR	to bristle up	GATHER (ס) - LIQUID (מ) - INSIDE (ר) [denotes the bristles of a brush]
5542	סֶלָה	SeeLaH	to praise	COMPLETEly (ס) – RAISED UP (ה) – STAFF or "Wings" [arms?] (ל) or possibly COMPLETELY- LIFT UP (GLORIFY) – HE WHO GUIDES THE FLOW of all things (God)
5537	סַל (modern) or סַל (Biblical)	SeL (modern) or Sal (Biblical)	basket	GATHER (ס) + to a CENTRAL POINT [or in one place] (ל) = BASKET
Modern Hebrew	סֶלָא	SeeLA	to weigh	BASKET (סַל) + SEPARATE (א) = to WEIGHT, as in the two separate baskets on each end of a balance scale. It may not be coincidence that SeyL and the English word SALE as the same phonetically.
from 5539	סָלַד	SeeLeyD	to praise, to bounce back, to rebound	COMPLETE ly (ס) - EXTENDED (ד) ↔ LEG (ל) (Hebrew syntax: adjectives come after the noun which it modifies)
5557	סָלַף	SaLaPH	to pervert	GATHER/COMPLETELY (ס) - LEAD/TAKE (ל) - DOWN/to a FALL (ף)
Modern & 5559 Biblical	סָלַק modern סְלַק Biblical	SeeLeQ (mod.) SLeQ (Biblical)	Mod.: to lift, to move, to put away Biblical: to come up, taken	GATHER (ס) - LEAD/TAKE (ל) – ACROSS/AROUND (ק)
5445	סָבַל	SaVaL	to bear a heavy load, sustain	**GATHER/UNIFY (ס) - BODY (ב) - LEAD/TAKE/SHEPHERD (ל)** [BEIT seems to indicate a person rather than an inanimate object - similar to the concept stated in Gal. 6:2 - "Bear one another's burdens…"]
8610	תָּפַשׂ but in Modern Hebrew תָּפַס	Tha-PHaS	to catch	The modern Hebrew spelling seems to be more correct: COMBINED/TOTAL [the catch/the "take" or "profit"] (ת) - FROM (פ) - **NET (ס)**
631	אָסַר	ASaR	to tie, bind, imprison, a prison	INDIVIDUAL (א) - **ENCLOSE** (ס) - INSIDE (ר)

Unlocking the Ancient Pictorial Code of the Hebrew Alphabet

Strong's Number	Hebrew Word	Trans-Literation	Word Definition	Explanation of Pictographical Meanings
5462	סָגַר	Sa-GaR	to close	CLOSED UP (ס) - NOT (ג) – INSIDE or poss. OPEN (ר)
5470	סֹהַר	SoHaR	a prison	**CLOSED UP (encircled) (ס) – RAISED UP (ה) – INSIDE (ר)**
2040	הָרַס	HaRaS	break down, overthrow… in English: harass	RAISED UP/GREAT [amplified] (ה) - CUT (ר) - COMPLETELY/ALL AROUND (ס)
2554	חָמַס	CHaMaS	treat with violence	PASSIONATE / ANGRY (ח) – [physical] BODY (מ) - **COMPLETELY (ס)**
2616a	חָסַד	ĤaSaD	to be good, kind, to show yourself kind	ALL AROUND (ח) - COMPLETELY (ס) - two GATHERED/JOINED (ד)
2616b	חָסַד	ĤaSaD	to be reproached, to be ashamed	ALL AROUND (ח) - COMPLETE (ס) - EDGE [lack] (ד)
5456	סָגַד	SaGaD	to prostrate oneself (in worship), fall down, falls down	COMPLETELY (ס) - BENDED (ד) ↔ LEG/KNEE (ג)
5383b	סוּס	SŪS listed as *prob. of foreign origin*	a horse, horses	ENCIRCLE/GATHER/CATCH (ס) + WAW between two SAMEKHS indicates to *GATHER* [SAMEKH] AGAIN or REPEATEDLY
5486	סוּף	SŪPH	to come to an end, to cease, completely removed	**COMPLETENESS (ס) - OF (ו) - DOWNWARD FLOW (ף)**
5493	סוּר שׂוּר	SŪR	to turn aside, departed	COMPLETENESS (ס) - OF (ו) - TURNing (ר) or CHANGE (שׂ) - OF (ו) - TURN (ר) [poss. an unplanned turn or something completely new]
5480a	סוּךְ	SŪK	to pour (in anointing), anointed	COMPLETENESS/GATHERED (ס) - OF (ו) – BLESSING / ANOINTING / COVERING (ך)
5521	סֻכָּה	SuKKaH	a thicket, Booths, temporary shelter	COMPLETELY (ס) - COVER (כ) – UP ABOVE (ה)

Chapter 16 – SAMEKH

Strong's Number	Hebrew Word	Trans-Literation	Word Definition	Explanation of Pictographical Meanings
5127	נוּס	NŪS	to flee, to escape, fugitive	MOVE [flee, escape] (נ) - FROM (ו) – NET (ס)
5462	סָגַר	Bib. Heb SaGaR Mod. Heb. SAGUR	to shut, close, isolate	ENCLOSE/CLOSED (ס) - NOT (ג) – INSIDE (ר) NOTE: The Biblical meaning does not seem to fit the use of the GIMMEL... which may have been originally a Ghayin. However, the word as used un modern Heb. fits amazingly well: closed up shops display the SAGUR sign in the window. It is possible that the Biblical meaning denoted that the prisoner's feet and/or legs (ג) were in stocks.
5465	סַד	SaD	stocks for securing the feet of prisoners [listed as prob. of foreign origin]	ENCLOSE/CLOSED (ס) – TWO GATHERED (ד) or CLOSED (ס) - EDGEs (ד)
6072	עָסַס	ASaS	to press, crush, tread down	FORCE (ע) **COMPLETELY (ס) GATHERED (ס)** or FORCE (ע) - GATHERING (סס) [poss. denotes compounding of force]
5473 also 5472	סוּג	SUG	fenced about, carefully fenced	ENCLOSEing/COMPLETE ENCIRCLing (ס) - of (ו) - FEET (ג) The use of the GIMMEL instead of a MEM or BEIT might indicate that the main concern addressed by this type of fence was to prevent a herd from running away. NOTE: SŪG is also listed as Strong's #5472 with an alternate meaning: "to move away, to backslide." In this case, the SAMEKH [net] pictograph would bring to mind the picture of a seining net being drawn back to its starting point... that is moving back to where it began.
6508	פַּרְדֵּס	PaRDDeS	a preserve park listed as "of for. or."	BLOSSOM OUT [prob. denoting blossoming trees and/or flowers] (פ) - INSIDE (ר) - the EDGES [prob. town limits] (דד) - GATHERED (ס)
4524	מֵסַב	MaSaV	that which surrounds or is round, table, surrounding area,	PLACE (מ) - SURROUNDING/ENCIRCLED (ס) - PERSON/HOUSE/LIVING BODY (ב)

Unlocking the Ancient Pictorial Code of the Hebrew Alphabet

Strong's Number	Hebrew Word	Trans-Literation	Word Definition	Explanation of Pictographical Meanings
3678	כִּסֵּא or כִּסֵּא	KeeSĀ	a throne, a chair	Hold (כ) - UP (י) - Gathered [non-standing] (ס) - Individual (א)
3680	כָּסָה	KaSaH	to cover, covering, covered (*casa* = house in Spanish)	COVER (כ) - GATHERED/COMPLETELY (ס) - RAISED UP (ה)
3697	כָּסַם	KaSaM	to shear [a sheep], clip	TAKE (כ) - COMPLETELY/GATHER (ס) - the BODY (מ)
3699	כָּסַס	KaSaS	to compute, to divide	TAKE (כ) - GATHERED (ס) - GATHERINGS (ס) prob. *To GROUP* or *TAKE GROUPINGS*
5577	סַנְסִן	SaNSiN	fruit stalk of the date tree, a fruit stalk	GATHER (ס) – MOVE (נ) - GATHER (ס) – MOVE (נ) or Gathering and Moving

Author's Side Note:

The ancient Phoenician fish gaff symbol for Samekh is the same symbol that the Slovakian Olympic hockey team has as the team emblem/logo on the fronts of their team jerseys during the 2010 Olympics in Vancouver, BC, Canada. It struck me as a strange co-incidence that the **S**lovakian team was wearing the equivalent of a big a silver **S** on a red background (with 3 blue hills underneath)… something akin to the classic Superman emblem.

Upon doing some checking on the Internet, apparently an ancient Slovakian king is credited with the first usage of this Samekh emblem. The king's name just happened to be named Stephen. The usage of the Samekh died out but was later revived by another Slovakian king. His name? **S**ebastian. The double cross, or patriarchal cross as the Byzantines called it, can be seen on Slovakian Euros as well as on their hockey jerseys.

Slovakian Coat of Arms [17]

---

[17] from http://en.wikipedia.org/wiki/Coat_of_arms_of_Slovakia

SAMEKH - Food for Thought
SaVaL סָבַל
Meaning: to bear a heavy load, sustain
GATHER/UNIFY (ס) - BODY (ב) - LEAD/TAKE/SHEPHERD (ל)

The Hebrew word *saval* means SUSTAIN, BEAR a BURDEN or SHEPHERD, but its pictographical meanings could be rendered as follows: GATHER or UNIFY (ס) – the BODY (ב) – LEAD and/or SHEPHERD (ל).

The letter BEIT is used in this word to indicate BODY rather than MEM (the letter more often used to indicate BODY). The BEIT could be rendered as a *BODY of BELIEVERS* or a *CONGREGATION*.

In the Christian book, *Letter to the Galatians,* we can find the following very Jewish sentiment:

> 1 Brethren, even if anyone is caught in any trespass, you who are spiritual, restore such a one in a spirit of gentleness; each one looking to yourself, so that you too will not be tempted.
> **2 Bear one another's burdens, and thereby fulfill the (TORAH)**
> 3 For if anyone thinks he is something when he is nothing, he deceives himself.
> - Galatians 6:1-3, NASB (author's emphasis)

How I wish that people of faith, (religious bodies and organizations of whatever type) would grasp tightly onto the core concept of the Hebrew word *saval* ! If only our burdens would be borne by one another in love.

The pictographical meaning of *SAVAL* indicates that if the bearing of burdens were being done properly today, we should be able to expect a *UNIFYING* effect upon the *BODY* of believers. Sadly, what too often occurs is judgmental and harsh treatment of anyone who does not toe the company line. What it means to "toe the line" might vary from group to group, but inevitably it comes down to is one person telling another that "wrong" means "disagreeing with me." Even more sadly, the person responsible for the harsh treatment of the flock may be the flock's shepherd himself. Too many times, it seems as though some leaders might have stopped reading the 6th chapter of Galatians part way though verse one, reading only "…you who are *spiritual*, restore such a one." Somehow, *restore* gets twisted into *rebuke*, and "*a spirit of gentleness*" if often neglected entirely.

The human frailty of self-importance threatens every heart. Psychologists agree that we all tend to see ourselves in a more favorable light than what others might say is justified by *reality*. For this reason, we all need to do our own *reality check* from time to time, especially whenever we hear ourselves speak ill of another.

There is no place for gossip and accusation within any body of believers who call themselves people of faith. Having faith in God's love and mercy means we accept the reality that, just like those blemished souls we see around us, we too are not perfect. Who are we to judge another? Who are we to accuse? For this reason Yeshua told his followers,

"Why do you look at the speck that is in your brother's eye, but do not notice the log that is in your own eye?" [18]

It is no coincidence that the Hebrew word for Accuser or Adversary is *Satan*.[19] I... and we... need to be careful with one another, especially when that other person is not as *strong* or *tough* or *spiritually mature* as we are. Rightly so does *Paul's Letter to the Galatians* state that those who are spiritually strong should be gentle when trying to **restore** anyone who has stumbled. And under no stretch of the word's intended meaning here does *restore*, as used here, mean *dropkick, accuse, shun* or *reject as being unworthy.*

The idea of loving one's neighbor goes back to the Hebrew scriptures (Lev. 19:8), which Yeshua (Jesus) is recorded as having quoted:

> 34 But when the Pharisees heard that Jesus had silenced the Sadducees, they gathered themselves together.
> 35 One of them, a lawyer, asked Him *a question,* testing Him,
> 36 "Teacher, which is the great commandment in the Law?"
> 37 And He said to him, " 'YOU SHALL LOVE THE LORD YOUR GOD WITH ALL YOUR HEART, AND WITH ALL YOUR SOUL, AND WITH ALL YOUR MIND.'
> 38 "This is the great and foremost commandment.
> 39 "The second is like it, 'YOU SHALL LOVE YOUR NEIGHBOR AS YOURSELF.'
> 40 On these two commandments depend the whole Law and the Prophets."
> - Matthew 22: 34-40

Let us fulfill the whole law (Torah). Love God, but also let us be sure to love one another!

* * *

---

[18] Matthew 7:3 and Luke 6:41
[19] שָׂטָן   See Strong's Concordance numbers 7853 through 7855.

Chapter 17
AYIN

LIFE FORCE - SPARK of LIFE - ALERTNESS

AYIN's pictograph (an open and alert Eye) represented *LIFE FORCE*
Note: NUN denoted living things and *LIFE*, while
AYIN denoted the SPARK of LIFE which causes someone to be ALIVE
TO KNOW (among the Semitic people, to *Know* = TO EXPERIENCE),
to AWAKEN or OPEN, ALIVE, to BECOME AWARE

AYIN's secondary meanings included
EXPOSE (CONDEMN), to PREVENT or RESTRAIN, DEMONSTRATE, BELOW,
UNDER, DOWN, TEARS, to SEPARATE APART, WITHIN, SATIETY

The post-Babylonian pictogram for AYIN is unclear.

AYIN's letter name means:
EYE (ע) - BRIGHT (י) - SIGN (י) - LIFE (ן)
(Signs of being Alert & Alive)
or
FORCE (ע) - CAUSING/INDICATING (י) - LIFE (ן) ↔ SIGN (י)
(*Signs of Life*)

AYIN

Action or Motion Indicated	Descriptive Form	Noun(s) Denoted	Prepositional Meanings
to open, to experience, to be aware, to watch to prevent or restrain to separate to take to expose *BEING* (State of Being)	Knowing, Experienced Aware Alert	A Force, *LIFE FORCE*, a Presence, Help or Helper, Awareness Consciousness poss. Spirit	Below, Under, Down

AYIN EXAMPLES:

Strong's Number	Hebrew Word	Trans-Literation	Word Definition	Explanation of Pictographical Meanings
5869 & 5870	עַיִן	'Ayin	Lit. an Eye 1. FORCE [including life force] of BEING... FORTITUDE "May the AYIN be with you." 2. AWARE, AWAKE 3. WATCH [over], LOOK OUTWARD, BE ALERT [the eyelids SEPARATE wider when one is alert] 4. to TAKE 5. to SET APART, DELIVER from, FORCEFULLY SEPARATE, 6. PRESENCE 7. to EXPOSE	EYE (ע) - BRIGHT (י) - SIGN (י) - LIFE (ן) (signs of being alert & alive) or FORCE (ע) – CAUSING/INDICATING (י) - LIFE (ן) ↔ SIGN (י) (signs of life)
7106a	קָצַע	Qa-TSA	across, take away, to scrape	ACROSS (ק) - TAKE (צ) – **SEPARATE** or **AWAY (ע)**
8628	תָּקַע	T'a-QA	to blow a trumpet, to give a blow, slap	ACTION (ת) - THROUGH/ACROSS (ק) - AWAY or OUT/AGAINST (ע)
Modern Hebrew	תֶּקַע	Tey-Qah	to plug	ACTION/APPLY (ת) - ACROSS (ק) - **OPENING** [or empty space] **(ע)**
Modern Hebrew	עוֹנֶן	'ŌNeN	an anchor	**SEPARATE (ע)** - FROM (ו) - MOVING (Double NUN: נן) or PREVENTING (עו) MOVING (נן)
see 5771 below	עוֹנָה	'ŌNaH	Sin	**SEPARATION/TAKING (ע)** - OF (ו) - LIFE (נ) and- (ה) [amplified] or PREVENTING (עו) LIFE (נ)
5746	עָג	'AG	1. to bake (Biblical) 2. to bake a cake (modern)	NOT (ג) ↔ SEPARATED (ע) [perhaps this denotes mixed ingredients... similar to the English language expression, "cake mix"]

Chapter 17 – AYIN

Strong's Number	Hebrew Word	Trans-Literation	Word Definition	Explanation of Pictographical Meanings
5692 from 5746 to bake	עוּגָה	ŪGaH [ooga]	Cake	NOT (ג) ↔ SEPARATED (עו) + RAISED (ה)
5750	עוֹד	'ŌD	still, yet, more, again	**PRESENCE (ע)** - OF (ו) - TWO JOINED (ד) [e.g. on the other hand, in addition] or **PREVENTING (עוֹ)** LACK (ד) [lacking nothing]
4581	מָעוֹז	MaŌZ From 5756 (עוז Ūz)	fortress, strong hold	PLACE OF (מ) - OPENING/SEPARATION (ע) - OF/FROM (ו) - FIERCENESS (ז)
5794	עוֹז	'ŌZ	to take refuge	1. to SEPARATE (ע) - FROM (ו) - VIOLENCE or AGRESSION (ז) or 2. poss. PREVENT (עוֹ) HARVEST (ז) (Perhaps an idiomatic expression denoting "**prevent being cut down/killed**")
5766	עָוֶל	A-VeL	injustice, wrong	SEPARATE (ע) - FROM (ו) - LEADERSHIP/CUSTOMS/LAW (ל) or NOTHING (עוֹ) + LEADERSHIP/LAW (ל) [lawlessness]
5766	עִוֵּל	Ee-VeL or EVIL	to do injustice	**SEPARATE (ע)** - FROM (ו) - LEADERSHIP/CUSTOMS/LAW (ל)
7167	קָרַע	QaRA	to tear, rend, torn	COMPLETELY (ק) - CUT (ר) - by FORCE (ע)
5927	עָלָה	Alah	to go up, to climb, ascend, brought	TAKE (ע) - WALK (ל) - HIGHER [lit. RAISED] (ה)
5975	עָמַד	AMaD	to stand, to take one's stand, to stand in place	TAKE (ע) - PLACE (מ) - STAND (ד) [to take a firm stand in one place]
6025	עֵנָב	ENaV	a grape	LIFE FORCE (ע) - LIVING/GROWING (נ) - BODY (ב) [see also 5107 NŪV] or poss. LIFE (נ) - FORCE (ע) - emBODYment (ב)
5769	עוֹלָם or עֹלָם	OLAM	perpetual, permanent, from antiquity, ancient	TAKEing (ע) OF (ו) - CENTRAL [established/permanent] (ל) - PLACE (מ) or TAKE (ע) - CENTRAL [established/permanent] (ל) - PLACE (מ)
Modern Hebrew	קָצַע	Qa-TSe-A	to trim	ACROSS (ק) - TAKE (צ) - AWAY (ע)

Unlocking the Ancient Pictorial Code of the Hebrew Alphabet

Strong's Number	Hebrew Word	Trans-Literation	Word Definition	Explanation of Pictographical Meanings
3444	יְשׁוּעָה	YeSHuAH	salvation, deliverance	is CAUSED TO BE (י) - ABUNDANCE (שׁ) - OF (ו) - SEPARATION/DELIVERANCE/LIFE (ע) ↔ GREAT (ה)
3443	יֵשׁוּעַ	Yeshua	Hebrew name [translated into Greek as Jesus]	CAUSE to BE (י) - the SUBSTANCE (שׁ) – of (ו) - LIFE FORCE or AWAKENING (ע)
Modern Hebrew	קָצַע	Qa-TSe-A	to trim	ACROSS (ק) - TAKE (צ) - AWAY (ע)
6805	צָעַד	TSAD	to march, to step	KNEE (ד) ↔ BEING (ע) ↔ at a FIXED PACE (צ)
6113	עָצַר	ATSaR	to restrain, bond, restrict, shut, refrain, held back	FORCE (ע) - CONFLICT/AGRESSION (צ) - from WITHIN (ר)
6026	עָנֹג	ANoG	soft, delicate, dainty	**LIFE FORCE of (ענ) – WEAK/DAINTY/MINIMAL/SMALL ? (ג)**
5756	עוּז	ŪZ	to take or seek refuge	SEPARATE (ע) - FROM (ו) - AGRESSION/DESTRUCTION (ז)
5783	עוּר	ŪR	to be exposed, bare	EXPOSE[ing] (ע) - OF (ו) – INSIDE or CHARACTER (ר)
5771	עָוֹן	AŌN or AVŌN	iniquity, guilt	EXPOSURE (ע) - OF (ו) - MOVEMENTs [poss. *deeds*] (נ)
5736	עָדַף	ADaPH	left over, excess prob. OVERFLOW	SEPARATE/AWAY FROM/BEYOND (ע) - the EDGE (ד) - FLOW (ף)
5774	עוּף	ŪPH	to fly away, flew, flying	**FORCE or AWAY FROM (ע)** - of (ו) - FLOW (ף) [lit. fly away]
5794 see also 5710 & 5810	עַז	AZ	strong, mighty, fierce	**FORCE/CONDITION (ע) - STRONG (ז)** lit. STRONG (ז) ↔ CONDITION/FORCE (ע)
5797	1. עֹז OR 2. עוֹז	ŌZ	1. strength, might, power 2. to take revenge	1. STRONG (ז) ↔ FORCE (ע) or CONDITION/FORCE (ע) - OF (ו) - STRENGTH (ז) Def. 2. FORCE OF DESTRUCTION/VIOLENCE

Chapter 17 – AYIN

Strong's Number	Hebrew Word	Trans-Literation	Word Definition	Explanation of Pictographical Meanings
5810	עָזַז	AZaZ	to be strong	STRENGTHENING (זז) - FORCE (ע) or STRONG FORCE (ע) from many WEAPONS (זז)
1197a	בָּעַר	BaAR	to burn, consume, remove, purge	EMPTY/HOLLOWing (ב) - CONDITION (ע) - INSIDE (ר) or INVISIBLE (ב) - FORCE (ע) - INSIDE (ר)
7491	רָעַף	RaAPH	to drip	ATTRIBUTE of (ר) - FORCE (ע) - FALL DOWN or DOWNWARD FLOW (ף)
7492	רָעַץ	RaATS	to shatter	ATTRIBUTE of (ר) - FORCE (ע) - MIGHTY FORCE or CHOP (ץ)
1830	דָּמַע	DaMA	to weep bitterly	GATHERED TOGETHER (ד) - WORD/SOUND (מ) - FORCEful (ע)
1847	דַּעַת	DaATH	Knowledge	TWO GATHERED (ד) [man and knowledge] - AWAREness (ע) - BECOME ONE (ת)
2111	זוּעַ	ZUA	to tremble	STRENGTH (ז) - OF (ו) - FORCE of ALERTNESS (ע) NOTE: The word prob. denotes the bodily effects of adrenalin
6760	צָלַע	TSaLaĤ	to limp, lame	FIXED [unbending] (צ) - LEG (ל) - **CONDITION (ע)**
6072	עָסַס	ASaS	to press, crush, tread down	FORCE (ע) COMPLETELY (ס) GATHERED (ס) or FORCE (ע) GATHERING (סס) [poss. denotes compounding of force]
6086	עֵץ	ETS	a tree	FORCE or CONDITION of BEING (ע) FIRMLY ROOTED (ץ) NOTE: AYIN might be the Hebrew equivalent of what we call "state of being" verbs in English: am, is, are, was, were, be, being, been.
6256	עֵת	ETH	1. OFTEN used to link a direct object & an action verb 2. time, appointed time, season	FORCE or CONDITION of (ע) BECOMing ONE (ת) NOTE: A direct object is a noun which receives the action of an action verb, e.g. "David slew ETH Goliath." Slew is the action verb and Goliath is the direct object, the recipient of the action SLEW. In English, we have no equivalent of the word ETH, which is almost always present in Hebrew before a direct object.

Unlocking the Ancient Pictorial Code of the Hebrew Alphabet

Strong's Number	Hebrew Word	Trans-Literation	Word Definition	Explanation of Pictographical Meanings
6326	פּוּעָה	PŪAH	MIDWIFE Listed as "of unc. der."	Possibly: BLOSSOM PRODUCING FRUIT [birth] (פ) - OUT/OF (ו) - EXTRA [raised up] (ה) ↔ FORCE/HELP (ע)
6544a	פָּרַע	PaRA	let go, let alone, neglect, uncover	CONDITION or **STATE of BEING** (ע) ↔ LET LOOSE [blossomed out like a HAND OPENING] (פ) - INSIDE (ר) or LET LOOSE (פ) - INSIDE (ר) – FORCE / CONDITION (ע)
5771	עָוֹן	AŌN or AVŌN	iniquity, guilt	EXPOSURE or FORCE (consequences) (ע) - OF (ו) - MOVEMENTs [poss. DEEDS] (נ)
5749a	עוּד	ŪD	to return, to repeat, go about, do again	FORCE (ע) - OF (ו) - TWO GATHERED (ד) The daleth seems to indicate repetition.
5749b	עוּד	ŪD	to bear witness, admonish, warn	FORCE (ע) - OF (ו) - EDGE (ד)
6212a.	עֵשֶׂב	ESeB	from an unused word; grass, herb, vegetation	FORCE of (ע) - GROWING (שׂ) - BODY (ב)
6212b.	עֲשַׂב	ASaB	(Aramaic) corr. to 6212a; herbage, grass	FORCE of (ע) - GROWING (שׂ) - BODY (ב)
6213a.	עָשָׂה	ASaH	do, make, accomplish, bring forth	FORCE of (ע) - GROWING (שׂ) - BEHELD or REVEALED (ה)
6213b.	עָשָׂה	ASaH	to press, squeeze	FORCE of (ע) - GROWING (שׂ) - BEHELD or REVEALED (ה)
2220	זְרוֹעַ	ZeROA	ARM, shoulder, foreleg of a lamb	RETURN (זר) - of (ו) – LIFE FORCE (ע) See Is. 53:1 To whom has the ARM (zeroah) of the Lord been revealed?
6279 but also 6280	עָתַר	ATHaR	to pray, supplicate	FORCE of (ע) - BECOMING ONE (ת) – INSIDE/WITHIN (ר) Note: Strong's 6280 is the same word but with a meaning of "deceitful." It seems impossible for one word to mean both PRAY and DECEITFUL, but a con man deceives his victims by using charm [his force of becoming one] to win their trust and confidence. The word "con" as used to mean "deceive" is lit. a shortened form of the English word "confidence." We also use the term **INSIDER** (ר) for someone who has the confidence of the people around them.

AYIN - Biblical Food for Thought
ATHAR עָתַר
Meaning: to Pray or to Supplicate

FORCE or POWER of (ע) – BECOMING ONE (ת) - WITHIN (ר)

To be quite honest, some of these *Biblical Food for Thought* sections have been more difficult to write than others. ATHAR, on the other hand, is a slam-dunk cinch!

If there was ever any doubt that the ancient Hebrews intentionally used specific letters, each letter with its own specific meaning, to form the 3-consonant roots of each Hebrew word, ATHAR should dispel all disbelief! The *power* of prayer is the very thing which causes us to *become one* with our Maker.

Only by spending quality time with someone do we actually get to know them. I could read a thousand books about Alexander the Great (or anyone), but I could never claim to really know him. The right of that claim belonged only to those who interacted with him in real life.

The same is true of knowing God. Only by communing with Him in prayer and by interacting with Him in our day-to-day existence can we ever really *know* Him. And remember, the Semitic concept of *knowing* was an *experiential familiarity,* and not simply *book learning*.

Believing in and *believing on* are two very different concepts. For example, when I was younger, I loved to play ice hockey. I can believe in *ice*. I can believe in the concept of ice. I can believe *ice* exists. I can testify that I have seen *ice* and skated on *ice*. I have often put *ice* into my soft drinks. But that is just *believing in* ice. I can do that without risking a single thing.

Believing on ice, however, would be to stand at the edge of a newly-frozen pond, skates and hockey stick in hand. In my mind I can tell myself that it has been cold enough for long enough and that the ice on the pond is thick enough for me to skate upon it safely. But until I actually "risk" skating out onto the pond, I have limited myself to only *believing* in ice, not *upon it* to support my weight.

OK, so maybe we want to see someone skate on that questionable ice first. No problem. Maybe we even need to see a multitude of people skate on the ice. Still no problem. But until we ourselves stand upon the surface of the ice and experience its full support, we are only spectators. Our skates are of no value to us.

Likewise, until we truly rely upon God to be a faithful provider and to be *our* Lord… until we fully trust Him with every aspect of our lives… we too are merely spectators in our walk of faith. Only by communion with God through prayer and by walking with Him actively in our daily life will we really, truly experience (*know*) Him.

* * *

Chapter 18
PEY or PEH

MOUTH & BLOSSOM with FRUIT — A Mouth or Side View of CURLED FINGERS & THUMB

Note: PEY and PHEY have significantly different meanings; therefore, PHEY will be the topic of Chapter 19.

PEY's Phoenician pictographs were a MOUTH and a FRUITFUL BLOSSOM.
PEY or PEH denoted the *bringing forth of fruit*.
The term *fruit* included everything from apples, oranges and various grains to the *fruit of the Spirit* which Paul wrote about in his letter to the Galatians[20]

The post-Babylonian pictogram for PEY is similar to the Phoenician pictograph.

Both a BLOOM on a tree and CURLED FINGERS were seen as having the same motion – BLOSSOMING OUTWARD.
PEY indicated BLOSSOMING OUT in order to PRODUCE FRUIT.
The dot in the center of the PEY indicates the FRUIT within the BLOSSOM.

PEY's meanings included the following:
to BLOSSOM OUT (EXPAND or DISPERSE), BREAK, SCATTER, RELEASE, LET LOOSE (the action of opening the hand… as pictured by the modern PICTOGRAPH which is the side view of a hand with curled fingers ready to open outward), BREATH, MOUTH, SPEAK, FRUIT (the dot inside PEY),
a PLACE of ORIGIN (such as a blossom), or a MESSAGE.

PEY's letter name means:
FRUIT (פ) - REVEALVED (ה)

PEY

Action or Motion Indicated	Descriptive Form	Noun(s) Denoted	Prepositional Meanings
to Blossom, to Expand, to Break, to Scatter, to Breathe, to Speak, to Release or Let loose	Fruitful Expanded, Scattered, Blown away poss. Filled	a Bloom with Fruit inside, A place of origin. Lit. PEH = a MOUTH	- NA -

---
[20] Paul's Letter to the Galatians 5:22

PEY EXAMPLES:

Strong's Number	Hebrew Word	Trans-Literation	Word Definition	Explanation of Pictographical Meanings
6310	פֶּה or פֶּא	PEH or PEY	A mouth	FRUIT (פ) REVEALED (ה), the word "PEH" lit. means "mouth" The modern (post Babylonian) letter is a side view of curled up fingers about to expand, indicating a motion of expanding outward into the space around… blossoming
6353	פֶּחָר	PeĤaR	a potter [Aramaic] Listed as "of unc. der."	BLOSSOM OUT (פ) - ALL AROUND (ח) - the INSIDE (ר) NOTE: Anyone who has watched a potter throw a clay pot on a pottery wheel knows exactly how this word came to be, as it perfectly describes the potter's fingers digging into the inside of the clay lump and the pot BLOOMING ALL AROUND the potter's hands.
6286	פָּאַר	PaAR	to beautify, glorify	BLOSSOMED OUT (פ) - INDIVIDUAL (א) - on the INSIDE (ר)
6288	פֹּארָה	PORaH	a bough, branches Listed as "of unc. der."	BLOSSOMED OUT (פ) - INDIVIDUAL PART (א) - on the INSIDE (ר) - up HIGH (ה)
6293	פָּגַע	PaGA	1. to meet, encounter, reach 2. attacked, kill and cut down	1. BLOOM [events fully developed] (פ) - GATHER for PLEASURE (GHAYIN) - [state of being… "it happened"] (ע) or 2. BLOOM [events fully developed] (פ) – OPPOSITION/AGAINST (GIMMEL) - FORCE (ע)
6296	פָּגַר	PaGaR	to be exhausted or faint	BLOOM of (פ) - RESISTANCE/OPPOSITION (ג) - INSIDE (ר)
6299	פָּדָה	PaDaH	to ransom, redeem	BLOOM [producing fruit] (פ) - EDGE [hunger or lack] (ד) - RAISED UP ABOVE or REVEALED (ה) Possible meaning: To open one's hand in charity [blooming of fruit] and help another rise above their hunger/lack [edge]
6313	פּוּג	PŪG	to grow numb, weariness	BLOOM (פ) - of (ו) - RESISTANCE (ג)

Chapter 18 – PEY

Strong's Number	Hebrew Word	Trans-Literation	Word Definition	Explanation of Pictographical Meanings
6315	פוּחַ	PūaĤ	to breathe, blow	BLOSSOM OUT [exhale] (פ) - OF or INTO (ו) - SPACE/VOID/AIR (ח)
6316	פוּט	PŪT	PUT - son of Ham Listed as "of unc. der."	This is just a wild guess here: BLOOM [poss. HAIR] (פ) - of (ו) - COILS (ט) The word PUT perhaps denotes a race of people whose distinguishing trait was Curly Hair
6321	פוֹל	PŌL	BEANS Listed as "of unc. der."	BLOSSOM [produce "fruit"] (פ) - on - POLE (ל)
6326	פוּעָה	PŪAH	MIDWIFE Listed as "of unc. der."	Possibly: BLOSSOM PRODUCING FRUIT [birth] (פ) - OUT/OF (ו) - EXTRA [raised up] (ה) ↔ FORCE/HELP (ע)
6327a	פוּץ	PŪTS	to be dispersed or scattered	SCATTER or BLOSSOM OUT [expanding outward motion] (פ) - of (ו) - FIRM ROOTS (fixed position) (צ)
6327b	פוּץ	PŪTS	to flow, overflow	BLOSSOM OUT [expanding outward motion] (פ) - of (ו) - FIRM ROOTS (fixed position) (צ)
6329	פוּק	PŪQ	to bring out, furnish, promote	BLOSSOM (פ) - OUT (ו) - COMPLETELY/THOROUGHLY (ק)
6332	פוּר	PŪR Listed as "of unc. der."	"a lot", plenty, bountiful... root word of feast name PURIM	BLOSSOM (פ) - OUT (ו) - the INSIDE (ר)
6335a	פוּשׁ	PŪSH	to spring about, skip about	BLOSSOM (פ) - OUT (ו) - ABUNDANTLY (שׁ)
6342	פָּחַד	PaĤaD	to dread, to be in awe, afraid	BLOSSOMing OUT (פ) - ALL AROUND (ח) - EDGE [fear or edginess] (ד)
6344	פָּחַד	PaĤaD	thigh, thighs Listed as "prob. of foreign origin"	BLOSSOMing OUT (פ) - ALL AROUND (ח) - KNEE (ד)

Strong's Number	Hebrew Word	Trans-Literation	Word Definition	Explanation of Pictographical Meanings
6357	פִּטְדָה	PiTDaH	Listed as "prob. of for. origin; (a precious stone) perhaps *Topaz*" Poss. a GEODE? Petrified Wood?	BLOSSOMing OUT (פ) - COILED or LAYERED (ט) - EDGE (ד) - MORE or REVEALED or RAISED ABOVE (ה) (A Swirling PATTERN?) AUTHOR's NOTE: Break out your old geology books… I have no great geological expertise. I recently saw a geode which was not crystallized inside, but instead had swirls, due to forming at a lower temperature. What is this mystery stone??? It remains a mystery to me still.
6362	פָּטַר	PaTaR	to separate, remove, set free, open	RELEASE (פ) - that which is CONTAINED (ט) - INSIDE (ר)
6508	פַּרְדֵּס	PaRDDeS	a preserve park listed as "of foreign origin"	BLOSSOM OUT [prob. denoting blossoming trees and/or flowers] (פ) - INSIDE (ר) - the EDGES [prob. town limits] (דד) - GATHERED (ס)
6509	פָּרָה	PaRaH	to bear fruit, to be fruitful	FRUIT (פ) - INSIDE (ר) - REVEALED (ה)
6523	פַּרְזֶל	PaRZeL	Aramaic: IRON	FACE [prob. denotes an axe head… a "face" with a BLOSSOMING OUT or widened cutting edge] (פ) -ATTRIBUTE (ר) - IRON (ז) - HANDLE [staff-like] (ל)
6524a	פֶּרַח	PaRaĤ	to bud, sprout, a shoot, blossom, budded	BLOOM/BLOSSOM (פ) - INSIDE (ר) - ALL AROUND (ח) or BLOOM/BLOSSOM (פ) - ATTRIBUTE (ר) - ALL AROUND (ח)
6524b	פֶּרַח	PaRaĤ	to BREAK out, broken, breaking, BROKEN	BREAK (פ) - INSIDE (ר) - ALL AROUND (ח) or BROKEN (פ) - ATTRIBUTE (ר) – ALL AROUND (ח) [attribute of *brokenness*]
6605	פָּתַח	PaTaĤ	To OPEN, RELEASE	RELEASE (break) (פ) - HOLD (ט swapped with ת) - ALL AROUND (ח)
6561	פָּרַק	PaRaQ	to tear apart or away	BREAKing APART (פ) ↔ THOROUGHLY (ק) - ATTRIBUTE (ר) or BREAKing APART [force] (פ) ↔ ACROSS (ק) - the INSIDE (ר)

Strong's Number	Hebrew Word	Trans-Literation	Word Definition	Explanation of Pictographical Meanings
6565a	פָּרַר	PaRaR	to BREAK, frustrate	BREAK (פ) - INSIDES (רר)
5301	נָפַח Bib. Hebrew / נָפַח Modern Hebrew	1. NaPHaḦ 2. Ni-PaCH	1. to blow, breathe, boiling 2. to swell	MOVE (נ) - **BLOSSOM out / BREATHE (פ)** - into the SURROUNDING VOID (ח)
3717	כָּפַל	KaPHaL	to double, folded over double	HAND or TAKE [poss. MAKE] (כ) - BLOOM (פ) - FOLD [lit. folds of linen] (ל) Poss. KAPH + PEY indicates to make a mouth-like fold
3721	כָּפַף	KaPHaPH	to bow down, to be bent	HOLD (כ) - MOUTH (פ) - DOWN (ף)
6529	פְּרִי	Pri [Pree]	fruit, result, offspring	FRUIT (פ) - INSIDE (ר) - CREATED/CAUSED TO BE (י)

PEY - Food for Thought

(פֶּה) PEH - A Mouth - FRUIT (פ) - REVEALED (ה)
(פְּרִי) PRI - FRUIT (פ) - INSIDE (ר) - CREATED/CAUSED TO BE (י)

When spring arrives, my fruit trees produce multitudes of beautiful blossoms. As beautiful as these flowers are, past experience has taught me that every blossom does not produce fruit. In fact, if conditions are not favorable (when the blossoms appear before the bees emerge from hibernation), there have been a few years when particular trees produced almost no fruit.

Paul's Letter to the Galatians lists what the writer considers to be the *fruit* of God's Holy Spirit working inside the believer: "… love, joy, peace, patience, kindness, goodness, faithfulness, gentleness, (and) self-control." [21] Like the beautiful blossoms on fruit trees, people of faith have the potential of bearing fruit. But… does our beautiful show of flowers on the outside have real fruit on the inside? How can we know what to look for as evidence of fruit?

Every God Fearer (whether Jewish, Christian, Muslim or whatever) could benefit from giving some thought to this list of *spiritual fruit*. Over a period of time,

---

[21] Paul's letter to the Galatians 6:22-23

often measured in years rather than in days and weeks, this fruit is produced by the working of God's Holy Spirit within us… but only if we give the Devine Spirit the freedom to work within us. Like the unpollinated blossoms on fruit trees, the showy flowers of *affected faith* (non-genuine faith) will eventually wither and drop of the tree. We must be genuine in our pursuit of God if we desire to bear spiritual fruit.

Once the fruit develops within the blossom, it still must be nourished from the deep roots of the tree. Before the young fruit can come to maturity, it needs the heat of the summer and the gentle rain to cause it to swell up and become sweet and juicy. Enduring fiery trials is the heat our spiritual fruit needs. The water which produces good fruit is God's Spirit, which rains down upon us and refreshes us… again… *if* we allow it to do so.

What else can I say? Let it rain!

* * *

Chapter 19
PHEY

BLOSSOM with NO FRUIT -   A Mouth or a
Side View of CURLED FINGER and THUMB

PHEY's pictograph (a FRUITLESS BLOSSOM) represented FALL.

The post-Babylonian pictogram for PHEY is similar to the Phoenician pictograph. The absence of a dot in the center of the PHEY indicates no FRUIT within the BLOSSOM.

PHEY's meanings included the following:
FACE, PLACE or LOCATION, MUCH, DROPLETS,
EXPANDING (uncurling or unrolling like a TORAH SCROLL),
FACE, poss. HAND (a common hand, not divine)

PHEY SOFIT denotes:
DOWNWARD FLOW, to FALL or DRIP DOWN, DROPLETS, FULLNESS,
FILLING, FRONT or SURFACE FACE (as used as a term in geometry), NECK,
FLOW DOWN, to DROP, or GO DOWN
(Similar to what occurs when fruit drops off the tree and ceases to live),
END of the GROWING SEASON
(The *FALL* season, leaves & fruit falling from trees ...
"FULLNESS OF TIME" is the idiom used in the Bible.)

PHEY's letter name means:
FLOW DOWN or FALL (פ) - INDICATED (ה)   or   HANDs (פ) - RAISED (ה)

PHEY

Action or Motion Indicated	Descriptive Form	Noun(s) Denoted	Prepositional Meanings
to Fall to Fall Down, to Drop to Go Down, to Die	Falling Much Dying	Neck (Phey Sophet) Fall (the season) Poss. *Death*	Down

Unlocking the Ancient Pictorial Code of the Hebrew Alphabet

PHEY EXAMPLES: ○ 7 ף פ

Strong's Number	Hebrew Word	Trans-Literation	Word Definition	Explanation of Pictographical Meanings
see PEY	פֶּה פֵּא	PHEH or PHEY	1. to flow/fall/drip down 2. ף = front or face [surface] 3. to breathe	FLOW DOWN / FALL (ף) + INDICATED (ה) PHEY denotes FACE, PLACE/LOCATION. PHEY SOFIT denotes DOWNWARD FLOW, to FALL or DRIP DOWN, DROPLETS, FILLING, FULLNESS, END of the GROWING SEASON [PHEY denotes the *fall* season, leaves & fruit *falling* from trees … **"FULLNESS OF TIME"** is the idiom used in the Bible]
1765	דָּחַף	DaHaPH	to drive, hasten [to PUSH in Mod. Hebrew]	EDGE (ד) - AGAINST (ח) - FLOW DOWN/FALL/PUSH (ף)
8199	שָׁפַת	Shaphat	to hand down, to govern, to judge (Mod. Heb.: put)	PROVISION/SUBSTANCE (שׁ) - **BLOSSOMING OUTWARD (פ)** – JOINED / DESIGNATED / MARKED [set on record] (ת)
Modern Hebrew	סָכֵף	SaKeF	to discourage	COMPLETELY (ס) - HOLD (כ) - **DOWN (ף)**
5557	סָלַף	SaLaPH	to pervert	GATHER (ס) - LEAD/TAKE (ל) – DOWN / to a FALL (ף)
7107	קָצַף	Qa-TSePH	anger, furious, provoke to wrath; Mod. Heb.: foam	THOROUGHLY (ק) – CHOPPED / AGITATED / PRESSED (צ) – FACE [surface] (ף) poss. something like having a "hard-pressed expression"
Modern Hebrew	זִיף	ZeeF	Modern Hebrew: bristle (the bristles of a paint brush) Biblical Hebrew: 2128 "uncl. der."	PICK (ז) - UP (י) - **DROPLETS (ף)** [a paint brush in Mod. Heb.] A name of one of Judah's sons: 2128
6884	צָרַף	TSaRaF	tried, refined	BECOME ONE (צ) - INSIDE/BEHIND (ר) - **SURFACE/FACE (ף)**
2643	חַף	HaF	to rub, to scrub, to be pure, innocent	SCRUB [washing, rubbing motion] (ח) – FACE or NECK (ף)
5736	עָדַף	ADaPH	left over, excess prob. OVERFLOW	SEPARATE/AWAY FROM/BEYOND (ע) - the EDGE (ד) - FLOW DOWN (ף)

- 128 -

Chapter 19 – PHEY

Strong's Number	Hebrew Word	Trans-Literation	Word Definition	Explanation of Pictographical Meanings
5774	עוּף	ŪPH	to fly away, flew, flying	FORCE or AWAY FROM (ע) - of (וּ) - FLOW (ף) [lit. fly away]
5003	נָאַף	NaAPH	to commit adultery	MOVEMENTs or ACTIONs of (נ) - a FALLEN (ף) ↔ INDIVIDUAL (א)
6687	צוּף	TSUPH	to flow, overflow, flowed, float	MIGHTY FORCE (צ) - OF (וּ) - DOWNWARD FLOW (ף)
Greek 5457	φῶς	PHŌS	Greek for LIGHT	DOWNWARD FLOW (ף = φ) – OF – (וּ = ῶ) – RESURRECTION / REBIRTH / RETURNing [SUN] (שׁ SIN = ς SIGMA)
7491	רָעַף	RaAPH	to drip	ATTRIBUTE of (ר) - FORCE (ע) - FALL DOWN or DOWNWARD FLOW (ף)
5486	סוּף	SŪPH	to come to an end, to cease, completely removed	COMPLETENESS (ס) - OF (וּ) - DOWNWARD FLOW (ף) end of blooming
3700	כָּסַף	KaSaPH	to long for, shame	TAKE (כ) - COMPLETE (ס) - FALL (ף) or TAKE (כ) - COMPLETELY (ס) - DOWN (ף)
3721	כָּפַף	KaPHaPH	to bow down, to be bent	HOLD (כ) – MOUTH / FACE (פ) – DOWN (ף)
6201	עָרַף	ARaPH	to drip, drop, drop down	FORCE (ע) – CHARACTERISTIC (ר) – FLOW DOWN (ף)
6202	עָרַף	ARaPH	to break the neck	FORCE (ע) – INSIDE of (ר) – NECK (ף)
6203	עֹרֶף	ORePH	back of the neck, neck, obstinate, stubborn, stiff-necked	FORCE (ע) – INSIDE of (ר) – NECK (ף) "stiff necked"
6566	פָּרַשׂ	PaRaS	to spread out, scatter, disperse,	SCATTER (פ) – CHARACTERISTIC (ר) – SPREAD OUT (שׂ)

PHEY - Biblical Food for Thought

(יָפֶה) YAPHE or JAFFE -
Meaning: BEAUTY

CLEAN (י) – [side view of curled] HANDs (פ) - RAISED (ה)

The pictographical meaning of the Hebrew word YAPHE shows us that *CLEAN HANDS RAISED* equals *true beauty* in ancient Semitic thinking. Job tells us, "He who has clean hands will grow stronger and stronger."[22] This paradigm is reiterated by King David:

> "3 Who may ascend into the hill of the Lord?
> And who may stand in His holy place?
> 4 He who has clean hands and a pure heart…
> 5 He shall receive a blessing from the Lord
> And righteousness from the God of his salvation."[23]

Have you ever done something which you completely regretted afterwards? Maybe you hurt someone, or did something you knew was just plain wrong. Guilt and remorse can weigh heavily upon a person's conscience.

I remember when I first repented of my sins before God. It was on April 11, 1970, about 10:30 at night. I remember asking God's Holy Spirit to search me inside and out, to show me my hidden sins (King David prayed in the same way in Psalm 139: 23 & 24). As they came to mind, one by one I asked God to forgive me for them. All of a sudden, it was like a dam bursting. They seemed to all flood out of me. In that instant I knew I was forgiven.

What a relief to the heart and soul it is to have clean hands! Since that time, there have been times when I wronged others or did something I knew was in disobedience to God and His commandments. Although I was forgiven back in April of 1970, I still had to come before God and repent, and in some cases I had to go to someone I had wronged to ask their forgiveness. Yet, because of the power of God's Holy Spirit which permanently resides within me, I now have additional, God-given strength (and courage) to ascend the hill of God in order to come before the Lord… even if it is because I feel a need to repent.

Joyfully, I am now able to come to God with clean hands. He gives those who come to him this gift simply because He wants His people to experience and to enjoy being in His Holy Presence. Do you desire true beauty within? Allow Him to give you clean hands. Experience the joy and freedom of coming before God with clean hands, hands He himself has made clean.

* * *

---

[22] Job 17:9, NASB
[23] Psalm 24:3-5

Chapter 20
TZADI, TZADE or TSADI

(FIXED IMAGE)
HUNTER STALKING PREY, GAFF – FIRMLY ROOTED TREE

TZADI's Phoenician pictographs represented ATTACHED at the SIDE.
The ancient pictograph is a side view of a creeping hunter w/spear, a TSADI, crouching as he stalks his prey. The second Phoenician pictograph is of a gaff hook, probably for catching fish by gaffing them by their sides in streams.

The post-Babylonian pictogram for TZADI shows a TREE with a STRONG TAP ROOT, indicating FIRMLY ROOTED or ATTACHED to the GROUND. The bottom of the letter represents the part of the tree that is underground.

TZADI's meanings included the following:
FIRMLY ROOTED - FIXED IMAGE,
TZadi is possibly a combination of TAV (become one) + ZAYIN (strength).
Secondary meanings: steady, control, on the side, catch, stealth: take from the side, affix(ed), STAYED, and lastly: BARBED [denoted by the GAFF HOOK pictograph].

The post-Babylonian symbol is a tree and thick main root: ATTACHED (צ) to the GROUND (ד) or FIRMLY ROOTED. Secondary meanings: CONSTANT, UNCHANGED, UNBENDING, PERMANENT,
SOLID & FIRM. [e.g. a mighty oak tree]

TSADI also denotes "MIGHTY" FORCE…
Including the array of meanings attached to the Hebrew word KAVOD:
HEAVY, GREAT, WEIGHTY, MIGHTY, SOLID, ESTABLISHED,
and UNBENDING.

TZADI's pre-Babylonian letter name denoted:
ATTACHED (צ) to the EDGE/SIDE (ד)
[STALKING]

TZADI's Post-Babylonian meaning became:
ATTACHED (צ) to the GROUND (ד)
[FIRMLY ROOTED]

TZADI

Action or Motion Indicated	Descriptive Form	Noun(s) Denoted	Prepositional Meanings
to *BE FIRMLY ROOTED* to Remain Motionless, to Stalk to Attach (to the side) to Chop to Stir up or Agitate	FIRMLY ROOTED, Weighty, Barbed, Stationary, Mighty, Solid, Established	FIXED IMAGE, DEEPLY-ROOTED like a tree	- NA -

TZADI EXAMPLES:

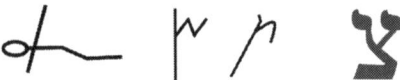

Strong's Number	Hebrew Word	Trans-Literation	Word Definition	Explanation of Pictographical Meanings
see 6718 below	צָדִי	TSaDI see 6718 below	AFFIXED, SOLID, STATIONARY, STILL or a FIXED PACE, a MIGHTY FORCE, PRESS, CONFLICT, DIFFICULTY, CONTEMPT, UNBENDING, poss. UNSTOPPABLE	1. *Tzad* means *to hunt*; therefore, a Tzadi צָדִי = a *Hunter*: FIXED POSITION (צ) - TO the SIDE (ד) plus the suffix YOD (י) to indicate a person. (e.g. Israel + Yod = Israeli) 2. STATIONARY /MOTIONLESS / UNBENDING, FIXED IN PLACE... the ancient pictograph is a side view of a hunter holding a spear and sneaking up on his prey: to STALK 3. CHOP 4. DIFFICULT or IMPOSING, probably a derivative meaning... from the steep, vertical angle made by a perpendicular chop (cut at a right angle). 5. SOLID [As TSADI morphed, it was associated with trees, which is what the modern symbol appears to be.] 6. MIGHTY [a MIGHTY or GREAT FORCE] 7. EXTREMELY HIGH HEAT [refining hot] 8. CONTEMPT

Chapter 20 – TZADI

Strong's Number	Hebrew Word	Trans-Literation	Word Definition	Explanation of Pictographical Meanings
6718	צַיִד	TSaYiD	hunter, hunter's game, provisions	FIXED PACE/MIGHTY FORCE (צ) - ON/UPON/OVER (י) - the EDGE (ד) [stalking prey]
Modern Hebrew only	קַץ	QaTZ	to loathe, to fear	NECK/COMPLETELY (ק) + FIXED MOTIONLESS (ץ) = fear
7093	קֵץ	QeTZ	end, limit	NECK/COMPLETELY (ק) + CHOPPED (ץ) = "CUT OFF" or ENDED
7092	קָפַץ	Qa-FaTZ	1. to close, to draw together 2. to chop	1. ACROSS (ק) - FRONT/FACE (פ) - ATTACHED/STRONG FORCE [bonded] (צ) or ACROSS - SURFACEs - ATTACHED 2. ACROSS (ק) - SURFACE (פ) - CHOPPED (צ)
Modern Hebrew	קַצָּב	Qa-TZaV	to butcher	COMPLETELY/AROUND/ACROSS (ק) - CHOP (צ) - BODY (ב)
6693	צוּק	TSŪQ	to constrain, press upon, oppress	COMPLETE (וק) ↔ MIGHTY FORCE (צ)
6699	צוּרָה	TZŪ-RaH	form, shape, image	FIXED IMAGE (צ) - OF (ו) - HIGHLY (ה) ↔ RECOGNIZABLE ATTRIBUTES (ר)
6713 & 6715	צֹחַר	Tsa-ĤaR Mod. Heb. TSAĤOR	White	CLEAR (צ) - EMPTINESS (ח) - APPEARANCE / RECOGNIZABLE ATTRIBUTE [COLOR ?] (ר)
6681	צָוַח	Tsa-VaĤ	to scream	MIGHTY FORCE (צ) - OF (ו) - THROAT (ח) [CHET denotes the throat because a throat is a place of clearly defined (limited) empty space]
6685	צוֹם	TSŌM	to fast, fasting, times of fasting	DIFFICULTY [poss. EMPTINESS] (צ) - OF (ו) - STOMACH or BODY (מ) TSOM came into Greek as SOMA... which means "body" and into English as part of the word chromoSOME.

Unlocking the Ancient Pictorial Code of the Hebrew Alphabet

Strong's Number	Hebrew Word	Trans-Literation	Word Definition	Explanation of Pictographical Meanings
6697	צוּר	TSŪR	a wall, a rock cliff	CHOPPED (צ) OFF (ו) -[steep / vertical / difficult] ATTRIBUTES (ר) or DIFFICULTY (צ) - OF (ו) – ATTRIBUTES (ר)
7112	קָצַץ	Qatsats	to cut, to cut off, cut into two pieces	COMPLETE (ק) - CHOPPING (צ + צ) [CHOP + CHOP = chopping]
Modern Hebrew only	קָצַץ	QaTSeTS	to mince, hash, chop, to sever, to fell (a tree) to agree upon	THOROUGH (ק) - CHOPPING (צ + צ) [CHOP + CHOP = chopping] or THOROUGH (ק) - PRESSING (צ + צ) [as in… to "hash out" an agreement]
7114	קָצַר	QaTSaR	to be short, to cut short, to reap, [Mod. Hebrew: insufficient funds]	ACROSS (ק) - FIXED IMAGE (צ) – CUT (ר)
7019	קָץ	QeeTS see Qitsah below	to awake	COMPLETELY (ק) - STIR (צ) [to rouse]
7096	קָצָה	QaT-SaH	to cut off, scraped	AROUND/COMPLELTY (ק) - CHOP (צ) - VERY MUCH (ה) Note: ה = AMPLIFIED (lit. raised up or elevated)
7106a	קָצַע	Qa-TSA	across, take away, to scrape	ACROSS/COMPLETELY (ק) - TAKE (צ) - SEPARATE/AWAY (ע)
7105	קָצִיר	Qa-TSeeR	to mow, to harvest	ACROSS (ק) - STATIONARY OBJECTS (צ) - MAKE (י) - CUT (ר)
7107	קָצַף	Qa-TSePH	anger, furious, provoke to wrath; Mod. Heb.: foam	THOROUGHLY (ק) – CHOPPED / AGITATED / PRESSED (צ) – FACE [surface] (ף) poss. something like having a "hard-pressed expression"
6884	צָרַף	TSaRaF	tried, refined	SOLID (צ) - INSIDE/BEHIND (ר) - SURFACE/FACE (ף)

Chapter 20 – TZADI

Strong's Number	Hebrew Word	Trans-Literation	Word Definition	Explanation of Pictographical Meanings
6975	קוֹץ	QOTS	a thorn bush	FULL (ק) - OF (ו) - THORNS/BARBS (צ)
6787	צָרַר	TSaRaR	distress, to suffer, to bring a rival wife into the home	CONFLICT/TROUBLE (צ) - on the INSIDE (ר) of the INSIDE (ר) or TROUBLE/CONFLICT (צ) at the INNERMOST CORE (ר)
6113	עָצַר	ATSaR	to restrain, bond, restrict, shut, refrain, held back	PREVENT [remove] (ע) - CONFLICT/AGRESSION/HOSTILITY (צ) - WITHIN (ר)
Word not in Tenach see 6734	צַיֵּת	TSee-YeT	OBEY! (imperative)	PERMANENTLY/CONSISTENTLY (צ) - HIT [strike] (י) - the MARK (ת) NOTE: (in the ancient pictographs) HAND (י) ↔ PERMANENTLY AFFIXED (צ) - to the MARK (ת)
6725	צִיּוּן	TSIYŪN	a signpost, a monument, marker	PERMANENT (צ) - SIGN [the sun and moon were set by God as permanent signs] (י) - OF (ו) - REMEMBERANCE (ן)
6687	צוּף	TSUPH	to flow, overflow, flowed, float	MIGHTY FORCE (צ) - OF (ו) - DOWNWARD FLOW (ף)
7169	קָרַץ	QaraTS	to nip, pinch, compress, wink	WRAP AROUND (ק) - INSIDE (ר) - FORCEFULLY (צ)
7061	קָמַץ	QaMaTS	to enclose with the hand, to grasp	WRAP AROUND (ק) - OBJECT (מ) - FORCEFULLY (צ)
5006	נָאַץ	NaATS	to spurn, treat with contempt	LIVING (נ) - INDIVIDUAL (א) - CONTEMPT (צ) [a DESPISED INDIVIDUAL]
7492	רָעַץ	RaATS	to shatter	ATTRIBUTE of (ר) - FORCE (ע) - MIGHTY FORCE or CHOP (צ)
7533.	רָצַץ	RaTSaTS	to crush, bruised oppressed See Is. 42:3	CHOPPING (צ צ) ↔ CHARACTERISTIC (ר)

Unlocking the Ancient Pictorial Code of the Hebrew Alphabet

Strong's Number	Hebrew Word	Trans-Literation	Word Definition	Explanation of Pictographical Meanings
6760	צָלַע	TSaLaĤ	to limp, lame	FIXED [unbending] (צ) - LEG (ל) - CONDITION (ע)
6703	צַחַח	TsaĤaĤ	dazzling, pure, scorching, clearly	MIGHTY FORCE (צ) - ALL AROUND (ח) - SPACE (ח)
6735b	צִיר	TSeeR	Swivel	FIXED (צ) - BECOMES [is caused to be] (י) - BENT [bendable] or CHANGED (ר)
3905	לָחַץ	LaĤaTS	to squeeze, to press, oppress	GUIDED FLOW/PURPOSEFUL (ל) - ALL AROUND (ח) - SOLID/FIRM/DESTRUCTIVE FORCE (צ) See 6743 immediately below, which uses the same 3 letters but in a rearranged order.
6743	צָלַח	TSaLaĤ	to break forth, to come upon mightily	STRONG/GREAT FORCE (צ) - GUIDED FLOW (ל) - ALL AROUND (ח)
4330	מִיץ	MITS (MeeTS)	To press, to squeeze, to wring	BODY (מ) – GREATLY/HIGHLY (י) - PRESSED (ץ)
6555	פָּרַץ	PaRaTS	to break through, break down	**BREAK**ing APART (פ) - the INSIDE (ר) - via **STRONG FORCE** or **CHOP** (צ)
6775	צָמַד	TSaMaD	to bind, to join (prim root)	**ROOTED** (צ) - BODY (מ) - TWO GATHERED (joined) (ד)
6781	צָמִיד	TSaMeeD	covering (prob. Denotes ground covering)	ROOTED (צ) - BODY (מ) - IN / ABOVE (י) - GROUND (ד)
6779	צָמַח	TSaMaĤ	to grow, spring forth, sprouted	ROOTED (צ) - BODY (מ) - GROWTH or GROWS into SPACE (ח) See 6784 below

Strong's Number	Hebrew Word	Trans-Literation	Word Definition	Explanation of Pictographical Meanings
6086	עֵץ	ETS	a tree	FORCE or CONDITION of being (ע) FIRMLY ROOTED (צ) NOTE: AYIN might be the Hebrew equivalent of what we call the "state of being" verbs in English: *am, is, are, was, were, be, being, been.*
6784	צָמַק	TSaMaQ	to dry up, to shrivel up	ROOTED (צ) - BODY (מ) – CONTRACTING or SHRIVELING SPACE (ק) See 6779 above

TZADI - Biblical Food for Thought

עֵץ   ETS -   a tree
LIFE FORCE/CONDITION of Being (ע) - FIRMLY ROOTED (צ)

The pictographical meaning of the Hebrew word for tree, *ETS*, means *FIRMLY ROOTED*, a phrase used many places throughout the Bible. In fact, the concept of being firmly rooted (firmly planted) provides the core idea of King David's first psalm:

> "1 How blessed is the man who does not walk in the counsel of the wicked,
> Nor stand in the path of sinners,
> Nor sit in the seat of scoffers!
> 2 But his delight is in the law of the Lord,
> And in His law he meditates day and night.
> 3 He will be **like a tree firmly planted by streams of water**,
> Which yields its fruit in its season
> And its leaf does not wither;
> And in whatever he does, he prospers."
> - Psalm 1:1-4

Arid land covers most of the area where the nation of Israel was established long ago. Any tree without deep roots will dry up, wither and die during the lengthy periods of drought. During the times when water cannot be found on the surface of the ground in the Middle East, there often remains sufficient moisture for plants and trees not too far below the surface.

In order to train a tree to set deep roots, Middle Eastern farmers and gardeners use a clever method of watering trees. They drive a long pipe into the ground; its bottom end rests a measured distance just below the roots of the tree they that are training. Water is then allowed to seep into the ground below the tree's root system. Responding to the deepening water source, the thirsty tree sends its roots further downward. As the roots grow ever deeper, the pipe is driven further into the ground, a little distance at a time.

Eventually, the farmer will have a tree with unusually deep roots. After that, whether water is scarce or not, the tree will usually be able to access all the water it needs. The result is a healthy tree which bears fruit of the highest quality.

As God's people, we may find ourselves suffering through difficult times, encountering a variety of spiritual trials and *dry spells*. If we set our spiritual roots deeply before we come upon difficult times, we will have the spiritual wherewithal to access the comfort and strength of the Holy Spirit when we are confronted with periods of extreme hardship.

This chapter on TZadi focuses on being a *FIXED IMAGE* and *FIRMLY ROOTED*; consider these following words penned long ago by the prophet Jeremiah:

> 7 "Blessed is the man who trusts in the Lord
> And whose trust is the Lord.
> 8 "For he will be like a tree planted by the water,
> That extends its roots by a stream
> And will not fear when the heat comes;
> But its leaves will be green,
> And it will not be anxious in a year of drought
> Nor cease to yield fruit."
> - Jeremiah 17:7-8

I find it fascinating that the two Phoenician pictographs which denote *ETZ*, **a firmly rooted tree**, are a *stalking hunter* and an *alert eye,* which are combined to show *the eye of the hunter*, one who has his gaze fixed upon his prize. I am reminded of the theme song for the movie Rocky II, *Eye of the Tiger*. The movie's theme is completely in step with what the ancient Phoenicians were trying to convey with the word *ETS*.

If we want the victor's crown in the race we run called *life*, then we must fix our gaze upon the prize and pursue it with all that is within us. Ancient hunters stalked game because they and their families were hungry, not because hunting was simply *sport* to them.

Is our faith rooted in a deep hunger? Or is our appearance of faith for appearances sake only? To *trust in the Lord*, the way Jeremiah meant *trust in the Lord*, is to be hungry for God. Like deeply-rooted trees which can access water even during the toughest of dry spells, we need to be ever seeking the Holy Spirit of God with all of our heart, with all of our soul and with all of our might (Deut. 6:5).

* * *

Chapter 21
QOPH (or KUPH)

NECK & BACK of the HEAD — SWELLING or FULLNESS
Setting Sun (completed day – fullness of time)

QOPH's Phoenician pictographs represented the NECK and BACK of the HEAD. QOPH denotes the transformation of the neck into a fully developed head, which is seen as SWELLING OUT from the neck at the head's base.

The post-Babylonian exile pictograph also seems to denote SWELLING, indicated by a pictograph again denoting FULLNESS of the NECK.

QOPH's various meanings include
FULLNESS of SWELLING [as in RIPE or MATURE fruit], FULLY DEVELOLPED, ENTIRELY MATURED, TRANSFORMED, COMPLETE, to FILL, CHANGE, ACROSS / THROUGHOUT (prep.), WRAPPED AROUND.

QOPH's letter meaning is
DEVELOPING (ק) - FLOW DOWNWARDS (ף)
… indicating the FLOW of TRANSFORMATION.

QOPH

Action or Motion Indicated	Descriptive Form	Noun(s) Denoted	Prepositional Meanings
to Swell up, to Develop fully, to Mature completely, to Wrap around to Cross over	Thorough, Completely, Fully developed Wrapped around Mature Ripe	Crossing over Transition Transformation Change Maturity Fullness of Time	Across Throughout Through

QOPH EXAMPLES:

Strong's Number	Hebrew Word	Trans-Literation	Word Definition	Explanation of Pictographical Meanings
Not in Tenach, but… it is interesting to note that Kopf does mean "head" in German	קוֹף	Qoph probably means: back of head	1. NECK, which also denotes JUDGEMENT 2. FULLNESS of DEVELOPMENT Or FULLNESS of TIME 3. WRAP AROUND 4. Back of head 5. CONTRACTING SPACE 6. Monkey or Ape (according to some sources)	NECK's (ק) - FULLNESS [swelled up/wide point] (ף) = FULLNESS [Wide Part] of the NECK = BACK of HEAD. FULLNESS also denotes complete and proper DEVELOPMENT. Lit. the name of the letter Qopf means "head" (specifically the back side) and came phonetically unchanged into the German language as Kopf. The primary meaning of QOPH is to SWELL, which denotes expanding or ballooning out in 3-D, but not in a full 360 degree fashion. Rather, QOPH primarily denotes the swelling upward and outward of things like heads of grain on stems or stalks, a person's head which "swells" on the neck, and even the "swell" of a person's body as they rise up from a crouched or seated position upon the stalks of the legs. Secondary meanings of Qoph denote the concepts of the prepositions ACROSS and THROUGH plus the concept of WRAPPED AROUND.
Modern Hebrew only	קָץ	QaTZ	to loathe, to fear	**NECK/COMPLETELY (ק)** + FIXED MOTIONLESS (ץ) = fear
7093	קֵץ	QeTZ	end, limit	**NECK/COMPLETELY (ק)** + CHOPPED (ץ) = "CUT OFF" or ENDED
7092	קָפַץ	Qa-FaTZ	1. to close, to draw together 2. to chop	1. ACROSS (ק) - FRONT/FACE (פ) - ATTACHED/STRONG FORCE [bonded] (ץ) or ACROSS - SURFACEs - ATTACHED 2. ACROSS (ק) - SURFACE (פ) – CHOPPED (ץ)
7094	קָצַב	Qa-TZaV	1. to cut off 2. to stipulate, to determine	1. **NECK/COMPLETELY (ק)** - CHOPPED/CUT (ץ) - [from] BODY (ב) or **ACROSS (ק)** - CUT (ץ) - BODY (ב). 2. [revolving/functioning] AROUND (ק) - FIXED [in place] (ץ) – BODY (ב) [to contract?]
Modern Hebrew	קַצָּב	Qa-TZaV	to butcher	COMPLETELY/AROUND/ACROSS (ק) - CHOP (ץ) - BODY (ב)

Chapter 21 – QOPH

Strong's Number	Hebrew Word	Trans-Literation	Word Definition	Explanation of Pictographical Meanings
8628	תָּקַע	T'a-QA	to blow a trumpet, to give a blow, slap	ACTION (ת) - **WRAP AROUND/ACROSS** (ק) - AWAY /OUT/AGAINST (ע)
Modern Hebrew	תֶּקַע	Tey-Qah	to plug	ACTION/APPLY (ת) - **ACROSS** (ק) - OPENING [or empty space] (ע)
Modern Hebrew	קֶצֶב	Qa-TZeV	1. rhythm 2. cut, shape	1. **ACROSS/WRAP AROUND** (ק) - FIXED PACED [established & patterned] (צ) - BODY (ב) [indicating a rhythmic PATTERN in music… to move across the page of music or through the song in quantified measures] 2. AROUND/ACROSS (ק) - CHOP (צ) - BODY (ב) = to cut, to shape
Modern Hebrew & 5559	סִלֵּק Modern סְלֵק Biblical	SeeLeQ (mod.) SLeQ (Biblical)	Mod.: to lift, to move, to put away Biblical: to come up, taken	GATHER (ס) - LEAD/TAKE (ל) - **ACROSS** or **WRAP AROUND** (ק)
7783	שׁוּק	SHUQ	to be abundant, overflow	SUBSTANTAIL ABUNDANCE (שׁ) + OF (ו) + **WRAPPED AROUND** (ק) or **COMPLETE** (וק) ↔ ABUNDANCE of PROVISIONS (שׁ)
Modern Hebrew only	קָצַץ	QaTS-TSeTS	to mince, hash, chop, to sever, to fell (a tree), to agree upon (as in… to "hash out" an agreement)	**THOROUGH** (ק) - CHOPPING (צ) [CHOP + CHOP = chopping] or **THOROUGH** (ק) - PRESSING (צ + צ)
7174	קָרַר	QaRaR	1. to be cold, to keep fresh 2. to tear down	1. **NECK** (ק) - BENDING (רר) or 2. COMPLETELY (ק) - CUTTING (רר)
7130	קֶרֶב	Qe-ReV	entrails, intestines, guts, inner parts, midst	**THROUGHOUT** [across] (ק) - INSIDE (ר) - BODY (ב)
7164	קָרַס	QaReS	to bow, to bend	**NECK** (ק) - BENT (ר) – COMPLETELY (ס)
7128	קְרָב	QRaV	to battle	COMPLETELY (ק) – FLEXIBLE [bendable] (ר) - BODY (ב)

Unlocking the Ancient Pictorial Code of the Hebrew Alphabet

Strong's Number	Hebrew Word	Trans-Literation	Word Definition	Explanation of Pictographical Meanings
7174 & 7175a	קַר or קֹר from קָרַר	QaR, QoR from QaRaR	7174: cold, coldness, 7175a breaking down, to tear down	**COMPLETELY/THOROGHLY** (ק) - CUTS (ר) - INSIDE (ר) or **COMPLETELY** (ק) - CUTTING (רר) [perhaps because cold weather cuts into & permeates the body]
7161 & 7162	קֶרֶן	QeRen	to have horns	**NECK** (ק) - **BENT** (ר) - **ARMs** (נ) or possibly **DEVELOP** (ק) - HEAD (ר) - ARMs (נ) [The "ARMS" meaning possibly came from observing horned animals bowing their necks and using their horns like arms.] **INTERESTING NOTE**: Moses is depicted in one of Michelangelo's works as having HORNS on his head due to the fact that this word was originally translated incorrectly as HORNS instead of RADIANT LIGHT [SEE FOLLOWING WORD. Link to more info: http://www.moseshand.com/studies/moses.htm]
7160	קָרַן	QaRan	to radiate light, beam of radiant light	**WRAPPED AROUND** [radiating] (ק) MOVING (נ) ↔ APPEARANCE (ר) [a halo of light] or possibly: **DEVELOP** (ק) - MOVING (נ) ↔ APPEARANCE (ר)
7114	קָצַר	QaTSaR	to be short, to cut short, to reap, [Mod. Hebrew: insufficient funds]	**ACROSS/WRAP AROUND** (ק) - FIXED IMAGE (צ) - CUT (ר) or **ALL the way AROUND** (ק) - CHOP (צ) - CUT or INSIDE (ר)
Modern Hebrew only	קַק or קָאָק	1. QaQ 2. Qa-AQ	swan, goose	1. NECKS (קק) or NECK (ק) - WRAPS AROUND (ק)
7106a	קָצַע	Qa-TSA	across, take away, to scrape	**ACROSS/COMPLETELY** (ק) - TAKE (צ) - SEPARATE/AWAY (ע)
Modern Hebrew only	קָצַע	Qa-TSe-A	to trim	**ACROSS/WRAP AROUND** (ק) - TAKE (צ) - AWAY (ע)
7105	קָצִיר	Qa-TSeeR	to mow, to harvest	**ACROSS** (ק) - STATIONARY OBJECTS (צ) - MAKE (י) - CUT (ר)

Chapter 21 – QOPH

Strong's Number	Hebrew Word	Trans-Literation	Word Definition	Explanation of Pictographical Meanings
7107	קָצֶף	Qa-TSePH	to be angry, anger, foam	**THOROUGHLY (ק)** - CHOPPED/AGITATED (צ) – FACE [surface] (ף)
Modern Hebrew only	טֶקֶס	Te-Qes	ceremony, protocol	ACTIONs (ט) - **THROUGHOUT** [across] (ק) - GATHERING (ס)
2706	חֹק	ÔQ	1. law, custom, statute, immutable law 2. portion, share, task	1. PORTION (ח) - **JUDGEMENT (ק)*** *Qoph, which means **NECK**, denotes **judgment**. PORTION (ח) - ACROSS (ק)
Word not in the Tanach	מַזִיק	MaZeeQ	evil spirit	ENTITY (מ) - VERY (י) ↔ STRONG (ז) - **WITHIN (ק)** or ENTITY (מ) - TAKE (ז) + UP (י) [possess] – MANIFESTS / DEVELOPS (ק) NOTE: The single dot under the Zayin is pronounced **EE** and typically is followed by a YOD.
7031	קַל	QaL	easy, swiftly	[move] **ACROSS (ק)** - COMFORTABLY (ל)
7032	קָל	QaL [Aramaic]	voice, sound	[move] ACROSS (ק) - COMFORTABLY (ל) or possibly FULLY/THOROUGHLY (ק) – GUIDED (ל)
6963	קוֹל	QOL	sound, voice	MOVE **ACROSS (ק)** - WITH (ו) – EASE (ל) or possibly the **MOVING ACROSS** or **FULLNESS (ק)** of GUIDANCE (ל)
7112	קָצַץ	Qatsats	to cut, to cut off, cut into 2 pieces	COMPLETE (ק) - CHOPPING (צ + צ) [CHOP + CHOP = chopping]
7000	קָטַר	QaTaR	to shut in, enclose	**COMPLETELY/SECURELY (ק)** - CONTAINed (ט) - INSIDE (ר)
7006	קִיא	QI	to vomit, that which is vomited up	**ACROSS/COMPLETELY (ק)** - CAUSE TO BE (י) - SEPARATED (א) This word seems to denote forceful, full projectile vomiting… **SPEW**
6975	קוֹץ	QOTS	a thorn bush	FULL (ק) - OF (ו) - THORNS/BARBS (צ)

Unlocking the Ancient Pictorial Code of the Hebrew Alphabet

Strong's Number	Hebrew Word	Trans-Literation	Word Definition	Explanation of Pictographical Meanings
Word not in the Tenach	מְקֻדָּם	MooQ-DahM	early	a THING (מ) - SWELLs/WIDENS/DEVELOPS (ק) - LACKING (ד) - SUBSTANCE (ם) [appearing on the outside to be fully develop but not developing properly inside, like fruit becoming large but remaining pithy] NOTE: The DALET (ד) is dotted [doubled] to indicate LACK-*ING*
7107	קָצַף	Qa-TSePH	anger, furious, provoke to wrath; Mod. Heb.: foam	THOROUGHLY (ק) – CHOPPED / AGITATED / PRESSED (צ) – FACE [surface] (ף) poss. something like having a "hard-pressed expression"
7169	קָרַץ	QaraTS	to nip, pinch, compress, wink	WRAP AROUND (ק) - INSIDE (ר) - FORCEFULLY (צ)
7061	קָמַץ	QaMaTS	to enclose with the hand, to grasp	WRAP AROUND (ק) - OBJECT (מ) - FORCEFULLY (צ)
7121	קָרָא	QaRA	to call, to proclaim, to read	FULLY DEVELOPED (ק) – INSIDE (ר) - SEPARATING AWAY (א)
7122 see 7136 below	קָרָא	**QaRaH**	to encounter, meet, befall	COMPLETE (ק) – CHANGE of FORTUNE (ר) – SEPARATE INDIVIDUALS YOKED (א) NOTE: This word appears to have become misspelled over time. See 7136 below for what appears to be a more logical and correct spelling.
7136 see 7121 above	קָרָה	**QaRaH**	to encounter, meet, befall	COMPLETE (ק) - CHANGE of FORTUNE (ר) - RAISED UP/BEHELD (ה)
7139	קָרַח	QaRaĤ	to make bald, to shave the head	COMPLETELY (ק) - CUT (ר) – ALL AROUND (ח)
7167	קָרַע	QaRA	to tear, rend, torn	COMPLETELY (ק) - CUT (ר) - by FORCE (ע)
7126	קָרַב	QaRaV	approach, come near, bring near, brought, offer	ACROSS (ק) - BEND/CHANGE (ר) - BODY (ב)
2388	חָזַק	ĤaZaQ	to be strong, to grow strong, strengthen	ALL AROUND (ח) - STRENGTH (ז) - FULLY DEVELOPED (ק)

Chapter 21 – QOPH

Strong's Number	Hebrew Word	Trans-Literation	Word Definition	Explanation of Pictographical Meanings
2389	חָזָק	ĤaZaQ	strong, stout mighty	ALL AROUND (ח) - STRENGTH (ז) – FULLY DEVELOPED (ק)
6693	צוּק	TSŪQ	to constrain, bring into straits, press upon, oppress	COMPLETE (וק) ↔ MIGHTY FORCE (צ)
7954	קָמָה	QaMaH	standing grain	AROUND (ק) - PLACE [poss. field] (מ) - RAISED ABOVE (ה) Note: ה = lit. raised up higher than…or elevated
6711	צָחַק	ZaĤaQ	to laugh, entertained, jesting	FORCE (ז) + THROAT (ח) [or THROAT FORCE] - SWELLING (ק)
6965	קוּם	QŪM	to arise, to stand up	SWELLing [to stand up, to ARISE] (ק) - OF (ו) - BODY (מ) Note: Just before a high jumper leaps, they take what is called a "gathering step," a step where the body sinks down & compresses so that it may spring upward into full extension. SWELL in this context would mean to uncompress the body from a crouched position [they had no chairs when this word was coined].
6561	פָּרַק	PaRaQ	to tear apart or away	BREAKing APART (פ) ↔ THOROUGHLY (ק) - ATTRIBUTE (ר) or BREAKing APART [force] (פ) ↔ WRAPPED AROUND (ק) – the INSIDE (ר)
6779	צָמַח	TSaMaĤ	to grow, spring forth, sprouted (prim root)	ROOTED (צ) - BODY (מ) - GROWTH or GROWS into SURROUNDING SPACE (ח) See 6784 below
6784	צָמַק	TSaMaQ	to dry up, to shrivel up (prim root)	ROOTED (צ) - BODY (מ) - CONTRACTING or SHRIVELING SPACE ??? (ק) See 6779 above In word 6784, QOPH seems to denote a meaning of to CONTRACT. This is the opposite of its typical meaning, which is to swell… but why???
7096	קָצָה	QaT-SaH	to cut off, scraped	AROUND/COMPLELTY (ק) - CHOP (צ) - VERY MUCH (ה) Note: ה = AMPLIFIED (lit. raised up or elevated)

Strong's Number	Hebrew Word	Trans-Literation	Word Definition	Explanation of Pictographical Meanings
7019a	קַיִץ	QeeTS	Awaken awakened, awake (prim. root)	COMPLETELY (ק) - STIR (צ) ↔ UP (י)

QOPH - Biblical Food for Thought

קַיִץ QeeTS
Meaning: to awake, to arouse
COMPLETELY (ק) - STIR (צ) ↔ UP (י)

The pictographical meaning of the Hebrew word to awaken, *QEETS*, means *COMPLETELY STIR UP*, to AWAKEN everything within. Isaiah exhorts Israel to arise from its slumber:

> 1 **Awake, awake,**
> Clothe yourself in your strength, O Zion;
> Clothe yourself in your beautiful garments, O Jerusalem, the holy city;
> For the uncircumcised and the unclean will no longer come into you.
> 2 Shake yourself from the dust, rise up, O captive Jerusalem;
> Loose yourself from the chains around your neck, O captive daughter of Zion.
> 3 For thus says the Lord, "You were sold for nothing and you will be
> **redeemed without money**."
> - Isaiah 52:1-3

For nearly 2000 years, Jerusalem rested under the control of non-Jews… basically in a state of slumber. On the 14th of May, 1948, the nation of Israel was reborn in one day, fulfilling a Biblical prophecy which lay dormant for more than 2600 years.[24] Then in June of 1967, the Old City of Jerusalem, where the Temple Mount is located, once again came under Jewish control after more than two thousand years of being "occupied territory" under the Romans, Muslims, Ottoman Turks, the British and the Jordanians.

We are at a time in history when God is most certainly moving! It is time indeed for Jerusalem to wake up from its slumber and stir itself! The signs of the time indicate that the day of the Messiah's appearance in Jerusalem may be very near.

* * *

---
[24] Isaiah 66:8

Chapter 22
RESH or REISH

OUTLOOK ON LIFE or DESTINY — BENT or CHANGED

REISH's Phoenician pictographs represented the PROFILE of the HEAD (ROSH) or possible an identifying flag which could easily be seen from afar.
REISH denotes a person's OUTLOOK on LIFE, which was seen as a DETERMINING or IDENTIFYING CHARACTERISTIC.

The post-Babylonian exile pictograph probably denotes
a BENT REED which CUTS (poss. *sawgrass*),
but also indicating one's BENT (natural tendencies).

Other meanings for the letter REISH include:
INSIDE ATTRIBUTEs, CHARACTERISTICs (profile of head),
PLAN, REASON, BEND, BENT OVER, CORRUPTED, CONTENTS,
CHANGE or make a TURN [bending is a change of direction],
APPEARANCE, ATTITUDE, BITTER (poss. a BITTER HERB[25]),
LESS, FOCUS ATTENTION UPON… , THOUGHT, BEGINNING, MIND (n.),
DESIRE, SHOUT, LINE, CHOICE, an exterior SHELL, RICH, ABOVE, OPEN,
PLACED OVER, poss. to WATCH or to SEE

RESH (*Rosh*, a *Head*) morphed to become REISH (a *Reed*).
REISH's pictographical letter names means
CHANGE of FORTUNE or OUTLOOK on LIFE's PROVISION…
to BEND or CHANGE (alter) one's DESTINY or possibly OUTLOOK
ergo the ancient pictogram of a head's profile "looking outward".

---

[25] The *bitter herb* is one of the items found on a Jewish Passover Seder plate.

REISH

Action or Motion Indicated	Descriptive Form	Noun(s) Denoted	Prepositional Meanings
to Bend, to Cut, Changing of fortune to Make a Turn - (a directional change) to Focus upon to Plan or Reason to Shout out to Radiate to Stare	**INSIDE**, Open, Bitter, Bent, Corrupted, Cut Radiating	Attribute of character, Reputation, Mental outlook, Attitude Contents, Core Distinguishing physical characteristics An arc (geometric term) Ray, Shout, poss. Poverty	Inside Within Behind OVER (see RAB) Above

REISH (RESH) EXAMPLES:

Strong's Number	Hebrew Word	Trans-Literation	Word Definition	Explanation of Pictographical Meanings
see also 7220b & 7389	רֵישׁ	**Reish** See Ya-RESH below	Bent or Cutting Strands REISH: Change of Fortune (Life's path is bent)	ATTRIBUTEs, CHARACTERISTICs, PLAN, REASON, BEND, CHANGE [bending is a change of direction], INSIDE, DESTINY NOTE 2: Rosh means "head" and this is the ancient symbol for the pre-Babylonian letter name; however, **Reish** (רֵישׁ), which was denoted by a pictograph of a *reed*, means *poverty* in Biblical Hebrew
3423	יָרַשׁ	Ya-ReSH	to seize, take possession, inherit, dispossess	CAUSE (י) – BEND / **CHANGE** (ר) – of EXISTENCE / POSSESSIONS / PROVISION (שׁ)
5534a	סָכַר סָכַר	SaKeR (modern) SaKaR (Biblical)	a dam (modern) to shut up, stop up (Biblical)	GATHER (ס) - HOLD (כ) - **INSIDE** (ר)
6529	פְּרִי	Pri [Pree]	fruit, result, offspring	FRUIT (פ) - **INSIDE** (ר) - CREATED/CAUSED TO BE/DEVELOPS (י)
6735b	צִיר	TSeeR	swivel	FIXED (צ) - BECOMES [is caused to be] (י) - BENT [bendable] or CHANGED (ר)

Chapter 22 – REISH

Strong's Number	Hebrew Word	Trans-Literation	Word Definition	Explanation of Pictographical Meanings
Modern Hebrew only	הָרַר	HaRaR	a corrupt person	Heh (ה) indicates AMPLIFICATION: VERY (ה) - BENT (ר) - INSIDE (ר)
6713 & 6715	צָחַר	Tsa-ĤaR Mod. Heb. TSAĤOR	White	CLEAR (צ) - EMPTINESS (ה) - APPEARANCE/**RECOGNIZABLE ATTRIBUTE [COLOR] (ר)**
6699	צוּרָה	TSŪ-RaH	form, shape, image	FIXED IMAGE (צ) OF (ו) - HIGHLY (ה) ↔ **RECOGNIZABLE ATTRIBUTES (ר)**
264	אָחוֹר	AĤOR	Buttocks	to SEPARATE (א) - PARTS (ח) - OF - **REAR/BEHIND (ר)**
1624	גָּרָה	GaRaH	stir up strife, provoke	NON (ג) - ELEVATED (ה) ↔ CHARACTER (ר) [lit. a person of **low character**... similar to the English term "**a low life**"]
8409	תִּגְרָה	TheeG-RaH	Strife	NON-UNITY (תג) - MORE (ה) - APPARENT (ר)
8446	תּוּר	TŪR	to spy, to tour, to explore	ACTION (ת... from ט) of LOOKING (ר) or ACTIVELY LOOKING NOTE: TAV & TET seem to have traded and inter-twined their meanings over time
2270 see also 2266	חָבֵר	ĤaVeR	friend, associate, united	PART/SECTOR [of] (ח) - HOUSE/BODY/COMMUNITY (ב) - RECOGNIZABLE (ר)
7174	קָרַר	QaRaR	1. to be cold, to keep fresh 2. to tear down	1. NECK (ק) - **BENDING (רר)** or 2. COMPLETELY (ק) - CUTTING (רר) (cold wind?)
7130	קֶרֶב	Qe-ReV	entrails, intestines, guts, inner parts, midst	THROUGHOUT (ק) - INSIDE (ר) – BODY (ב)
7164	קָרַס	QaReS	to bow, to bend	NECK (ק) - **BENT (ר)** - COMPLETELY (ס)
7174 7175a	קֹר קָרַר	QaR, QoR fr. QaRaR	7174: coldness, 7175a: to tear down	COMPLETELY (ק) - CUTS (ר) - INSIDE (ר) or COMPLETELY (ק) – CUTTING (רר) - [perhaps because cold weather permeates the body]

Unlocking the Ancient Pictorial Code of the Hebrew Alphabet

Strong's Number	Hebrew Word	Trans-Literation	Word Definition	Explanation of Pictographical Meanings
6884	צָרַף	TSaRaF	tried, refined	SOLID (צ) - **INSIDE/BEHIND** (ר) – SURFACE or FACE (ף)
2094	זָהַר	ZaHaR a) is also for ZoHaR	a) radiant light b) a warning cry	STRONG (ז) – RAISED UP (ה) – RAY (ר) see 7160 below re Resh meaning *RAYS of Light* STRONG (ז) – RAISED UP (ה) – SHOUT (ר)
7160	קָרַן	QeReN	To send out rays, to radiate light	AROUND (ק) – **RAY**s (ר) – MOVE (נ) Wrongly translated as **horns** during the Middle Ages, so Michelangelo mistakenly put horns on the head of Moses when he made the statue.
2022	הַר	HaR	Mountain	RAISED/HIGH (ה) – ATRIBUTE, APPEARANCE or CURVE (ר) or OPENed (ר) ↔ UP (ה)
738	אֲרִי	ARI	a lion	GREAT/HIGH/MIGHTY (י) ↔ INDIVIDUAL/LEADER (א) - ATTRIBUTES/CHARACTER/REPUTATION or PERSONALITY "BENT" (ר)
1921	הָדַר	HaDaR	to honor, to adorn	EXTOL / HONOR (ה) - EXTEND (ד) - ATTRIBUTED CHARACTERISTICS (ר) or REPUTATION (ר) - EXTENDED (ד) - UPWARD (ה)
7000	קָטַר	QaTaR	to shut in, enclose	COMPLETELY/SECURELY (ק) - CONTAINed (ט) - **INSIDE** (ר)
7105	קָצִיר	Qa-TSeeR	to mow, to harvest	ACROSS (ק) - STATIONARY OBJECTS (צ) - MAKE (י) - **CUT** (ר)
2737	חָרוּז	CHaRUZ	string of beads	SEGMENTS (ח) - **INSIDE** (ר) - OF (ו) – ARC (ז)
6113	עָצַר	ATSaR	to restrain, bond, restrict, shut, refrain, held back	PREVENT [restrain, remove] (ע) - CONFLICT/HOSTILITY (צ) – WITHIN (ר)
7169	קָרַץ	QaraTS	to nip, pinch, compress	THOROUGHLY (ק) - **INSIDE** (ר) – PRESS (צ)
2026	הָרַג	HaRaG	killed, slay	RAISED UP/GREAT [amplified] (ה) – **CUT** (ר) - AGAINST (ג)
2040	הָרַס	HaRaS	break down, overthrow… in English: *harass*	RAISED UP/GREAT [amplified] (ה) - **CUT** (ר) - COMPLETELY/ALL AROUND (ס)

Chapter 22 – REISH

Strong's Number	Hebrew Word	Trans-Literation	Word Definition	Explanation of Pictographical Meanings
5783	עוּר	ŪR	to be exposed, bare	EXPOSE[ing] (ע) - OF (ו) - **INSIDE (ר)**
7126	קָרַב	QaRaV	approach, come near, bring near, brought, offer	ACROSS (ק) - **BEND (ר)** - BODY (ב)
8388a	תָּאַר	TA-AR	to incline, curved	MARKed (ת) - OUT (א) – BEND / CURVE (ר)
1642	גְּרָר	GeRaR	city in Gaza which may have influenced Essau's character	NOT (ג) - INSIDERS/WITHIN (ר)(ר) GERAR denotes people not like the people of Israel. GER denotes a foreigner... so the town's name could lit. be translated FOREIGNERS [double RESH makes FOREIGNER plural]
7122 see 7136 below	קָרָא	QaRaH	to encounter, meet, befall	COMPLETE (ק) - CHANGE of FORTUNE (ר) - SEPARATE INDIVIDUALS YOKED (א) **NOTE:** This word appears to have become **misspelled** over time. See 7136 below for what appears to be a more logical and correct spelling.
7136 see 7121 above	קָרָה	QaRaH	to encounter, meet, befall	COMPLETE (ק) - CHANGE of FORTUNE (ר) - RAISED UP/BEHELD (ה)
7139	קָרַח	QaRaĤ	to make bald, to shave the head	COMPLETELY (ק) - CUT (ר) – ALL AROUND (ח)
7167	קָרַע	QaRA	to tear, rend, torn	COMPLETELY (ק) - CUT (ר) - by FORCE (ע)
7806	שָׁזַר	SHaZaR	to be twisted	ABUNDANT (שׁ) - STRENGTH (ז) - BEND (ר)
1197a	בָּעַר	BaAR	to burn, consume, remove, purge	EMPTY/HOLLOWing (ב) - CONDITION (ע) - INSIDE (ר) or INVISIBLE (ב) - FORCE (ע) - **INSIDE (ר)**
1481 a	גּוּר	GUR	to sojourn, strangers, aliens	NOT (ג) - OF/ON (ו) - the INSIDE (ר) lit. not an insider
1481b	גּוּר	GUR	to stir up strife, quarrel	NOT (ג) - OF/ON (ו) - the INSIDE (ר) lit. not an insider or OPPOSITION (ג) - OF/ON (ו) – the INSIDE (ר)

Strong's Number	Hebrew Word	Trans-Literation	Word Definition	Explanation of Pictographical Meanings
966	בָּזַר	BaZaR	to scatter, distribute	BODY (ב) - ARC (ז) - AROUND [bent] (ר)
7491	רָעַף	RaAPH	to drip	ATTRIBUTE of (ר) - FORCE (ע) - FALL DOWN or DOWNWARD FLOW (ף)
7492	רָעַץ	RaATS	to shatter	ATTRIBUTE of (ר) - FORCE (ע) - MIGHTY FORCE or CHOP (ץ)
5493	סוּר שׁוּר	SŪR	to turn aside, departed [turn as used here means *a change in direction*]	COMPLETENESS (ס) - OF (ו) – **TURN**ing (ר) CHANGE (שׁ) - OF (ו) - TURN (ר)
5462	סָגַר	Sa-GaR	to close	CLOSED UP (ס) - NOT (ג) – **OPEN (ר)** or CLOSED UP (ס) - NOT (ג) – **INSIDE (ר)**
6279 but also 6280	עָתַר	ATHaR	to pray, supplicate	FORCE of (ע) - BECOMING ONE (ת) - **INSIDE (ר)**
6362	פָּטַר	PaTaR	to separate, remove, set free, open	RELEASE (פ) - that which is CONTAINED (ט) - INSIDE (ר)
6509	פָּרָה	PaRaH	to bear fruit, to be fruitful	FRUIT (פ) - INSIDE (ר) - REVEALED (ה)
6565a	פָּרַר	PaRaR	to break, frustrate	BREAK (פ) - INSIDES (רר)
2213	זֵר	ZeR	circlet, border (round), molding	STRONG (ז) - **BEND/ARC (ר)** See 2219 above for comparison; notice how the letters' meanings have changed over time, especially after the Babylonian exile c. 500 BCE. **IMPORTANT NOTE**: ZER is a 2-consonant root that indicates a sharp turn or arcing motion [including up to a **180 degree U-turn**]
2232	זָרַע	ZaRA	to sow, to scatter seed	STRONG (ז) - BEND/ARC (ר) - FORCE (ע) See 2213 above. ZER indicates an **arc** and *AYIN* denotes *a force*. Scattering or sowing seed is done by throwing it in an arcing motion.

Chapter 22 – REISH

Strong's Number	Hebrew Word	Trans-Literation	Word Definition	Explanation of Pictographical Meanings
Modern Hebrew	חֹזֵר	ĤŌ-Zer	to return, to turn around	AROUND (ח) - TURN (זר)
3733	כַּר	KaR Listed as "of unc. der."	1. a basket-saddle 2. a pasture	HOLD (כ) - INSIDE (ר)
2220	זְרוֹעַ	ZeROA	ARM, shoulder, foreleg of a lamb	RETURN (זר) - of (ו) – LIFE FORCE (ע) See **Isaiah 53:1** To whom has the ***ARM (zeroah)*** of the Lord been revealed?
7462a	רָעָה	Ra-AH	shepherd, keeper, tend, feed	WATCHFUL (ר) - FORCE (ע) – AMPLIFIED or AUGMENTED (ה) A state of high alert, keen watchfulness
7239	רִבּוֹ or רִבּוֹא	RiBBŌ fr. 7231	ten thousand, myriad	[set] **OVER or IN EXCESS OF** (ר) - a 1000 or a MULTITUDE (ב) - OF (ו) – INDIVIDUALS (א)
7231	רָבַב	RaBaB	to be or become many or much prim root	[set] OVER or IN EXCESS OF (ר) - THOUSANDS or a MULTITUDES (ב ב = plural)
8269	שַׂר	SaR	prince, chief, commander, ruler,	EXPANDING (ש) – INFLUENCE [being set over as a ruler] (ר)
7227	רַב	RaB	many, much, great, captain, chief	[set] OVER or IN EXCESS OF (ר) - a 1000 or a MULTITUDE (ב)
7442	רָנַן	**Ranan**	to give a ringing cry (shout)	MOVING (נן) ↔ Radiating SHOUT (ר)
7451	רַע	**RA**	bad, evil, wicked, adversity	BENT (ר) – FORCE (ע) or FORCE of ADVERSITY
7456	רָעֵב	**RAeV**	Hunger	BENT or INSIDE (ר) – FORCE (ע) – BODY (ב)

REISH - Food for Thought

ZER זֵר and ZEROA זְרוֹעַ
RETURN (זר) – OF (ו) – SPARK of LIFE [life force] (ע)

The Phoenician pictograph ZAYIN denotes AN ARCHING MOTION. The word stem ZER (זֵר) indicates a 180° arc – much like the path of a boomerang, which returns to its original starting point (if thrown properly). ZER is a word stem in many words involving motions that would cover a circular area, such as casting seed by hand while standing in one place (ZaRA). In fact the Hebrew word meaning both seed and offspring is zera. זֶרַע

ZEROA appears in the opening lines of Isaiah 53, "To whom has the *arm* (zeroa) of the Lord been revealed?" The *Strong's Concordance* number for *ZEROA* is 2220, and it is defined as meaning an *arm*, a *shoulder*, *strength* or *power*. OK... so there is nothing eye-opening about that.

However, to a Jewish nation where a vast majority of the people celebrated Passover every spring, ZEROA denoted something much more than just a strong arm. The Passover meal (called a Seder) is an ordered meal, some might say ritualistic, others might say highly symbolic throughout. Certain items must be present on the table, and these special items are placed on the Seder plate. The head of the household, as part of the Seder meal, must present and briefly describe the significance of each item on the Seder plate.

The central item on the Seder plate is the ZEROA- the unbroken foreleg of a lamb. Perhaps the foreleg of a lamb was seen as being powerful and had an arced shape to it, ergo the original word ZEROA; we can never know for sure. ZEROAH can also mean *seed*, as seed that is scattered when it is sown into the ground.

ZEROAH can be read in the pictographical original form as *RETURN* of (זרו) - the *Spark of Life* (ע). The nation of Israel is like the ZEROAH. For 2000 years it ceased to exists, but like Ezekiel's dry bones, the spark of life is returning to Abraham's *seed*, and to the nation of Israel. The dry bones, the Jews from the Diaspora are being returned to the Land, and they are showing signs of life once again!

* * *

Chapter 23

SHIN

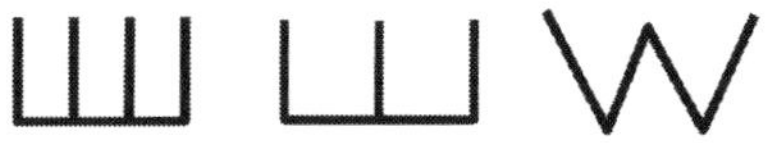 שׁ

Graph of the SUN's PATH indicating RESURRECTION

SHIN's pictographical letter names means
RESURRECTION (ש) – TO (י) – LIFE (נ)

The post-Babylonian exile pictograph is the same as the original Phoenician symbol.

Other meanings for the letter SHIN include:
PUFF OUT, PUFF UP, EXPAND in all directions, BREAD (rising),
SHIN's Phoenician pictographical meaning is the RETURN or RESURRECTION of the SUN to LIFE each day, lit. SUN's ↔ RESURRECTION to LIFE.

The ancient pictograph is not TEETH (as some have posited)...
SHIN's Phoenician pictographs represented a 3-day (2-night) graph of the sun's movement.
The sun was thought to die each night and be resurrected to life again each morning.
Secondary pre-Babylonian meanings include:
SYMMETRY of LIFE or REOCURRING MOVEMENT.

SHIN's post-Babylonian meaning is PUFF UP or PUFF OUT like BREAD RISING.
This meaning originates from the rising bread, which happened by "resurrecting" a bit of leavening from the previous day's bread and mixing it with the new dough... the sourdough leavening method.
SHIN represented the leftover sourdough (yeast) starter that made it possible to *REPEAT AGAIN* (another meaning of SHIN) the bread making process.

Shin also denoted EXPAND, a PUFF (of air), EXHALE, DISBURSE (up or out),

Secondary post-Babylonian meanings include:
TAKE, CONSUME, PLENTIFUL SUBSTANCE or PROVISION(s), ABUNDANCE, WEALTH, FORTUNE, PROVISION(s).

Tertiary derivative meanings include AGAIN, TEETH, GRIND, PRESS UPON, to SEPARATE OUT [teeth biting down], DESTRUCTION, DIVERSE STRANDS or POSSIBILITIES.

SHIN

Action or Motion Indicated	Descriptive Form	Noun(s) Denoted	Prepositional Meanings
To resurrect To puff up or out To expand outward (in all directions) To exhale To grind To press To separate out (oil) To provide / to give	Again Diverse Expanding Abundant Plenty Comparable	Resurrection Bread (Rising) Re-occurring movement Symmetry Abundance Prosperity Wealth Destruction Provision	With

SHIN EXAMPLES:

Strong's Number	Hebrew Word	Trans-Literation	Word Definition	Explanation of Pictographical Meanings
not a Biblical word	שִׁין	Shin	1. RETURN, REBIRTH, RESURREC-TION 2. PUFF (שׁ) – UP (י) MOVEMENT (ן) or **HIGHLY SYMMETRI-CAL MOVEMENT** [to expand like rising BREAD] **WEALTH, CONSUMABLE** PROVISIONS POSSESSIONs, **RETURN, SYMMETRY** of MOVEMENT, EQUAL to,	1. SHIN's most ancient pictograph [jagged **W**] indicated the rising and setting pattern of the sun... which to the Egyptian & many other primitives was thought to be the daily, reoccurring death and **RESURRECTION of the SUN.** SHIN originally denoted RETURN, REBIRTH or **RESURRECTION.** 2. After the 40 years in the desert with Moses, SHIN evolved to denote the **MANNA,** which sustained them and was REBORN every morning, similar to the sun. Over time, however, SHIN morphed to denote PROVISION of SUSTENANCE [ABUNDANCE and PROSERITY] rather than the CONSUMING of sustenance: SUBSTANCE (שׁ) - CAUSING or CREATIING (י) - LIFE (ן). Secondary meanings included PUFF UP, EXPAND [like bread rising], ABUNDANCE of PROVISION, and BREAD. Provision / to Provide /to Give EXPAND, BREAK, SEPARATE, FRACTURE

Chapter 23 – SHIN

Strong's Number	Hebrew Word	Trans-Literation	Word Definition	Explanation of Pictographical Meanings
2-letter root	נ+שׁ	nas or nash	to take	MOVE (נ) + SUBSTANCE (שׁ) = to take (SEE BELOW)
5375	נָסָה נָשָׂא	1. Biblical: NaSA 2. Modern: NaSHA	to take away, to bear, carried	MOVE (נ) + SUBSTANCE (שׁ) – AWAY (א) = take away
Modern Hebrew	נָשׁוּל	Nashul	eviction, ousting	nun + shin = take **possession**, nashul = TAKING + OF (ו) + COMFORT (ל)
7783	שׁוּק	Shuq	to be abundant, overflow	**SUBSTANTIAL ABUNDANCE (שׁ)** + OF (ו) - WRAPPED ALL AROUND (ק) or COMPLETE (ק) ↔ ABUNDANCE of PROVISIONS (שׁ)
5391	נָשַׁךְ	Nashak	to bite, to take interest (on a loan), creditors	**TAKE** (נָשׁ) + a HANDFUL (כ) [similar to the English idiom "take a cut"]
5377 & 5386	נָשִׁי	N'shi	to loan, a debt	**DISBURSE** [motion going out in all directions] (נָשׁ) + YOD (yod indicates "*high*" or "*above*") = disbursed with *interest*
5387	נָשִׂיא	Nashiah	lifting up, carrying, raising, leaders, prince, chief	**TAKE** (נָשׁ) + ABOVE/HIGH (י) + AWAY (א) + RAISED UP (ה)
Mod. Heb. from 5386b	נְשִׁ'מָה from נָשִׂיא	Nashima fr. NASIA	breath, exhale	movement (נ) + puff up (שׁי) + body (מ) + raised or lifted up (יה)
8034	שֵׁם	SHeM	a name, fame, renown	**EXPAND/GROW (שׁ)** - FORM/IMAGE () [one's name is known apart from the person in an expanding circle within the community]
5378	נָשָׁא	Nasha	1. to lead astray 2. to exact payment	1. MOVEMENT (נ) - PUFF UP (שׁ) - SEPARATE/AWAY (א) also 2. MOVEMENT (נ) - DISBURSE (שׁ) – SEPARATE / AWAY (א)
Modern Hebrew	הִשִׂיא	Hi-SIA	to give in marriage	RAISED (ה) - LIFTED UP (שׂי) + AWAY (א) (a Jewish bride was traditionally carried to the groom) [שׂ also denotes **CHANGE**]

Unlocking the Ancient Pictorial Code of the Hebrew Alphabet

Strong's Number	Hebrew Word	Trans-Literation	Word Definition	Explanation of Pictographical Meanings
Modern Hebrew	הִשִׁיא	Hi-shia	to deceive	RAISE (ה) - **SUBSTANCE** [hope/faith] (שׁ) - HIGH (י) - SEPARATE (א)
5380	נָשַׁב	Nashav	to blow	MOTION (נ) - **EXPANDING/PUFFING UP** (שׁ) - BODY (ב)
3423	יָרַשׁ	YaReSH	to seize, take possession, inherit, dispossess	CAUSE (י) - CHANGE (ר) - of WEALTH / PROVISION / POSSESSION (שׁ)
3426	יֵשׁ	YeSH "uncl. der."	1. being, existence, fact, substance 2. there is/are	CAUSE (י) – EXISTENCE/SUBSTANCE (שׁ)
7725	שָׁב or שׁוּב	Mod. SHaV or Bib. SHŪV	return, again, bring back,	CONSUMEd/DESTROYED (שׁ) - OF (ו) - HOUSE (ב) or CHANGE/RETURN (שׁ) - OF (ו) – a PERSON (ב)
7673	שָׁבַת	SHaBaT	Sabbath	**PROVISION/RENEWAL** (שׁ) - for the HOUSE/FAMILY (ב) - MARKED/OBSERVED (ת)
1644	גָּרַשׁ	GaRaSH	to drive out, to cast out	NOT (ג) - INSIDE/WITHIN (ר) - CHANGE/PROVISION (שׁ) [change to non-inclusion] NUN-/NON- (ג) - BENDING/FLEXIBLE (ר) - CHANGE/PROVISION (שׁ)
1657	גֹּשֶׁן	Goshen	The land of Goshen in Egypt	GATHER for a POSITIVE PURPOSE (*ג) - PROVISIONs/SUBSTANCE/BREAD (שׁ) – LIFE or MOVE [the Hebrews' move to Egypt?] (נ) (*ג) denotes that Ghayin (the letter which disappeared from the Hebrew alphabet c. 500 BCE) was probably replaced with GIMMEL.
8199	שָׁפַת	Shaphat	to hand down, to govern, to judge (Mod. Heb.: put)	PROVISION/SUBSTANCE (שׁ) - BLOSSOMING OUTWARD (פ) - JOINED/DESIGNATED / MARKED / RECORDED [set on record] (ת)
Modern Hebrew	שׁוּם	SHŪM	nothing important, not noteworthy, "no biggie"	SHIN + WAW = WITHOUT (שׁו) MEM = SUBSTANCE (ם)

Chapter 23 – SHIN

Strong's Number	Hebrew Word	Trans-Literation	Word Definition	Explanation of Pictographical Meanings
3443	יֵשׁוּעַ	Yeshua	Hebrew name [translated into Greek as Jesus]	CAUSE to BE (י) - the SUBSTANCE (שׁ) – of (ו) - LIFE FORCE or AWAKENING (ע)
7805	שָׁזַף	SHaZaPH see below: 7583 SHaAH	1. to catch sight of, look on 2. burned	1. STRONG (ז) ↔ GAZE (שׁ) – FALL UPON (ף) [the Zayin seems to indicate more than just a passing glance] 2. STRONG/VIOLENT (ז) ↔ CONSUMSUMPTION (שׁ) – FALL DOWN (ף)
7585	שְׁאֹל שְׁאוֹל	SheŌL	the underworld, place to where the dead descend	SUBSTANTIAL/EXPANSE (שׁ) - SEPARATE (א) - of (ו) - COMFORT (ל)
7965	שָׁלוֹם	Sha-LŌM	peace, completeness, soundness, safely	**ABUNDANT** (שׁ) - COMFORT (ל) - OF (ו) - QUIET BEING [STILLNESS] (מ)
7806	שָׁזַר	SHaZaR	to be twisted	STRONG (ז) ↔ GRASP (שׁ) - BEND (ר) or ABUNDANT (שׁ) - STRENGTH (ז) - BEND (ר)
3888	לוּשׁ	LUSH	to knead bread	GUIDED FLOW (ל) - OF (ו) – BREAD or SUBSTANCE (שׁ)
7623	שָׁבַח	SHaVaḦ	Biblical – to soothe, to laud, praise Mod. – to improve, to grow in value,	EXPAND (שׁ) - PERSON/HOUSE (ב) - ALL AROUND (ח) [e.g. "magnify the Lord" or to enlarge the house]
7818	שָׂחַט	SaḦaT	to squeeze out	GRASP (שׂ) - ALL AROUND (ח) - MOTION (ט) Note: It is likely that this word was spelled with a SIN instead of a SHIN (with indicates GRASP) to differentiate it from 7819 below.
7849	שָׁטַח	SHaTaḦ	to scatter, spread out, scatter abroad	EXPAND/SCATTER (שׁ) - MOTION (ט) - ALL AROUND (ח) or EXPAND/SPREAD OUT (שׁ) - MOTION (ט) - ALL AROUND (ח)

Unlocking the Ancient Pictorial Code of the Hebrew Alphabet

Strong's Number	Hebrew Word	Trans-Literation	Word Definition	Explanation of Pictographical Meanings
7819	שָׁחַט	ShaḦaT	to slaughter, beat, slay	GRASP (שׁ)- ALL AROUND (ח) – MOTION (ט) [to seize, to lay hold of, to put one's hand to]
7660	שָׁבַץ	SHaVaTS	to weave in a checkered pattern	ABUNDANT or SYMMETRICAL (שׁ)- [geometric] BODYs (ב) – FIXED POSITIONs (ץ)
7737a	שָׁוָה	SHaVaH	to agree with, resemble	SYMMETRY/SIMILARITY (שׁ) of (ו) - LEVEL/AMOUNT/IMPORTANCE (ה)
7743	שׁוּחַ	SHUaḦ	to sink down	CONSUMED (שׁ)- BY/OF (ו) - SURROUNDINGS (ח)
1653	גֶּשֶׁם	GeSHeM	torrential rain, downpour	TRAMPLE (ג) - **SUBSTANCE** (שׁ)- BODY [esp. Body of Water] (מ) prob. Lit. a BODY of WATER that **SUBSTANTIALLY** TRAMPLES or PELTS the earth… this is definitely a HEAVY RAIN.
7583	שָׁאָה	SHaAH	to gaze	VOICE/NOISE (שׁ) - SEPARATED AWAY (א) - MORE (ה) [intensity elevated] NOTE: In 7582 and 7580, SHIN denotes the sense of SOUND, yet in 7583 it clearly indicates SIGHT.
7582	שָׁאָה	SHaAH	to make a din, crash, rumble	VOICE/NOISE (שׁ) - SEPARATED AWAY (א) - MORE (ה) [intensity elevated] NOTE: In 7582 and 7580, SHIN denotes the sense of SOUND, yet in 7583 it clearly indicates SIGHT.
7580	שָׁאַג	SHaAG	to roar, to roar mightily	VOICE/NOISE (שׁ) - SEPARATE AWAY (א) - TRAMPLEs/PELTS/POUNDS (ג)
7602a	שָׁאַף	SHaAPH	to gasp, pant after, long for	CONSUMED (שׁ) - SEPARATED (א) - FALL DOWN or to the END (ף)
3847	לָבֵשׁ	LaVaSH	to put on, wear, clothe, be clothed	[GUIDED FLOW] for the PURPOSE (ל) - BODY (ב) - PUFF UP (שׁ) [The intended function or purpose of clothes is to PUFF UP the BODY and retain heat]

Chapter 23 – SHIN

Strong's Number	Hebrew Word	Trans-Literation	Word Definition	Explanation of Pictographical Meanings
6566	פָּרַשׂ	PaRaS	to spread out, scatter, disperse,	SCATTER (פ) – CHARACTERISTIC (ר) – SPREAD OUT (שׂ)
7641	שִׁבֹּלֶת	SHiBo-LeTH	ears of grain	PUFFED UP SUBSTANCE (שׁ) - BODY/FIELD (ב) - GUIDED FLOW (ל) - BECOME ONE (ת) lit. field of flowing grain heads
7665	שָׁבַר	SHaVaR	to break, to break into pieces, shatter, fracture	BREAK/SEPARATE/SPREAD OUT (שׁ) - BODY (ב) - INSIDE (ר)
8121	שֶׁמֶשׁ	SHeMeSH	Sun	EXPANDING OUTWARD (שׁ) – MATTER (מ) – EXPANDING OUTWARD (שׁ)
6211	עָשׁ	ASH	a moth, moth-eaten	CONSUMing (שׁ) ↔ FORCE (ע) Author's Note: I find the pictorial meaning of this word to be as clever as it is amusing.
7945	שֶׁל	SHeL	*SHEL* indicates ownership, e.g. That is the house *SHEL* David.	POSSESSION (שׁ) - GUIDED FLOW/CONTROLLED (ל) [denoting anything of value under the control or **ownership** of a person]
7953	שָׁלָה	SHaLaH	to draw out, extract	SUBSTANCE, GROW or EXPAND (שׁ) - GUIDED FORCE (ל) - UPWARD (ה)
7971	שָׁלַח	SHaLaĤ	to send, sent, go, stretch, spread	EXPANDing (שׁ) - GUIDED FORCE (ל) - [into] VOID/SURROUNDING EMPTY SPACE (ח)
8104	שָׁמַר	SHaMaR	to guard, to watch "brother's keeper" in Gen. 4:9	EXPANSION (outpost) (שׁ) - of the BODY or GROUP (מ) - INSIDE or WITHIN (ר)
7636	שָׁבִיס	SHaBIS	headband [listed as unc. der.] See 3847 above	PUFF UP (שׁ) - BODY (ב) - UP/HIGH, ABOVE (י) - ENCIRCLED (ס) *PUFF UP BODY* is prob. an idiom for *putting on clothes* for warmth

Strong's Number	Hebrew Word	Trans-Literation	Word Definition	Explanation of Pictographical Meanings
7618	שְׁבוֹ	SHeBŌ See Ephod Specs. Below	Listed in Strong's as "unc. der.(a precious stone) perh. **agate**" SHEBO most likely denotes **AMBER**, which is formed by tree sap and sometimes **encases** the **body** of an insect	PUFF UP (שׁ) - OVER (וֹ) ↔ BODY (ב) or EXPAND OUTWARD OVER [surround] BODY

Specifications for making the high priest's *ephod*, taken from *Exodus*:

17 "You shall mount on it four rows of stones; the first row shall be a row of ruby, topaz and emerald;

18 and the second row a turquoise, a sapphire and a diamond;

19 and the third row a jacinth, an *agate* [author's translation would read- *AMBER*, see 7618 above] and an amethyst;

20 and the fourth row a beryl and an onyx and a jasper; they shall be set in gold filigree.

21 "The stones shall be according to the names of the sons of Israel: twelve, according to their names; they shall be like the engravings of a seal, each according to his name for the twelve tribes."

- Exodus 28:17-21 (NASB), author's emphasis added

- -

⊔⊔ SHIN - Biblical Food for Thought W

שׁ SHIN, the symbol of RESSURECTION

RETURN or RESURRECTION (שׁ) - of the SUN [the Creator] (י) - to LIFE (ב)

SHIN's pictographical meaning later morphed to take on the meaning of
EXPANDING (שׁ) - UPWARDS (י) - MOTION (ב)
(literally: PUFF-UP MOTION)

The SHIN symbol permeates Judaism. The SHIN adorns every mezuzah (placed upon the door posts of Orthodox Jewish homes and upon their gates). The *SHIN* also appears on the prayer tellafin (the leather pouches worn on the foreheads of Orthodox Jews when praying). But why the letter *SHIN*?

Anyone who has made challah, the traditional sweet Sabbath bread which is woven of either three or four strands, has seen the SHIN when the dough is laid out in ropes for braiding. Why is challah, a symbol of the Sabbath, braided? Again, why the letter *SHIN*? What does *SHIN* have to do with Judaism that it should appear so often in its symbolism and its imagery?

Initially, before the time of Abraham, SHIN referred to the up-down-up pattern of the SUN in the sky. "Magically," the sun was reborn every morning. To the ancient peoples, the sun was thought to die each night when it united with the horizon and went into the underworld. It was a long-held belief among these agrarian people of the Middle East (and elsewhere as well) that the Sun was the *Creator* of all things; surely this "must" be true, as the sun obviously gave life to all growing things. A quick look at some of the Middle Eastern gods tells it all. Egypt's chief god was RA, the sun god. Shamash and Shemesh were variations of the sun god among the peoples stretching from the Canaanites in the west to the Babylonians in the east. *Shemesh* is the exact Hebrew word for the *sun*. Yes, even the Hebrew people, long ago, were probably sun worshippers. It took the LORD quite a while to reveal Himself to these people, but at least they grasped the idea of resurrection long before their sojourning in Egypt.

After the 40 years in the desert with Moses, *SHIN* evolved to denote the **MANNA,** which also sustained the Israelites in the wilderness desert and was REBORN (RESURRECTED to LIFE) every morning, similar to the sun. Over the millennia, the Semitic concept of the Creator sun being resurrected was replaced with the concept of God's provision, His *manna*, being resurrected and renewed each morning. The Israelites began making progress in their understanding of who Yahweh really was.

The Jewish sages teach that the *Shin* possibly symbolizes MANNA (because the TORAH is their MANNA, their daily bread). Or perhaps *Shin* represents their **PRAYERS** of **FAITH** rising up to God and being the BREAD OF LIFE.

Then, about 1400 years after Moses, came Yeshua. And guess what? The *Shin* was still a prominent symbol among Jewish people. Understanding the pictographical meanings of the letters S*HIN-YOD-NUN*, which spell the name of the letter *SHIN*, opens up a whole new world of understanding towards both the meaning of the letter *Shin* and towards many of the obscure sayings which Yeshua spoke.

An Alternate Meaning for SHIN's Letter Name Could Be:
BREAD (שׁ) - which CAUSES to BE (י) - LIFE (ן)
or
"Bread of Life" [26]

The letter *Yod* denotes the hand of the *CREATOR*... the hand of God Almighty, who will someday resurrect the dead.

Count the number of days the letter Shin represents; remember it is a graph of the movement of the sun.

W

---

[26] John 6:48

According to the Christian tradition and the *New Testament* gospel accounts, Yeshua was in the grave for three days and two nights (although the Matthew, chapter 12 account states *three nights*). Long before the time of Jesus, there were other ancient mythological accounts from pagan cultures, each of which claimed that their sun-god was also resurrected after three days. The resurrection story is actually quite common among cultures who worshipped a sun god (Mithras, Attis, Krishna, and Osiris, to name a few). Interestingly, Jonah was in the belly of the whale for the same period of time.

How many days and nights did you count when you read the graph depicted by Shin, the letter which represents *RESURRECTION?* If you counted 3 days and 2 nights, you counted correctly.

Perhaps God's task of weaning His Chosen People away from sun god worship was a bit harder than we can imagine today. To me, the lesson He gave the Israelites in the Wilderness with the daily portions of manna like may have been a very essential step in helping them to correctly perceive Him as their Provider. It is quite probable that the Israelites had to be weaned off the pagan sun-god-resurrection beliefs they had been exposed to (and perhaps embraced) while living among the Canaanites and the Egyptians. If so, the daily portion of "resurrected" manna might have been as much of a spiritual lesson as it was God's hand of provision.

* * *

Chapter 24
SIN (pronounced Seen)

 CHANGE — GROWTH

SIN's pictographical letter names means the same a SHIN's

Meanings specific to the letter SIN include:
Change, Growth, Sharp, Clever, and **Pointed**

SHIN EXAMPLES: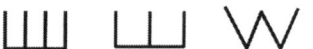

Strong's Number	Hebrew Word	Trans-Literation	Word Definition	Explanation of Pictographical Meanings
-NA-	שִׁין	Sin	21st Hebrew Letter	CHANGE, LIFT, POINTED/SHARP, CLEVER, POVERTY, HUNGER, NEED/LACK [of provision] Sin's letter name means POINTED (שׁ) - MOVING (נ) - SHARP POINT (י) [poss. a spear tip or arrowhead]
7899	שֵׂךְ	SeKH	Thorn	SHARP/POINTED (שׁ) - FINGERs (ך)
Modern Hebrew	שִׂכָּה	SuKHaH	barb, thorn, spear	SHARP/POINTED (שׁ) - FINGERs (כ) - RAISED UP/ELEVATED (ה)
1719	שָׂכֵל	Sa-KHeL	to be prudent, wise, to have insight	**SHARP [clever] (שׁ)** - OUTSTRETCHED HAND (כ) - LEADING/GUIDING (ל)
Modern Hebrew	שָׂב	SaV	old man	CONSUMED/CHANGED (שׁ) - BODY (ב) or poss. SHARP (שׁ) [wise] PERSON
Modern Hebrew	שׂבוּל	See-BŪL	reversing, crossing (legs), folding (arms)	CHANGE (שׁ) - PLACE/POSITION (ב) - of (ו) - STANCE/LEGS/ARMS (ל)

Unlocking the Ancient Pictorial Code of the Hebrew Alphabet

Strong's Number	Hebrew Word	Trans-Literation	Word Definition	Explanation of Pictographical Meanings
5493	סוּר שׂוּר	SŪR	to turn aside, departed	COMPLETENESS (ס) - OF (ו) - TURNing (ר) or CHANGE (שׂ) - OF (ו) – TURN or DIRECTION (ר) [an unplanned turn]
6212a.	עֶשֶׂב	ESeB	from an unused word; grass, herb, vegetation	FORCE of (ע) – GROWING/SPREADING (שׂ) - BODY (ב)
6212b.	עֲשַׂב	ASaB	(Aramaic) corr. to 6212a; *herbage, grass*	FORCE of (ע) – GROWING/SPREADING (שׂ) - BODY (ב)
6213a	עָשָׂה	ASaH	prim. Root - do, make, accomplish, bring forth	FORCE of (ע) - GROWING (שׂ) - BEHELD or REVEALED (ה)
6213b	עָשָׂה	ASaH	to press, squeeze	FORCE of (ע) - GROWING (שׂ) – BEHELD or REVEALED (ה)
8269	שַׂר	SaR	prince, chief, commander, ruler	GROWING (שׂ) – INFLUENCE [being set over as a ruler] (ר)
8055	שָׂמַח	SaMaĤ	to be glad, to rejoice, cheer, merry, to rejoice, to give happiness	JOYful (שׂ) – BODY (מ) – ALL AROUND (ח)

SIN (*Seen*) - Biblical Food for Thought

שׁ SIN, a symbol of JOY, and SAMEAĤ (שָׂמַח) - to be Merry, to Rejoice

> "A *merry* heart doeth good like a medicine,
> but a broken spirit drieth the bones."
> - Proverbs 17:22, KJV [27]

SAMEAĤ can mean *to rejoice, to be merry, glad* or *happy*. The Hebrew word for *merry* used in the quote above from Proverbs is *SAMEAĤ*. It is the word used in Psalm 104 which says that *"wine... makes man's heart **glad**"*:

> 14 He causes the grass to grow for the cattle,
> And vegetation for the labor of man,
> So that he may bring forth food from the earth,
>   15 And **wine** which makes man's heart **glad**,
> So that he may make *his* face glisten with oil,
> And food which sustains man's heart.

Wine is part of the Jewish weekly ceremony for welcoming the Sabbath (Shabbat). Why? We are to rejoice in the Sabbath of the Creator. We are to rejoice not only in the 7th day of the week, when we have rest, but also the coming days of the next week, even if we do not find these days restful. Even in the face of adversity, we are to rejoice, because life is precious; it is God's gift to us.

* * *

---

[27] Proverbs 17:22, *The Holy Bible : King James Version.*, Pr 17:22. Oak Harbor, WA: Logos Research Systems, Inc., 1995.

Chapter 25
TAV or THAV

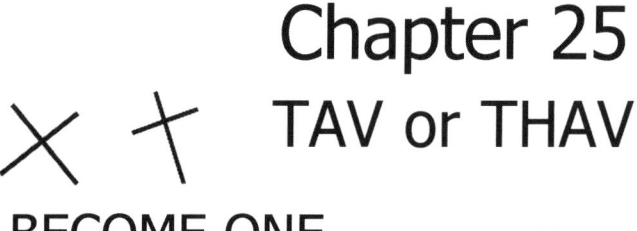

BECOME ONE   –   **PURE**

The Phoenician pictograph is literally 2 sticks crossed... a CROSS.

THAV's pictographical letter names means
PURE (ת) – FLOW (ו)
or
BECOME ONE (ת) – FLOW TOGETHER (ו)
or
PRESS DOWN (ת) – FLOW INTO (ו)

Meanings specific to the letter THAV include:
BECOME ONE, PURITY,
PRESS DOWN (e.g. a coin minting stamp or wine/olive press),
MARK of CERTIFICATION (e.g. 24k),
COVENENTAL AGREEMENT, CONSENSUS

Secondary meanings include:
a signature, also a letter of the alphabet or any symbol.

NOTE: THAV and TET seem to have interchanged meanings as the writing system evolved over time, so that THAV can also mean *MOTION* or *JOINED*
(MOTION and JOINED were originally concepts primarily indicated by TET)

THAV (or Thaw)

Action or Motion Indicated	Descriptive Form	Noun(s) Denoted	Prepositional Meanings
to Become One to Purify	Pure; Joined or Merged inseparably into one	A *mark* signifying an agreement or *covenant*, Action	- NA -

THAV (TAV) EXAMPLES:

Strong's Number	Hebrew Word	Trans- Literation	Word Definition	Explanation of Pictographical Meanings
8420	תָּו	Thav/Tav Or Thaw / Taw	to press down, to make a mark	1. to COME TOGETHER or to COMBINE 2. to **PRESS DOWN** (ת) - FLOW TOETHER (ו) like a minting stamp. THAV also stood for a mark of purity, much like **24k**. Furthermore, a "THAV" could be any mark (written or not), such as a letter of an alphabet.
1660	גַּת גַּת	GaTh (Biblical) or GeTH (modern)	an olive or wine PRESS	UN- (ג) + COMBINE (ת) ... evolved into **press** (e.g. to **separate** out olive oil and grape juice)
1003	בֵּת	Beth, BeiTh or BeIT	house, temple, between	FAMILY (RESIDENCE) (ב) - MARKED/DEFINED/INDICATED (ת)
Modern Hebrew	תַּת	Tet	under, below sub-	PRESS (ת) – DOWN (ת)
8628	תָּקַע	T̲a-QA	to blow a trumpet, to give a blow, slap	ACTION (ת) - WRAP AROUND/ACROSS (ק) - AWAY /OUT/AGAINST (ע)
7673	שָׁבַת	SHaBaT	Sabbath	PROVISION/RENEWAL (שׁ) – for the HOUSE/FAMILY (ב) – MARKED/OBSERVED (ת)
1660	גַּת	Gath	A wine press or Olive press	TRAMPLE or FOOT (ג) - PRESS DOWN (ת)
6279 but also 6280	עָתַר	AThaR	**to pray**, supplicate	FORCE of (ע) - BECOMING ONE (ת) - INSIDE (ר) FORCE of (ע) - BECOMING ONE (ת) – in ATRIBUTES (ר)
8420b	תּוֹאָם	TŌ-AM	a twin	CONNECTION (ת) - OF (ו) – Separate INDIVIDUALs (א) - IMAGES (ם) poss. meaning "identical"
8610	תָּפַשׂ or תָּפַס	Tha-PHaS	to catch	COMBINED/TOTAL [the catch / the *take* or the *profit*] (ת) - FROM (פ) - NET (ס)

Chapter 25 – THAV or TAV

Strong's Number	Hebrew Word	Trans-Literation	Word Definition	Explanation of Pictographical Meanings
Modern Hebrew from 8409	תִּגֶּר	TheeG-GeR	to haggle, to bargain	UNITY (ת) - RESISTED (ג) - INSIDE (ר) or poss. UNITY (ת) - NOT (ג) - APPARENT (ר)
see below	תִּגָּר modern / תִּגְרָה Biblical	ThiG-GaR (modern) / ThiG-RaH (Biblical)	1. complaint (Mod. Hebrew) 2. contention, strife, hostility, opposition (Bib. Hebrew)	lit. NOT MADE ONE (תג) - APPARENT (ר) Note: GIMMEL functions like the English word NOT or the prefixes UN- and NON-
8409	תִּגְרָה	TheeG-RaH	Strife	NON-UNITY (תג) - MORE (ה) - APPARENT (ר) or UNITY (ת) - RESISTED (ג) - INSIDE (ר) - EVEN MORE (ה) Note: The Hebrew word for *more* (*meod*) always follows the word it amplifies.
8199	שָׁפַת	Shaphat	to hand down, to govern, to judge (Mod. Heb.: put)	PROVISION/SUBSTANCE (שׁ) - BLOSSOMING OUTWARD (פ) – **JOINED / DESIGNATED / MARKED / RECORDED** Set on Record (ת)
4969	מָתַח	MaTHaĤ	to spread out, spreads	PLACE (מ) - JOINED (ת) - ALL AROUND (ח) or THING (מ) - JOINED (ת) - ALL AROUND (ח)
Not in Tenach see 6734	צִיֵת	TSee-YeT	OBEY! (imperative) [poss. from TSITS-TSIT, the tassels on Jewish prayer shawls]	PERMANENTLY/CONSISTENTLY (צ) – HIT [strike] (י) - the MARK (bull's eye)(ת) NOTE: When written in the ancient pictographs: HAND (yod) - PERMANENTLY AFFIXED (TSade) - to the MARK of PURITY (thav)
2856	חָתַם	ĤaTaM (Chatham)	sealed, to seal	ALL AROUND (ח) - ATTACHED/JOINED (ת) - SUBSTANCE (מ) [prob. denotes a wax seal]
8446	תּוּר	ThŪR	to spy, to tour, to explore	ACTION (ת... from ט) of LOOKING (ר) or ACTIVELY LOOKING NOTE: TAV & TET seem to have traded and inter-twined their meanings over time
8420b	תּוֹאָם	TŌ-AM	a twin	CONNECTION (ת) - OF (וֹ) – INDIVIDUALs (א) - IMAGES (מ) [poss. meaning "identical"]
8373	תָּאַב	TA-aB	to long for	**MERGED [become one] (ת)** - SEPARATED (א) - PERSONS (ב) [to desire to **become one**]

Unlocking the Ancient Pictorial Code of the Hebrew Alphabet

Strong's Number	Hebrew Word	Trans-Literation	Word Definition	Explanation of Pictographical Meanings
8376	תָּאָה	TA-aH	to mark out	MARK (ת) - AWAY/OUT (א) - AMPLIFIED [poss. MADE OBVIOUS] (ה) or INDIVIDUAL/SEPARATE (א) ↔ MARK(s) (ת) - INDICATED (ה)
8388a	תָּאַר	TA-AR	to incline, curved	MARKed (ת) - OUT (א) - CURVE (ר)
8382	תָּאַם	Tha-AM	Bib. Hebrew: double, to bear twins. Mod. Hebrew: to combine	JOIN(ed)/COMBINE(d)/UNITE(d) (ת) - INDIVIDUAL/SEPARATE (א) - PARTS/COMPONENTS (מ)
1847	דַּעַת	DaATH	Knowledge	TWO GATHERED (ד) [man and knowledge] - AWAREness (ע) - BECOME ONE (ת)
8551	תָּמַךְ	ThaMaK	to grasp, uphold, take hold	BECOME ONE / MARKed [specific?] (ת) - OBJECT (מ) - GRASP (כ)
8537	תֹּם	THoM or TOM	completeness, integrity	PURE (ת) - BODY/OBJECT (מ)
6256	עֵת	ETH	1. ETH is often used to link an action verb to a direct object 2. time, appointed time, season	FORCE or CONDITION of (ע) BECOMing ONE (ת) NOTE: A direct object is a noun which receives the action of an action verb, e.g. "David slew ETH Goliath." *Slew* is the action verb and *Goliath* is the direct object, the recipient of the action *SLEW*. In English, we have no equivalent of the word ETH, which is almost always present in Hebrew before a direct object.
8478	תַּחַת	TaḤaT	underneath, below, instead of, place	ONE SUBSTANCE (ת) - EMPTY SPACE (ח) - ONE SUBSTANCE (ת) prob. from… LAYER (ט) - SPACE (ח) - LAYER (ט) Note: THAV indicates 'become one' [substance] or "pure." The word TaḤaT indicates a void sandwiched between two solid masses whether a TET or THAV is used; however, TET- CHET- TET would be a better spelling, as TET indicates a stacked layer. TET-CHET-TET would then indicate a layer below another layer. TET and THAV seem to have interchanged their meanings over time, possibly during the Babylonian exile.
8481	תַּחְתּוֹן	TaḤ-TŌN	lower, lowest	From 8478 above LAYER (ת) - SPACE (ח) - LAYER (ת) - OVER (ו) - BOTTOM (ן)

Chapter 25 – THAV or TAV

Strong's Number	Hebrew Word	Trans-Literation	Word Definition	Explanation of Pictographical Meanings
8401	תֶּבֶן	TeBeN	chaff, straw	PRESS (ת) - BODY (ב) - MOVE (ן) This is a perfect image of *separating the wheat from the chaff* by pressing and then tossing the crushed mix up so that the breeze could blow away the chaff.
225	אוֹת	ŌTh	a mark, a sign, also the Hebrew translation of the Greek: ALPHA AND OMEGA	YOKED TOGETHER (א) - OF (ו) –TWO BECOME ONE (ת) or ALPHA and (VAV = *and*) OMEGA [*Aleph* א and *Thav* ת are the first and last letters of the Hebrew alphabet, just as *Alpha* and *Omega* are the first and last of the Greek alphabet].

TAV (*or THAV*) - Biblical Food for Thought

אוֹת   ŌTh (like the English word *oath*)
Meaning: a mark, a sign, a covenantal signature

According to the Christian book called *Revelation*, Yeshua referred to himself as the *ALPHA AND OMEGA*, the *Beginning and the End*.[28] Although it is true that the New Testament was written in Greek, the events and conversations documented within its pages took place primarily in Hebrew and Aramaic, not in Greek. Because Yeshua's mother tongue was probably Aramaic, and because He would have also known Hebrew from his study of Torah during his upbringing as a Jewish son, the Messiah's conversations with both his disciples and with the average inhabitants of the nation of Israel would have been in Aramaic and/or Hebrew.

With this in mind, let's consider the three places in the book of Revelation. Revelation 1:8-18, 21:6, and 22:13 each state that Yeshua refers to himself as the *Alpha and Omega*, **the beginning and the end**.

Although the New Testament was written in the Greek language, Hebrew and Aramaic were still the predominant languages of Israel when these books were written. Again, it stands to reason that these events actually took place with little, if any, Greek being spoken. Instead, the majority of these conversations would have been in Hebrew and Aramaic. Therefore, it also seems likely that John was translating his conversations with Yeshua from Aramaic and/or Hebrew into Greek when he wrote both the Gospel of John and the book of Revelation.

The alphabet used in the original conversation makes a huge difference in the implications of what Yeshua was telling John. If Hebrew letters were actually used by

---

[28] Revelation 1:8-18; Rev. 21:6 and Rev. 22:13

Yeshua, rather than Greek, Yeshua would **not** have said that he was the *Alpha and the Omega, the beginning and the end.* The word *and* in Hebrew phrase *Aleph and Thav* would have been represented by a single *WAW* placed between the *ALEPH* and the *THAV*. Instead, using the first and last letters of the Hebrew Alphabet, Yeshua would have called himself the *ALEPH WAW (and) THAV, the AOTH* (אות). In this light, it becomes apparent (or at least plausible) that the writer of the Book of Revelation to John, if Jewish, saw Yeshua as a SIGN from God, as a Messiah.

The Hebrew letters ALEPH – WAW – THAV spell out the Hebrew word *AŌTH*, which means a *mark*, a *sign*, *a covenantal seal* or *signature*. Interestingly, the word ALEPH-WAW-THAV is translated many times as the word the *MARK* by author Gustav Mahler in his book T*he Sealed Book of Daniel Revealed: the Linear Bible Code.* Mahler used a computer to reverse the letter order for the entire book of Daniel, making the last letter of the book the first letter of the translation, and so on. What he found after reversing the letter order for Daniel is that huge sections of the book read perfectly in reverse order. Furthermore, many lines and even whole paragraphs specifically refer to the Messiah as the MARK… the *ŌTH*.

The ancient Phoenician pictograms for the word *ŌTH* (אות) would have been as follows:

THAV's individual Phoenician letters mean **INDIVIDUAL** *(aleph)* - **OF** *(waw)* – **PURITY or ONENESS** *(thav)*. *Purity* is another common theme in the Bible. We begin this life more as distinct individuals, who must alter make the personal choice as to whether or not we wish to bind ourselves to God's laws and desires. Clearly, we are instructed to bind ourselves to the Law of God, to His commandments, so that He can begin the process of refining us, purifying us. For those who chose the light of God's Laws (His Torah), much purification and refinement then begins to take place.

THAV can also mean BECOME ONE. We shall become one with God if we are yoked with TORAH. As God is pure and holy, then we too will become pure and holy by contact with Him. We will be transformed through our close relationship with him, thus fulfilling the words of Leviticus 11:45 and 19:2, both of which state, "You ***shall be*** holy, for I am holy." In both cases, the verb form of HAYA (to be) is in the imperfect, not the command form. This is not a command; it is a promise! IF we bind ourselves to God through His Torah, just by "rubbing elbows" with God through prayer, study of Torah and implementing Torah's guidance (the mitzvoth) in our daily lives, we will become ever increasingly like Him.

* * *

Chapter 26
The Mysterious Name of God

   יהוה

YAHWEH

The Phoenician pictographical letter's of God name mean
CAUSE to (י) – STAND AGAIN (הוה)
or
CAUSE to BE (י) – RAISED UP AGAIN (הוה)

YAHWEH is the name God revealed to Abraham long ago. The exact correct pronunciation of the word is not actually known with 100% certainty by anyone, because Hebrew was not originally written with the vowel points placed under, over and/or inside the letters. The picture meaning of the words was the important thing to the Phoenicians and Hebrews, not the pronunciation.

As discussed in previous chapters, the letter WAW (ו or Υ), when inserted between two identical letters (in this case, HEY: ה or 𐤄) indicates *to repeat again* the action indicated by HEY. HEY means to *RAISE UP* or to *STAND*; therefore, *HEH-WAW-HEY* means to *STAND AGAIN* or to *RISE UP AGAIN* (Hey means *Raised* or *Heaped Up Above*).

STAND AGAIN is a term worth noting. Much of the alphabet and language structures, as well as every-day information, were exchanged between the Phoenicians and the Greeks. The Greek word *anastasis* (ἀνάστασις, *Strong's* number 386) literally means *stand again* (the prefix *ana* indicates *again*, and *stasis* means *to stand*). However, neither *YAHWEH* nor **anastasis** actually means *to stand again*.

HEY-WAW-HEH should be translated into the same English word that *anastasis* is consistently translated into. In all of the major English versions of the New Testament *anastasis* is translated into the following English word: **resurrection**. In Ancient Greek, *standing again* was an idiom for being raised from the dead or *resurrected*. The same must have been true for Phoenician and ancient Hebrew.

With this information, we can now get the true ancient meaning of God's revealed name to Abraham. The letter YOD (׳ or) means *CAUSE TO BECOME* or *CREATE*. The name YAHWEH, therefore, translated from the pictographical meaning of the letters, means:

CAUSE to STAND AGAIN or CAUSE to be RESURRECTED.

It's almost as if God had intended from the beginning to show that there really is life after death. Of course, this could all be merely coincidence or just another fiction devised by Constantine to get people to buy in to the ideas he and his lackeys presented at the Council of Nicaea in 325 A.D.
Or perhaps it is no coincidence at all. Remember the ancient pictogram for SHIN?

W

Once again… how many days was Jonah in the belly of the whale? Three days? You don't think God (YAHWEH) had may have been trying to tell us something by His revealed divine name, do you? It's sure something to think about in my book. (Bad pun *intended*.)

* * *

Chapter 27
But Wait! There's More...

Most of us have seen those annoying info-mercials on TV that show you all the magical things their product can do. After turning a common radish into the likeness of the Mona Lisa, we are offered this *amazing* product at an *amazingly* low price. Wow… amazing! And if that is not enticement enough, there is always the loud and excited proclamation, "But wait; there's more!" We are then told with cries of glee and wildly waving hand gestures that we will get two for the price of one, or that we will get add-ons that make it possible to do otherwise impossible things… all for just $19.95!

Having given that first caveat, plus one more in the following two paragraphs, I want to suggest something that sounds a bit on the unbelievable side, even to me. However, feel free to rip the last chapter out of my book if what I am about to suggest seems just a bit over the top.

My second caveat is that the Phoenicians lived in and just north of what is now northern Israel. They were primarily sea traders, and they really got around: Greece, Egypt, Turkey, perhaps Italy (not the countries, but the geographic locations). Some have postulated that the Phoenicians were actually northern tribes of Israel. Others have suggested that the Phoenicians might be the same group of people as the mysterious ancient people known as the Scythians. Nobody really knows for sure. And the Scythians probably traded and intermingled with a group of people north of them, the Huns. For all I know about the Scythians, it may have been this mysterious tribe of people who invented both the amazing radish chopper and info-mercials.

Much more is known about the Huns, who evolved into the German-speaking people groups of Europe. For those who did not know it, English and German are linguistic cousins. Many of the most common words in English came from Germanic roots. Brown came from Braun; white came from weiss; milk came from milch. There are hundreds, perhaps thousands, of words in the two languages that are quite similar.

From what I have observed while examining the Phoenician-Hebrew alphabet system, it seems quite possible that the Phoenicians, or the Scythians (…or *somebody out there…* perhaps some of the lost tribes of Israel even, who knows?) showed the pre-Germanic Huns how to write down their spoken language using the Semitic letter meanings as the base of a writing system. Obviously, the Germanic tribes use a different alphabet (it's almost the same alphabet that English speaker's use). But there are strong linguistic hints that the a multitude of Germanic words may have been developed using the Phoenician-Hebrew letter meanings, at least many of the Germanic word stems, especially those word stem comprised of only three consonants with a few vowels scattered in.

Why would I suggest such a thing? Because the pictographic letter meanings work with Germanic words (even some English words) as well as with Semitic words. Although the Germanic letters of the alphabet are quite different from Semitic letters, the sounds of the two alphabets seem to carry the same meanings, with only a few differences. Yet, even the differences are regular enough that it is possible to make "educated" guesses at which Semitic letters morphed in sound when they translated over into the Germanic languages.

In English we call the letter system the alphabet… which in Greek begins *Alpha Beta* and in Hebrew begins with the letters *Aleph Bet*. We too begin our English alphabet with the letters and sounds *A* and *B*. This alone is certainly not compelling evidence. But wait; there's more.

Linguists have stated that the use of double consonants is not indigenous to the Germanic languages (German, English, Flemish, Swedish, Danish and Norwegian). In English, however, we have words like *better*, *fill*, and *manner*, just to name a few.

In Hebrew, there are two T sounds, Tet and Thav, but THAV means *pure*. I strongly suspect that doubling the *T* consonant in Germanic languages indicated *MORE pure*. Now remember, E and A vowel sounds were not written using consonants, although long I, long O and long U vowels were written in Hebrew using YOD and WAW. I think the β symbol in German (S-set) might be the Germanic version of the THAV as distinguished from the TET or a Germanic alphabet indication of the English language's doubled T found in the middle on many words.

Just for the sake of "what if" contemplation, here is a chart of possible Germanic family words that may have originated based on Semitic letter meanings:

English Word	German Word	Explanation of Pictographical Meanings
Better	Besser	**BODY** (B = Beit) – **PURER** (Dbl. T or Dbl. S in German = Dbl. Thav) – **INSIDE** (R = Reish)
Best	(Am) Besten	**BODY** (B = Beit) – **COMPLETELY** (S = Samekh) – **PURE** (T = Thav)
Bird	Vogel	BODY (B for Beit) – CHARACTERISTIC or INSIDE (R) – EXTENTIONs (D) [wings] BODY (V for BEIT) - OF (O) - OPPOSING (G) – WINGs (L)
White	Weiß	FLOW INTO (W = WAW) – BRIGHT (I – YOD) – PURER (T & ß = Dbl. Thav)

Chapter 25 – THAV or TAV

English Word	German Word	Explanation of Pictographical Meanings
Flow	- NA -	An OW letter combination in Germanic languages may represent the WAW when WAW is used at the end of a word in Hebrew. F-L-OW could be rendered: FLOW (F as in Phey) – THAT WHICH GUIDES THE FLOW (L as in Lamed) – OF (ו) - FLOW INTO (OW as in WAW which shows connectedness or flowing from one thing to another).
Fill	Füllen	In Hebrew the doubled Lamed consonant meant the *void* between 2 soft folds of linen. Phey meant to *flow down*. Yod sometimes indicated INTO. The English word FILL could be rendered: FLOW (F as in Phey) – INTO (I as in YOD) – VOID (doubled L as in Lamed). Add MOVING (N = nun) in German.
Black	- NA -	*CK* in Germanic languages seems to be the equivalent of the letter Kaph, the palm of an open hand which meant a *covering*. BODY (B) – GUIDED FLOW (L) – COVERING (CK as in Kaph)… which may be the concept of the covering of night, a concept that appears to exist in Hebrew pictographical word meanings.
Cork	Korken	COVER (C or K = Kaph) – ON (O = Waw) – INSIDE of (R = Reish) – COVER (K)… perhaps the bottle would be seen as the outside cover and the cork the cover or stopper on the inside of the container.
Man	Mann	ENTITY (M = Mem) – ALIVE (N) ENTITY (M = Mem) – LIVING (NN)
Dog	Hund	DOG could be rendered: TWO GATHERED (D as in Dalet… meaning a man and the dog) – at the FEET (G as in Gimmel)… indicating the dog will stay close to the heels of its owner. 　In German, HEAPED UP (Hu = Hey WAW) - LIFE (N = Nun) – Two Gathered (D = Daleth)
Cart	Kart	CART might be COVER or HOLD (C as in Kaph) – INSIDE (R as in Resh) – CONTAIN (T as in THAV)
Tree	Baum	The word *TREE* is interesting, when pictographically broken down. MARKs (T as in THAV) – INSIDE (R as in REISH) – CAUSED to BE (EE as in YOD when used as a vowel place holder). I know that evergreen trees, when cut straight across, have rings showing on the inside, one ring per year of growth. Could these be the *MARKS INSIDE*? 　In German the meaning would be BODY (B = MEM) – of (U = WAW) – MASSIVE STUFF (M = Mem)
Sun	Sonne	The word SUN could be rendered GATHERED (S as in Samekh) – UPON (U as in WAW) – LIFE (N as in Nun). The Dbl. N in German = Dbl. Nun = LIV**ING**

English Word	German Word	Explanation of Pictographical Meanings
Leg	Bein	LEG could be rendered: OPPOSING (G as in Gimmel) ↔ GUIDED FLOW (L as in Lamed).
Foot	Fuß	FOOT could be rendered: FLOW (F as in Phey) – OF (OO as in WAW) – MARKs (T or ß as in THAV)... perhaps indicating *foot prints*.
Shoe	Schuh	EXPAND (Sh or Sch = Shin) – OVER (OE or UH = WAW)
Water	Wasser	FLOW INTO (W = WAW) – BECOME ONE (T or SS = Thav) – CHARATERISTIC (R = Reish)
Fish	Fisch	FISH could be rendered: FLOW (F = Phey) – CAUSES (I = Yod) – EXPANDING or ABUNDANCE (SH or SCH = SHIN)... perhaps indicating a school of fish or an abundant food source.
Sail	Segel	GATHER (S = Samekh) – CAUSE (I = Yod) – GUIDED FLOW (L = Lamed) GATHER (S = Samekh) – GATHERED for a GOOD PURPOSE (G = Ghayin) – GUIDED FLOW (L = Lamed)
Lake	See	DIRECTED FLOW (L) – COVERs (K = Kaph) GATHER (S = Samekh) – EE (perhaps EE = YOD as a vowel, CAUSE to BE or CREATES)
Ocean	Ozean	FORCE (Ō = Ayin) – EXPANSE (C = Shin) – MOVE (N = Nun) FORCE (Ō = Ayin) ↔ STRONG (Z = Zayin) – MOVES or OF LIFE (N = Nun)
Hot	Heiß	RAISED UP (H = Hey) – PURITY (T or ß = Thav) Poss. denoting the metal smelting process, where the heat is raised up and the dross rises to the surface where it can be skimmed off.

As I mentioned in the forward of this book, while attending graduate school in southern California, I had an outstanding Greek professor, Professor McDougal, who one day came into class and excitedly told us about the information regarding primary word stems such as *STA* that he had gathered for his doctoral dissertation.

Building upon the line of thinking he began, I believe *TSA*, the sound **TZA**DE represents, seems to have come into Indo-European languages as *STA*. Perhaps *TSA* was too cumbersome for many Indo-European language speakers to pronounce correctly so they changed the sound to *STA*. **TZADE means a FIXED IMAGE. STA, according to my professor, also denotes something which is fixed in place. Sta** + R means a FIXED RAY. In Hebrew, TZadi + Resh (TSAR) would indicate the same meaning, based on the Hebrew Alphabet Code. **Sta**re (STA+RE) could be rendered as a FIX GAZE. *Sta*tue (**STA**TUE) could be rendered as a *FIXED* (STA as in Tzade) - *MARK* (T as in Thav).

Other sounds seem to have made their way from Phoenician to English. FL (Phey + Lamed) would indicate FLOW in Phoenician pictograms. Phey and Peh are the same letter, so PL might indicate FLOW long with FL in some English words: PLAN (Flow of Movement), and PLANT (Flow of LIFE CONTAINED). PLACE (Peh + Lamed + Sameck) would be FLOW GATEHERED (The area of gathering?).

Particularly interesting is the word KNOW. K (KAPH) is FINGERS. N (NUN) is MOVEMENT. The OW sound in English seems to denote FLOW, in addition to the FL combination. K-N-OW might be rendered FINGERS – MOVEMENT – FLOWS, again supporting the Semitic concept of *knowing* denoting hands-on e*xperiential knowing*, not just head knowledge.

There is much study yet to be done by others who find an interest in the possibility of a link between the Phoenician alphabet and the Germanic languages. I eagerly hope others will pursue this concept further.

The Languages with which this System will Not Work:

I tried applying this system to a few Romance languages (Latin based languages) such as French, Italian and Latin. I can see no correlations whatsoever. Spanish was greatly influenced by the presence of the Arabic-speaking Moors in southern Spain from roughly 1000 to 1500, so there are Spanish words which, because of their **Semitic** origins, do work with this system. A few Greek words I checked out worked too. As for most Latin-based words, the system seems to fall apart and not work.

I doubt this system works with Russian, Polish or similar Slavic languages either. I leave that for someone else to figure out. The same goes for Asian languages, about which I know very little. And again, truthfully, I have no idea why it seems to work with German and English.

Thoughts on the Hebrew Letter System & Germanic Languages:

That the Phoenician/Hebrew pictographical letter system works with Germanic languages is really only supposition on my part, plus it is well outside the scope of this book and the limits of my studies. However, I offer it as a possible springboard to some eager linguist who wants to pursue the concept further. Without a doubt, I find the possibility that the Phoenician/Hebrew Alphabet Code system might be applicable to other languages fascinating.

This all makes me wonder how much underlying truth there actually might be to the Genesis account of the language confusion caused by God during the building of the Tower of Babel. To me it seems quite plausible that there was an original language, at least one language that was a common ancestor to most Semitic and many Indo-European languages. What if this original language was written with a form of the Phoenician alphabet? Once they became scattered all over the world, they may have likely continued to form new words based on the meanings of a clearly-understood system of pictographical letter meanings.

Whatever the case may be, I am convinced the meanings behind the ancient letter pictographs used by the Phoenicians and the Hebrew peoples were indeed a linguistic mystery just waiting to be unlocked. I shall never again read Hebrew in plain black and white. When Biblical Hebrew words are read using this pictographical system, they now appear to me as living entities, alive with deep meanings and cultural perspectives. After months of painstaking research and investigation, the letters of the Hebrew alphabet have become like close friends to me; hereafter, shall they burst forth from the pages of the Bible in full living color. My wish for you is this - may you too be able now read Hebrew in color!

Concluding Thoughts Regarding the Phoenician Alphabet:

The term *phonetics* exists in the English language because the alphabet use by English speakers evolved from the Phoenician alphabet. The fundamental concept of phonetics, where each voiced sound is represented by a specific letter which denotes that particular sound, reinforces the belief that languages will developed spoken vocabulary first and then subsequently those words were written phonetically according to their voiced sounds. However, I wish to suggest a radically different possibility here.

The evidence, at least for Hebrew, seems to point to a completely new reality… that in Hebrew (as well as in several other languages) words were formed BASED upon the meanings and concepts of the letters which were used to write them; the pictographical alphabet system seems to have dictated (or at least determined) which 3 root letters would be used in the formation of many vocabulary words. It is quite possible that many of the earliest Semitic languages grew out of the Phoenician and Hebrew alphabets' pictorial meanings. Specific combinations of three letters and their corresponding meanings determined how concepts and ideas would be voiced. In short, *phonetics* is something of a misnomer. Hebrew words were not represented in print by letters; the letters themselves determined the combination of sounds which formed the basic words of Semitic languages.

This would suggest that at least some primitive languages were very right-brained (pictorial) in their inception and not as linear as Western thinkers might like to believe. Sounds were not transcribed after-the-fact onto paper using the letters; rather, the picture images and concepts represented by the pictographical letters were actually the foundational basis for the formation on the spoken languages among ancient peoples of the Middle East. At least among the Hebrews and Phoenicians, the written language shaped their spoken language.

* * *

About the Author

J. Steven Babbit began studying Hebrew in 1971 while living and working on Kibbutz Gevulot in Israel. For years afterwards, his keen interest in Hebrew motivated him to study the language on his own, especially during his years as an undergraduate student at Western Washington University.

As a graduate student at Talbot Theological Seminary in 1984, he had the opportunity to continue his Hebrew studies under Dr. Richard Rigsby, one of the leading Biblical Hebrew scholars in America and a contributing translator to the *New American Standard Bible*. In 2004, Babbit studied Modern Hebrew at The Hebrew University of Jerusalem, Israel.

Since 1975, Babbit has worked as a secondary public school teacher. Over a period spanning three decades, he has studied at eight different universities and has amassed nearly nine years of university-level studies in a wide variety of subjects. After retiring as from public school teaching at the end of the 2007-2008 school year, Babbit has devoted the bulk of his time to studying the Hebrew alphabet and writing system, as well as teaching adult Hebrew class at Temple Beth El in Tacoma, Washington. In the fall of 2010, Babbit and a close Israeli friend, Mark Gershom, hope to begin leading tours in Israel.

Detailed information about Babbit's books and/or future tours to Israel can be found the author's website:

www.ReadHebrewInLivingColor.com

(This information was previously located on **livingtabernacles.com**)

The author currently resides in Gig Harbor, Washington, but continues to spend extended periods of time in Israel. Please feel free to contact Steve any time through the above-listed web site.

Look on-line for author J. Steven Babbit's
Hebrew in Living Color series –

The first book in the series will be the book of **Ruth**. *Genesis* through *Deuteronomy* will follow.

Books will become available in the **summer of 2010.**

The *Hebrew in Living Color* Series Features…

- **Each book will have fully colorized Biblical Hebrew text in large, easy-to-read print.**

- **To the right of each line of Hebrew text will be a corresponding fully colorized English word-by-word translation.**

- **Hebrew word prefixes, suffixes, word roots and all other parts of speech will be individually colorized, so readers can discern each specific individual part of complex Hebrew words.**

- **The Hebrew in Living Color books will provide the perfect study aid for both beginning and intermediate Hebrew students who desires to read Biblical Hebrew.**

Made in the USA
Charleston, SC
01 March 2016